T0379162

Imposing Fictions: Subversive Literature and the Imperative of Authenticity

Thomas Phillips and Cate Rivers

Imposing Fictions: Subversive Literature and the Imperative of Authenticity

Thomas Phillips and Cate Rivers

Academica Press
Washington~London

Library of Congress Cataloging-in-Publication Data

Names: Phillips, Thomas (author). Rivers, Cate (author).
Title: Imposing fictions : subversive literature and the imperative of
authenticity | Phillips, Thomas (author), Rivers, Cate (author).
Description: Washington : Academica Press, 2024. | Includes references.
Identifiers: LCCN 2023949407 | ISBN 9781680535358 (hardcover) |
9781680535365 (e-book)

Contents

Introduction

– The Question Concerning Authenticity

French novelist and playwright, Marie NDiaye, whose mother is French and whose father Senegalese, gained notoriety at a relatively young age and has become one of France's most celebrated contemporary writers. Amid this success, she has (historically, at least) been adamant about staking no claims in her subject-position as female, Black, or relatively privileged. As Warren Motte observes, when asked if this view had shifted with time, she asserted "'I can't see myself, for my part, as a black woman'" (quoted, *French* 28), choosing instead to foreground her cultural position as one who writes first and foremost. Though her work often addresses the complexities of race in Western culture, this is nonetheless a bold assertion, eschewing as it does the cultural tendency toward identity politics under the gaze of probing others. Motte concludes "one may read [in her 2005 novel *Autoportrait en vert* (*Self-Portrait in Green*)] NDiaye's will to define herself in a rather different manner, as the person she wishes to *be*, quite apart from the expectations of others, and strictly on her own terms" (our italics, ibid.). Perhaps the most immediate question to ask in response to the author's position concerns the degree to which it is tenable, not to mention ethical, in the context of both 21st century racial atrocities and the milieu's unparalleled immersion in what we might loosely call personal essence. Other significant lines of inquiry include: Does public eschewal of racial identity edge too close to some detestable, reactionary stance? Is a central investment in Being necessarily overridden by subject-position, and are these mutually exclusive or intimately entwined? Black lives, on any continent, unquestionably matter, in the specificity of their historical heritages, in the inherent right to equal treatment under the law, especially insofar the latter is wielded by all-too-often contemptable police *in flagrante delicto* (the crime, of course, being deadly bigotry), and in their access to cultural empowerment and recognition. Yet what is at stake in our reading of NDiaye's stance is the challenge and potentiality of *being* authentic, not simply as another identity marker to tack on to one's otherwise unyielding sense of self (as in "behold my authenticity, world!"), but at the level of immediate ontological, psychological, and, by extension, somatic experience. Consequently, one of our aims is to address the questions above more or less overtly and broadly to include a number of marginalized subject-positions as a means of reckoning with the individual's perception of and engagement with Being and becoming.

Race obviously has a deeply pertinent bearing on each of these three overlapping levels of existence, though it is also molded by evolving, cultural narratives. Given the immense power of such narratives, as Paul Smith puts it, to "cern" the subject/individual whose lack of agency may in turn be "dis-cerned" with the aid of critical theory and developing self-awareness (*Discerning* 5), the general premise of this study is that authentic Being is a profoundly elusive quality, particularly in the context of a populist technocracy, and proportionately essential to cultivate for the sake of a given intellectually and psychologically healthy self and the peopled context in which one functions. It is such health that may potentially constitute the fulcrum of individual and communal ethics, be they applied to the everyday of people struggling to survive or to one's grappling with Julia Kristeva's "subject-in-process" and every modality in between. At any point on this continuum, we argue, literature, in addition to specific philosophical frameworks, is useful to the recognition, structuring, and deployment of ethical Being.

NDiaye's *Self-Portrait in Green* is certainly invested in the color green, the hue in which most of the self-portrait's characters are adorned, that defines them. It signifies struggle, women's struggle amidst selfish men and a culture that nurtures the same in its women. Green is also attached to a monstrous vision of nature, as in the river Garonne that periodically overflows and devastates an adjacent community that invariably chooses to remain there, the narrator explains in the novel's first paragraph. To solidify the parallel, she asserts that "*la Garonne's* essence is feminine" (Ndiaye, *Self-Portrait* 4). Women are hardly lionized here;

they are implicated in an equation of social customs, nature, and monstrosity.[1] "Green" ultimately assumes any form in order to enact its real, its Otherness that is equally mundane, and all the more unsettling for its banality. And yet, the women in whom green is most apparent are also necessary, "at once real beings and literary figures, without which, it seems to me, the harshness of existence scours skin and flesh down to the bone" (82).

As narrator, Ndiaye is more or less one such woman, both flesh and character, particularly when she confuses her daughter (Marie) with herself, thereby distinguishing, albeit ambiguously, between lived experience and literary narrative. Her concern, as she asserts, is on her characters first and foremost, "in what sort of situations I can place them, and, above all, about the moral issues they'll have to face, as opposed to the meaning these moral issues might have in contemporary society. I don't want any of my books to be described with words ending in '-ist,' whether that be humanist, feminist, socialist... I can be all of those things as a citizen, but not as an artist" (Ndiaye "Interview"). In an era of high-stakes identity coordinates and necessarily pronounced efforts toward social justice, it is difficult to imagine a more culturally subversive stance beyond one that is overtly reactionary.

That the term 'subversive' is typically used in relation to the collapsing of political systems is certainly relevant to this study, though no more so than the broader significance the term has to cultural hegemony. The former, of course, cannot exist without some degree of the latter; even fully totalitarian systems require culturally informed complacency, if not active support of their agendas. Political behavior follows ideological, and finally, psychological states of Being. Hence our effort to examine Being as an ontological space *behind* thought, speech, and emotional expenditure, not anatomically but empirically discernible, the minutiae of Being accessible only when identity is temporarily, at least, bracketed. Byung-Chul Han asserts that "relinquishing the imaginary identity of the ego and suspending the symbolic order to which it owes its societal and social existence represents a weightier death than the end of bare life" (*Agony* 25). Here bracketing and suspension are synonyms for the essential, metaphorical death insofar as Being is invariably diminished or concealed by the ego of identity with which one must contend if an authentic engagement with the immense variety of life is to take precedence in lived experience.

Of course, literature is inscribed in the symbolic order, Jacques Lacan's term for the inevitable compulsion of language and other social phenomena. Where it is assumes the form and sensibility of subversion, however, is in its power to resist the authority of certain dominant symbols, thereby communicating, if not embodying, the radicalism of a symbolic dis-order. The latter has less to do with disorganization than transgression, of conventional literary structure, content, and expectation in terms of how literature is typically conceived, by writer and reader, to make one feel. In other words, subversiveness reaches its psychological and cultural heights in achieving organic, rather than prescribed or culturally sanctioned alterity, while convention is edification, even in cases of harsh realism that nevertheless proffer regenerative closure. Convention is also a mode of indoctrination that lends itself well to the most paradoxically unfeeling operations of capitalism and to the bizarrely overlapping political strains that have quite possibly accelerated Oswald Spengler's decline of the West beyond anyone's howling imagination.

Right-wing ideology and the religious fundamentalism with which it often conspires are easy targets of any effort to distinguish authenticity from inauthenticity. Despite what is doubtless sincere commitment, its adherents (particularly those who have formed into extremist cabals religiously, nihilistically devoted to hatred and violence) must inevitably bump up against a level of speciousness or contrivance by virtue of their core reactionary values in the face of progressivist cultural forces galvanized by evolving ethics and science. Racism, misogyny, religious intolerance, and homophobia, however micro- or macro-aggressive, don't quite pan out when one's life, or that of another one cherishes, is on the line and in the hands of an "other" one would ordinarily repudiate in the privacy of thought or the (virtual) public arena of discourse. The ego is typically forced to step down from its throne at the center of one's fortress in these situations and accept its walls as the rather stupid (or impractical, for the staunch believer) constructions they are. One may chastise or simply ignore the intellectual, female writer of color (and do not get the American right started about the French...), but find oneself stuck alone in an elevator with her for hours on end (no mobile reception) and one may learn something positive, even beautiful, about the human condition.

The left, however, presents a different set of problems, divergent lines of inquiry. Or not. At the most basic, psychological level, the two poles have the capacity to dovetail in ways inconceivable to both but may appear jarringly apparent to relatively objective observation. Anyone can be complicit in constructing the citadel against those who might tread upon a treasured "me," outside, of course, overtly prejudiced, violent antagonism. Moreover, the presentation of self may act not only as a bastion of security but as a "screen" upon which the performance of one's identity is projected to all who would watch, listen, and applaud, 21st century crippled attention spans notwithstanding. There is nothing particularly new or provocative in this observation until the issue of authenticity is raised and called into question relative to the individual, whereupon gloves, bare knuckles, or vicious tweets may be roused. Examining the role of authenticity in the context of lived, progressivist ideology poses numerous difficulties for one seeking to both write and embody those advancing forces that compel us to be genuinely compassionate and intellectually modern. Embracing this challenge, among others, is a central aim of this study in terms of illuminating the imperative around authentic modes of Being apparent in subversive literature. The ambition is not, then, to further offend those who are historically and currently derided by what Kaja Silverman calls the "dominant fictions" (*Threshold* 85) of hegemonic culture. We are not interested in presenting some reactionary screed, but in making a sincere effort to elucidate the value of authenticity and genuine, as opposed to merely presumed or performed alterity as the central precondition for the former. Any effort to reify increasingly antiquated social structures emblematizes the antithesis of authenticity; it generates a paradoxical void of *excess* Being in the sense that the fortress, however mighty and over-stuffed with aggregates of self, is invariably a prison in which inmates are eventually nullified by the unforgiving world outside. For progressivism to thrive, we maintain, it must impose the discipline (the ethic) of psychological self-examination on its own potentially debilitating, and critically, *universal* proclivities, an act that more often than not seems inconceivable to a narcissistically-inclined right-wing sensibility.

Our sense of the authentic (that exerts its force or its edifying failure in the literary and other texts that follow) has nothing to do with fortifying the self. Instead, it offers another, healthier paradox, that of a fluid essentialism as the central, procedural medium of potential agency, the self as nexus of Being *and* becoming, capable of shifting its orientation according to the exigence of a given moment while maintaining a core awareness or *remembrance* of immediate, psychosomatic *Dasein*. For Martin Heidegger, "in the anticipatory revealing of this potentiality-for-Being, *Dasein* discloses itself to itself as regards its uttermost possibility … that is to say, the possibility of *authentic existence*" (*Being* 307). Authenticity necessitates an ongoing process of "revealing," or "unconcealment," as the philosopher puts it in "The Question Concerning Technology," of that which is to some degree already present in the self (*Basic* 319). Nevertheless, in keeping with the horror-as-subversion texts that concern the first half of this study, achieving the real of oneself inevitably comes with sacrifice. "The ontological constitution of such existence," Heidegger asserts in *Being and Time*, "must be made visible by setting forth the concrete structure of anticipation of death" (307). Death may be (and is ideally, of course) as figurative as it is literal, though the "setting forth" here signifies an entirely explicit, materially substantial effort on the part of one so inclined to transcend identity, or at least to expand its scope to a point of minimizing its importance in the context of what Alain Badiou refers to as an "event" that provokes a particular mode of ethics. It is an effort that transforms one into a murderer of sorts, of the self that occupies – with pride, elation, humiliation, audacity, or fatality – Being and time without awareness of actually doing so. Death is the fluidity, the essential becoming of Being, that requires that Herculean effort which Terry Eagleton distinguishes as "radical sacrifice" of the self to which one may be tethered as though by nature in all of its glory and its sticky, problematic certainties. The only martyr here is the one who, in the best-case scenario, steps back from the carnage – or peaceful passing in slumber – and quietly celebrates being what J.D. Salinger recognizes as "an absolute nobody" (*Franny* 30) at the center of all experience. Such are the philosophical foundations of our examination of and advocacy for authenticity that concern the opening chapter.

Undertaken with committed sincerity, as done by numerous individuals in our roster of literary characters, sacrifice and death become the precursor to a dissident alterity. This is alterity shorn of pretense and performativity, though it does not necessarily evade marginalization, another reality borne out by the horror genre. To be the willing recipient of the aesthetic articulation of "potentiality-for-Being" means to be intensely "other," though, significantly, one's response to this condition determines in large part the measure of said potential. In a 1905 letter to Oskar Pollak, Franz Kafka crafts his understanding of the primary function of literature in this way: "I think we ought to read only the kind of books that wound and stab us. If the book we're reading doesn't wake us up with a blow on the head, what are we reading it for? So that it will make us happy, as you write? Good Lord, we would be happy precisely if we had no books, and the kind of books that make us happy are the kind we could write ourselves if we had to. But we need the books that affect us like a disaster, that grieve us deeply, like the death of someone we loved more than ourselves, like being banished into forests far from everyone, like a suicide. A book must be the axe for the frozen sea inside us. That is my belief " (Zagava, *Booklore*). There are plenty of "disasters" and "frozen seas" walking the aisles of grocery stores, parenting children, teaching, attending political rallies, and deciding which gun to buy next, but to allow that axe to fall, to walk of one's own accord into that forest of solitude and grief can only result in the kind of alterity that a Kafka praises and a reactionary (of any political stripe) may be inclined to repudiate. Or we might think of Andre Tarkovsky's aesthete, Alexander, in *The Sacrifice* (1986) who laments the daily assault of "words, words, words!" and finally, at the behest of a profound (perhaps even occult) intuition, confines himself to silence and madness, the loss of his family, career, and home, for the sake of saving the planet from nuclear war. His is an alterity that stems from a father's love, established by the film's conclusion when his son, Little Man, alone with a newly planted tree, speaks the final line: "In the beginning was the Word. Why is that, Papa?" Tarkovsky's "event" is indicative of an existential love that challenges discursive representation, and thus the common substance of identity, at the same time that it reveals an imperative of difference, to use Badiou's general terminology. We might say that the self is always already a medium of alterity; what matters is the degree of recognition, and the benevolence or enmity of spirits conjured.

Aesthetic practice and utilization, then, are not without limits given the elasticity of words, sounds, images, so any examination of authenticity is ultimately engaging with psychological, philosophical, and, as Alexander discovers, metaphysical imperatives. Though this study is certainly concerned with material circumstances of lived experience, its point of origin is finally unrelated to the vicissitudes of a subject-position and centered around obscure but resonant conditions of selfhood. To employ another essential, extended passage, this one from the non-dualist Hindu teacher Sri Nisargadatta Maharaj: "You cannot possibly say that you are what you think yourself to be! Your ideas about yourself change from day to day and from moment to moment. Your self-image is the most changeful thing you have. It is utterly vulnerable, at the mercy of a passerby. A bereavement, the loss of a job, an insult, and your image of yourself, which you call your person, changes deeply. To know what you are, you must first investigate and know what you are not. And to know what you are not, you must watch yourself carefully, rejecting all that does not go with the basic fact: "I am." ... Our usual attitude is of "I am this." Consistently and perseveringly separate the "I am" from "this" or "that." All our habits go against it and the task of fighting them is long and hard sometimes, but clear understanding helps significantly. The more clearly you understand that on the level of mind you can be described in negative terms only, the more quickly you will come to the end of your search and realize your limitless being" (*I Am* 54). It may be especially egregious in this epoch to suggest "rejecting" all that one is on and just beneath the surface when so many venomous ideological forces are intent on subjugating the person. But again, such eschewal is not a matter of dropping out of life and the responsibilities it necessitates. Nisaragadatta's assertion is operating "on the level of the mind," which, as it happens, literature in particular is quite good at interrogating. The rest – the intentionality of undertaking a practice of clearly directed self-observation – is both contemporary to and post-aesthetic experience. While "limitless being" is beyond the scope of our project, its potentiality is nevertheless an undercurrent that comes more or less into focus at certain junctures in so far as it is indicative of truly radical alterity. Access to such Being unfolds, we suggest, at the pivot between one's "mind-level" conception of oneself and a psychological/somatic experience of immediate, core awareness.

Here on the world's surface, the current American epoch is still, astoundingly, witnessing the indiscriminate murder of people of color, rejection of gender and sexual orientation, and the haughty dismissal of women's sexual abuse claims and the right to their own bodies, in addition to the general leveling of basic facts. Alterity is most commonly associated with politically (and maliciously) reinforced abjection, a reality of which we are not unaware. And yet, the line between abject and agentic is thin. As framed by Julia Kristeva, the subject, "weary of fruitless attempts to identify with something on the outside, finds the impossible within ... finds that the impossible constitutes its very *being*, that it *is* none other than abject" (*Powers* 5). "Impossible" may be understood here as "a deep well of memory that is unapproachable and intimate" (6), "a land of oblivion that is constantly remembered" (8), and "is above all ambiguity" (15). It is the fact of a corpse, of one's inescapable trajectory toward this absence, and yet abjection also signifies "a resurrection that has gone through death (of the ego). It is an alchemy that transforms death drive into a start of life, into a new significance" (15). So, one of our intentions is to foreground the toxicity of prescribed otherness and to then exemplify the power of (re)claiming alterity, not as a badge or a flag asserting the beleaguered or cavalier self, but as an enduring, contemplative practice of "resurrection," or *Dasein*. To accomplish this, we have divided the study into two sections, each addressing levels of subversiveness in literature. The first looks at horror or weird fiction texts as homeopathy, that medical treatment involving consumption of the very poison one seeks to avoid. Whether one is on the right or the left of the political spectrum, or some hazy, indifferent position in between, it behooves one to stare at length into the mirror reflection on occasion, with no distraction, no Photoshop or Instagram "reality augmentation," in order to distinguish between what is relatively integral in that image, and in the immediate, psychological perception of oneself, and what is forgery, written ideologically on the body and in the mind, as though posthumously. At its most sophisticated and nuanced, what Phillips has identified elsewhere as "critical horror"[2] is that mirror.

One particular reflection, a quietly vicious story of child molestation and murder, "The Frolic," finds horror writer Thomas Ligotti's narrator referencing the "contamination" and "psychic imposition" of the prison, the "imposing structure" (5) that houses the central perpetrator, a man whose voices are many and whom it is not hyperbole to call legion. The protagonist, a prison psychologist, senses the weight of this architecture and its inhabitants bearing down on his relatively posh, suburban home where safety is all but guaranteed and the abject is presumed to be kept at bay. It is his wife, however, who first encounters the creeping disquiet in the very quietude of their new home that will eventually serve as the bleak space of their young daughter's abduction and, presumably, grisly molestation and death. The evil has gotten inside. Such is the general program of subversive, and particularly horror literature. At its critical best, such fiction brings disorder to a domineering symbolic, imposes itself on the psyche, well beneath the skin, and contaminates delusional presuppositions where they are at their most potent. Gilles Deleuze claims of authorship and concomitant texts, "it's a strange business, speaking for yourself, in your own name, because it doesn't at all come with seeing yourself as an ego or a person or a subject. Individuals find a real name for themselves, rather, only through the harshest exercise in depersonalization, by opening themselves up to the multiplicities everywhere within them, to the intensities running through them" (*Negotiations* 6). Potent presuppositions (ego, person, subject) give way here to a relentless, aesthetic undoing of their conventional force in the life. Finding "a real name," then, is a novel, exceptional "business" (especially in this milieu of social media saturation) in which the individual comes to terms with a self-in-process, as opposed to codified identity. Deleuze continues, however, to suggest that this mode of writing (and reading) is "depersonalization through love rather than subjection"

(7).³ Subversive literature's *raison d'etre* is the evocation of the real (the thing/monster/deceptively innocent phenomenon that enters or is already inside the self) that stretches, we argue, beyond politics and into ontological depths that have a capacity for provoking compassion, respect, even tenderness.

Based in Rebecca Janicker's two-fold notion of liminality wherein one may emerge from liminal experience "at a higher stage of personal or cultural development *or* encounter a place of threat" (*Literary* 125), section one adheres to the latter as essential provocation. Section two presents readings of similarly subversive, non-genre texts in which the horror is relatively mundane (and therefore, paradoxically, perhaps, more threatening) but more overt and consistent in advocating for Heidegger's "potentiality-for-Being" in the cultivation of organic difference, and thus authenticity. Such texts yield what Kristeva refers to as a "purification" (*Powers* 17) or a "sublimation" of the abject "without consecration" (26), without, that is, a rigid, sacral declaration of Being that would limit the subject beyond the inevitability of death, and thus aid in the development of said subject into a self aware of both its "impossibility" and its potential for creative fulfillment in the lived life. In each case, it should become clear, contrary to longstanding prejudices, that a venerated notion of the literary is securely persistent in much horror fiction and vice versa. Moreover, and remarkably, the foregrounding of authenticity operative in certain examples of horror and other subversive literary texts creates the seemingly incongruous conditions for a way of being that some, including Deleuze, call love. If the current or any era is to push beyond vainglory and infantilism, authenticity must be taken to task (or "revealed," in Heidegger's terms) in the individual lives of its participants and in its collective, monumental force, so as to be observed, remembered, dissected, and quite possibly, for those who believe their monopoly on Being, sacrificed for the sake of far lesser evils.

Part I

The Subversiveness of Death, Morbidity, and Being

Chapter 1

– Heideggerian Diagnoses
and the Possibility of Dissent

In "It Will Be Here Soon," famed horror writer Dennis Etchison characterizes the American milieu as "a time of leisure and deadly boredom, of investigation and inconclusion, of heat waves and chills under an effluvia sky; of cancer research and chemical juggernauts, of Tac Squads and the Basic Car Plan, of God freaks and camper cities; of no longer suppressed unrest. Assassination, mass murder, ascension to office; the bomb in the backyard and the cop in the woodpile" (*Dark* 145). In most every respect, this particular time (the story was originally published in 1979) is hardly removed from that of early twenty-first century America. Bizarre weather patterns, disease, militaristic interventions, rabid consumerism, religious fanaticism, social turmoil, inconceivable seizure of office, and literal death, always death, occupy prominent positions in the current epoch. The opening section title of Etchison's story, "Something Strange in Santa Mara," references the town being "not what it used to be" (145), or so says an aging father, recently recovered following surgery, to his visiting son, Martin, recently divorced and considering a class reunion. Perhaps the "something strange" is the mundane fact of life's inevitable vicissitudes, despite the resilience of certain core components of the human experience, or at least of life in the United States as the characters experience it. Etchison's story, however, like the fundamental tropes of horror, transcends nationality and culture insofar as amid the discombobulating multiplicity of contemporary life, the retired father has become deeply engaged in audible signs of the paranormal, a real beyond the mundanity of conventional borders. He has used his knowledge of electronics to record "Spirit Voice Phenomena"

(151), especially after having encountered creatures in his hospital room. "They started coming for me from the walls," he claims. "They came out of the wardrobe. They'd stand and watch. Waiting. I thought they wanted me to go with them" (154). The father is fixated, perhaps delusionally so, on manifestations of what might very generally be called profound otherness.

As it happens, between aging, frailty, discontent, and pop culture absorbed via television ("A used-car salesman with freeze-dried hair flickered to life on the screen … like he's ready to eat us right where we sit," the elder notes [150]), "It Will Be Here Soon" is ultimately offering a domestic snapshot of life pushing inexorably toward the great Otherness of mortality. The father dreams of his time expiring and his son observes him outside "at the curb, waiting like an animal for the exterminator" (158). Specifically, then, the "it" that appears imminent is death, the relativity of "soon" fostering the horror with or without sounding, lurking creatures, no matter one's age or social rank. It is the horror that takes us all, in dignified, abysmal, or commonplace termination. And yet no being is wholly and completely stock cardboard, including Etchison's characters navigating the end in one way or another. By the story's conclusion, Martin surreptitiously records a "Spirit Voice" (his own) on a tape his father has yet to hear. It's a poignant moment, unsettlingly tender in the son's effort to love in the face of death. Early on, we learn of his potential for love in the notion that had he "been able to love anyone, he would have loved his father" (145), in addition to his general need for "contact" (149) as he ventures out one evening in search of a woman, any woman, with whom he went to school during what was presumably a formative period of his life. Even in his skepticism regarding his father's preoccupation, the son is compelled to think "maybe, just maybe there is a key to some kind of truth in the asking, in the questioning itself; maybe, maybe there is, after all. I want to be out there, he thought [from inside the house, staring out], to be there with him, next to him" (159). Etchison avoids judging the reality or unreality of paranormal entities and thus leaves this question open; only to foreground *humanitas* in everyday life.

This is one way to read the text, in terms of what it signifies, what it means, what wisdom, pathos, or horrifying knowledge it imparts to a reader. Another approach might consider the story as a functionary of the larger category and practice of literature and ask the question: what does it do? How does it reveal further, radical vistas of human experience beyond what mass culture with its hungry salesmen and populist authoritarianism enforces? Deleuze scholar Bruce Baugh asserts that "great [literary] works intensify life, and life is intensified in us as we encounter them" ("How" 52) to the degree that a collaboration between text and reader is inaugurated and the everyday invested with potentially transgressive insight. In the case of horror, this intensification endows life with an acute, immediate (or slow burn) awareness of death. One way or another, death ravages the self, the reality that is easily – too easily – abetted by the garden-variety aggression, unconsciousness, and narcissism of other people, of warring nations or couples isolated on the island of home who nevertheless inadvertently expose their dysfunction when operating in the public sphere. The "they" that ostensibly seek to haunt and possibly abduct the father in "It Will Be Here Soon," for example, intrigue as much as they disturb him, along with, presumably, the reader whose own lived sense of otherness is confirmed and titillated. The story entertains with paranormal speculation while, more importantly, provoking an awareness of alterity, in both its uncanniness and its inevitability, that lies not in the future but in the intensive now of people engaging with other people before the specter of death.

"They" are equally affecting and trenchant in the very different context of Heidegger's distinctive philosophical discourse. In *Being and Time*, he examines how "the real dictatorship of the 'they' ['*Das Man*'] is unfolded. We take pleasure and enjoy ourselves as *they* (*man*) take pleasure; we read, see, and judge about literature and art as *they* see and judge; likewise we shrink back from the 'great mass' as *they* shrink back; we find 'shocking' what they find shocking. The 'they,' which is nothing definite, and which all are, though not as a sum, prescribes the kind of Being of everydayness" (164). Here "they" are comparable to the amorphous collective that inhabits such a common phrase as "they say that…" to indicate authority on given subject matter. It is a claim that we all recognize as at once reasonably accurate and potentially fallacious, just as Heidegger's argument speaks to the mass conformity we instinctively know dominates a culture at large while finding it difficult, perhaps, to abandon our sense, however erroneous, of individual integrity amidst the collective. Yet this "nothing definite" carries immense power. It is "Das Man" on television, selling, *influencing* online, provoking superfluous desire; or the communal groan of a school class itching for prompts and formulas, or for nothing at all, that stymies and redirects the individual student's access to radical literature or art; or the religious or political fanaticism that prescribes fear, paranoia, and vitriol in the everyday landscape of beings insulated from Being.

Heidegger goes on to explicate the "distantiality, averageness, and leveling down, as ways of Being for the 'they,' [that] constitute what we know as 'publicness,'" by which "everything gets obscured, and what has thus been covered up gets passed off as something familiar and accessible to everyone" (165). Instantly, we are at several removes here from the paradoxical equipoise of Etchison's story relative to the philosopher's vertical, hierarchical model of Being's value with terms such as "averageness" and "leveling down." That said, reducing this model to the level of the individual at the mercy of the "they" aligns the philosophical argument with the generally unsettling orientation of horror. As the aversion to depart from normative social mores, "publicness" has a kind of diabolism about it, an unseemly, interiorized fascism, something to avoid when substantial life choices are on the line. Likewise, the "familiar" and the "accessible" aren't always preferable, as anyone who has been cajoled into a film or concert of the bubblegum variety can attest. What is finally at issue in Heidegger's critique is the developmental *Dasein* of a being who participates in the world of other people, objects, and ideological structures. Its central conflict is the general condition, as he understands it, of being "lost in the 'they'" (312), or to put it another way, being "homeless," a state that "is coming to be the destiny of the world" (*Basic* 243). And it is this diagnosis that returns us to the Etchisonian "it-will-be-here-soon" as a foreboding insight that prognosticates both a compromised present and an intellectually, spiritually crippled future, the overarching condition of which Heidegger implies as inauthenticity.

Another problematic term, to be sure. Who determines such a category and to what end? Etchison perceives a malevolent, capitalistic "hunger" in the condition that is not far removed from Heidegger's perspective wherein "the essential happenings in this darkening [the debasement of authenticity] are: the flight of the gods, the destruction of the earth, the reduction of human beings to a mass, the pre-eminence of the mediocre" (qtd. in O'Brien 72). Etchison's car salesman's "freeze-dried hair" is surely mediocre, but far more damning in the seemingly innocuous commercial is the viewer's commandeered attention, and by extension, the eschewal of mythical time and heritage, the displacement of awareness around oil dependence, the cattle-prodding into mass consumerism, and the bigger picture of cultural mediocrity in terms of addiction to the screen, be it televisual or otherwise. Inauthenticty is "dark" in the sense of a negative void, a darkness that erases the illumination of wisdom or intuitive knowledge, a deafening noise that cancels the aural and cognitive spaciousness of critical thought-producing, or quietly meditative silence. "In this darkening" may be found, arguably, justification for terminology the impetus behind which is not to disenfranchise individuals or communities but to provoke a relatively sensitive and sophisticated relationship to the being of *Dasein*, such that the subject of a self is granted the possibility of not being tethered to a prefabricated identity.[4] Heidegger seeks to avoid the scenario of "everyone [being] the other and no one [being oneself]" (O'Brien 58), or in his own words, "the final delusion" whereby "it seems as though man everywhere and always encounters only himself" (*Basic* 332). It is a degraded form of solipsism, in the final analysis, that best characterizes the state of inauthenticity, one governed by the mundane egotism of people absorbed into the machinery of the much-decried culture industry.

While there's nothing particularly novel in the application of Heidegger (or Theodor Adorno, for that matter) to issues germane to cultural theory, it is worth pursuing a Heideggerian examination into how the "industries" of culture inform certain momentous tendencies in the current cultural climate of the US, especially insofar as they have emerged from particular histories, ply their trades in the present, and will doubtless have an impact on future, cultural, ontological dispositions. Due to its prominence in both Heidegger's oeuvre and, naturally, in cultural development, technology is a crucial starting point. In his "Letter on

Humanism," he warns "the greatest care must be fostered upon the ethical bond at a time when technological man, delivered over to mass society, can be kept reliably on call only by gathering and ordering all his plans and activities in a way that corresponds to technology" (*Basic* 255). We'll return to the nature of Heidegger's ethics later, but what stands out in this passage for our present purposes is the system of "delivery" through which the individual becomes assimilated into the masses. One is compelled to be "reliably on call" as natural resources are considered fair game for the industrialists of the world no matter environmental consequences. By virtue of this unfailing availability, the individual may blithely become-subject to mass ideology, "gathered" into the fray of mass behavior, discourse, thought, and "ordered" in the domain of time, an ongoing process whose "correspondence" to technology likely evolves – in force and conspicuousness – in tandem with the latter's own advancement.

Current examples are abundant and deviously entwined: the inconceivability of being without one's phone as raw, bodily and psychological addiction, as in object fetishism; addiction to the identity that develops in corresponding behavior via social media, constructed from cute, or clever, or merely regurgitated soundbites, images, "likes," tirades, and laments; the emerging impossibility of not being "on call," of missing out on yet another piece of information, or an invitation to join, follow, or mimic. The technology of entertainment also generates addiction by way of Hollywood screens, of course, compulsive viewing that sculpts the addiction according to ontological fashions, ways of being and connecting in the modern world. Physical, intimate contact between people can even assume the form of what Badiou calls online dating site/app "propaganda" that "reflects a safety-first concept of love" (*In Praise* 6) in that chance and risk are reduced as users pinpoint their needs and desires according to a consumer/product model.

In each instance, technology has a tendency to "set upon," in a manner of "regulating and securing" (Heidegger, *Basic* 320, 322) the individual on its own terms, as opposed to thought processes and behavior developing out of a relatively capacious, conscientious, freely improvisational agency. Heidegger refers abstractly to the implementation of such cultural, technological phenomena as "enframing," "the rule [of which] threatens man with the possibility that it could be denied to him to enter into a more original revealing [of Being] and hence to experience the call of a more primal truth" (333). The "primal truth" that is elided in voicing one's identity (the exteriorized, interior scaffolding of desire and repudiation) through technological means is that "technological man" is not the self encountered in Being. In other words, despite the pervasive delusion mentioned above, "precisely nowhere does man today any longer encounter himself, i.e., his essence" (332). The implication here is that there has in fact been a period, or there are periods, of communal or individual life, in which the encounter with self is genuine rather than fanciful. "Essence," of course, is the key – and, as with "truth," dubious – term, connoting as it does an unalterable, fundamental component of selfhood that, post-Heidegger, is rightfully submitted to the dangers of essentialism (who determines what is essential to encapsulating self, and based on what potential power dynamic?). If we align "essence" with authenticity, however, the term assumes a compelling and pragmatic legitimacy in its signification of groundedness in Being *in*, or perhaps even outside, time, whereby thought is flexible and intuitive in the immediacy of its embodiment. And it is this primary, human mode of being qua *Being* that the regulating effects of technology inhibit when the latter sufficiently "set upon" the self, the culture, the species.

Obviously, the Heidegger passages call attention to their dated, exclusive, male pronoun in the twenty-first century, which complicates any effort to bring his arguments to bear on the lived experience of contemporary individuals and communities. The philosopher was a product of his time, to be sure; time in the sense of both discursive and relational mores. [5] How might we utilize this unfortunate reality, this perfunctory, linguistic dismissal of women and non-binary people beyond calling attention to its archaism? The correlation between contemporary restrictions and imperatives around language and in/authenticity offers an illuminating and quite charged answer, alongside the question of what role technology plays in this link. To specify even further, we might ask how "they" inform language and how language informs "Das Man." How are "essence" and "primal truth" (as hallmarks of potential Being in or outside the immediacy of time, what T.S. Eliot refers to in "The Four Quartets" as

"the still point of the turning world" [*Complete* 119]), to be navigated by
identity coordinates immersed in "publicness," technologically mediated
or otherwise? To what degree can *Dasein* cultivate and maintain a level of
authenticity when "they" govern what can and cannot be said (or thought)?

Heidegger's "they" is clearly fascistic in orientation, the kind of
fascism that, with or without a toothbrush mustache, burrows into the
interior self and becomes established as normative. "They" say … so it
must have veracity. "They" as an indicator of gender fluidity, while
precipitating a conundrum for English educators, including those of us
who fully support one's right to tailor discourse to suit one's inherent sense
of self, speaks to and for productive, organic alterity in the face of the
abominable history, still slowly and painfully unraveling, of LBGTQIA+
discrimination. When wielded in a context of grounded, integral being, it
assumes the power of minoritarian functionality, the seizure of dominant,
potentially fascistic language for the sake of reinvention, of discourse, of
a people to come.[6] That said, beyond every such term that is invested with
as much generosity and self-knowledge as its proponent is capable, this
study maintains, there lies the possibility of selfhood requiring no
culturally-mandated re-presentation at all; an active, politically
transgressive, abjectively amelioritive self without a self. At stake is a
project of self-development in the service of disabling *all* identity insofar
as the identificatory nature of self may be negatively constructed –
"regulated," "secured" – so as to stabilize, to whatever ephemeral degree,
in what Virginia Woolf calls relatively authentic "moments of being."[7]

Woolf's Julia Craye, in the short story of that title that we will examine
in chapter eleven, is a singular character, a woman defined by the
insistence on cultivating her passions (music, solitary walks in nature,
waking and navigating her days on her own time, etc.) but suffers a
profound lack at the core of her life. She desires love, the passion of
intimacy. That she is gay in a milieu when coming out was hardly feasible
situates this lack as all the more poignant, particularly as her beloved piano
student, Fanny, imagines into the awkwardness of unwanted marriage
proposals and depression. The story builds to a blazing, erotic climax in
which Julia's (and quite possibly Fanny's) authenticity of desire is
fulfilled, at least in a *moment* of unbounded liberation, though her

discriminating, idiosyncratic way of being is also on display, with a confident, "queer" laugh, suggesting that wherever the moment leads, nothing of her individualism will be sacrificed. One may seize moments of ontological weight, participate fervently in life, in its endless inter-personal, inter-cultural dramas and requirements of justice, critical thought, though in Julia's case, nothing is as important as occupying a singular existence.

It is the danger of homogeneity, then, rather than any moral compass as to what is or is not acceptable, that is the issue here. It goes without saying that there are authentic, radical subject-positions, an endless array of deeply felt orientations in life that deserve only respect. Where any marginal orientation unfolds out of, or is shaped by, an ironically populist form of "alterity" (as inspired by raw conformity or a pervasive need to belong), however, is where both authenticity and respect become diluted. Delusional alterity is just as easily applied to privileged social positions as abjection is to those that are historically marginal: the out of touch upper-class; preppy white supremacist; "Trump girl" (a bumper sticker); evangelical; digital humanist; art school student; philosopher/theorist; Man, etc. Any identity conceptualized around a supercilious sense of becoming obsolete, or standing above cultural or intellectual "inferiors," especially in a milieu governed by the masking potentiality of online "textual transvestism," as Marc Guillaume puts it in conversation with Jean Baudrillard (*Radical* 36), is inauthentic. This assertion is as germane to the tatted-up hipster who, born earlier, may have unconsciously embraced the bright lights/big city, cocaine-fuelled, country club self-absorption of a previous generation, as it is to the woman who votes awkwardly, perversely, against her own best interests. Heidegger's notion of "homelessness," like genuinely, profoundly sensed, embodied alterity, is also very real.

So as an extension of its philosophical foundations, another premise of this study is that inauthenticity and the crude irony that can surround misrecognized alterity are pervasive enough to warrant the contributions of a Nazi. Granted, with Badiou and Cassin we observe that Heidegger was "not a very important Nazi, just an ordinary one, a provincial petite-bourgeois Nazi" (*Heidegger* 14); and further, we may agree that "philosophy [or literature] is a distinctive kind of activity whose unavoidable relationship with a sort of encyclopedic [or aesthetic] desire also happens to be the privileged site of errancy" (2). To Badiou and Cassin's list of errant philosophers, we might add writers such as H.P. Lovecraft and his racism, Ezra Pound's fascism, Harlan Ellison's initial misogyny, or Michel Houellebecq's many (though questionably) controversial statements and behaviors. These writers endure because they have something valuable to contribute on the subject of authenticity or the lack thereof, among other topics. We will return to the particular authors (all doubtless problematic in their own, humanly peculiar ways) who carry on this tradition in the present study, though for now it is enough to address the errancy that is most pressing, beyond even a philosopher's mid-twentieth century National Socialism: the frailty of being at the center of modern life that Heidegger refers to as "monstrousness" (*Basic* 121). His equation of the monstrosity of natural resources being "set upon" with people being technologically "on call," or subjects of "enframing," is hardly melodramatic, especially in the context of the century that would follow his own. In the marriage between technological subservience and the often amorphous, exigent libertarianism of contemporary identity formation, there lies the capacity for and lived reality of severe abuse – of language, people, of Being, and time. Advocacy for some mode of "divorce" seems vital.

Alternatively, Kristeva and Philippe Sollers, in their *Marriage as a Fine Art*, frame their own exceptional marriage "without shame or shirking, without altering the past or embellishing the present, and [steer] very clear of the flaunting of sentimental fixations and erotic fantasies so prevalent in the current 'selfie' memoir. We shall also avoid," Kristeva continues in her preface, "overstatement and the gothic pulp that covers for unspoken grief" (*Marriage*, IX). For his part, Sollers begins with a view of their wedlock "as social critique and poetic apology for freedom against every form of obscurantism" (VII). He suggests we, as readers, "try it," referring to said liberation (ibid.). The proposition is certainly compelling, particularly as it comes from a couple that has managed to remain both open (in the sense of allowing for additional lovers) and solidly, individually (and if the postcard-like photo on the book's cover is any indication, quite happily) unified. Their spoken/written portrait is bold without being sensational. It rejects sentimentality but recognizes the realities of affirmation, tenderness, and anguish. It renounces self-centeredness, self-performativity, but remains psychologically and aesthetically aware. It unfolds, in life and in print, in defiance of the corruption and foreclosure of knowledge. If this portrait, this metaphor, were assigned to the human being, the latter would most likely assume a quality of authenticity, and thus, genuine, productive, dissident alterity in a milieu too often governed by the faux individuality and vertiginous, ego-maniacal "ethics" of countless "selfies" addicted to re-presentation.

It will be fruitful to remain a bit longer within the sphere of a French (and part Bulgarian, in the case of Kristeva) sensibility by examining Badiou's ethical program and what it posits around inauthenticity and the "fine art" of contravention. In his *Ethics: An Essay on the Understanding of Evil*, Badiou identifies what he calls the common run of Western "ethical ideology" that "prevents itself from thinking the singularity of situations as such, which is the obligatory starting point of all human action" (14). This ideology is "the symptom of a disturbing conservatism" that relies on "abstract [generalities]" to determine behavior (16) and is thus directed by a modus operandi of "insularity" (33), the need to believe that one already knows how to respond to various (perhaps superficially) similar situations, and thus the impulse to maintain a sense of self as one who can withstand micro- or macro-incursions into one's "ethical" identity, one who can be consistent and recognizable. What is so immediately arresting in this argument is its calling into question the ethical orientation regarding human rights that most Westerners take for granted (along with calling it out as conservative). This is not to say that Badiou eschews human welfare and justice. Rather, his aim is to dismantle and reconstitute the *center* of ethics by removing the notion of universal laws applicable to a universal human Subject so as to allow the ethical *moment* to reveal itself as a singularity, the "truth" of a given circumstance enacted by individuals in response to the needs of this moment. Being and time are of the essence here, unfolding in what he calls the "truth-process" that is "heterogeneous to the instituted knowledges of the situation" (43). Such institutionalism obviously cuts to the heart of obscurantism by

limiting the *potentiality* of said situation, the core features of which Badiou
will distinguish as "event," "fidelity," and "truth." The first of these
designations marks the passage of an anomaly in the context of standard
opinion or "common knowledge" regarding a state of affairs. It acts as a
"hazardous, unpredictable supplement [to the situation], which vanishes
as soon as it appears" (67). "Fidelity" "amounts to a sustained
investigation of the situation, under the imperative of the event itself"
(ibid.), a way of "thinking ... the situation 'according to' the event" (41)
that may depart from any imperious, generalized, universalist ethics with
its "prevailing language and established knowledge" (43). "Truth" or "a
truth" is "the real process of fidelity to an event: that which this fidelity
produces in the situation" (42).

Why "truth?" That much exalted and maligned category that
ostensibly ends the argument, or provokes deconstructive tendencies, or
exposes its user from either camp as being over-zealous in trafficking a
dogmatic agenda – why reduce ethics to such a problematic term? The
qualifying article is doubtless crucial to Badiou's claim, the way it
jettisons certitude for solubility, "a truth" among others, always already
amenable to variation, as opposed to *the* rigid, unchanging absolute. And
yet it remains, in its adherence to the event, singular, in the sense of
signifying one thing or situation as unique, unprecedented. For Badiou, a
truth of an event encapsulates the essential requirement(s) of that event, it
"punches a 'hole' in [ethically prescribed] knowledges, it is heterogeneous
to them, but it is also the sole known source of new knowledges. We shall
say that the truth *forces* knowledges" (70). A truth that is produced by an
event, then, is *organic* to the situation relative to an "established" ethics;
hence the event's "hazardous" nature that supplements, with a kind of
neutral aggression, by generating a necessary, forceful line of thinking and
acting that "breaks" with conventional, ethical ideology. Ethics is relative.
This becomes especially clear when an event manifests a "simulacrum of
truth" (73) that in turn creates a "simulacrum of the subject" (74), the
human being who is faithful not to the event, the moment and whatever
new knowledge it may produce, but to a mere simulation. As Badiou
observes, "fidelity to a simulacrum, unlike fidelity to the event, regulates
its break with the situation ... by the closed particularity of an abstract set

(the 'Germans' or the 'Aryans'). Its invariable operation is the unending construction of this set" (ibid.).

The Aryan fantasy of the Nazis is obviously a "simulacrum of truth." As a faulty reproduction – to say the least – it produces its own hazard, the malevolent divergence from organic truth being the artificiality of its cultural mandates that invariably produce Evil. Evil, for Badiou, is ultimately "the process of a simulation of truth. And in its essence, under a name of its invention, it is terror directed at everyone" (77).[8] This powerful statement speaks to a familiar "terror," the one from the history books that decimated so much of Europe and, astonishingly, continues to rear its head in contemporary public discourse and behavior; such a terror whose familiarity – even for those who currently wield its name for the sake of their own simulated, adolescent embellishment – is itself a simulation, as all history finally is for those who weren't there. And yet we are all here, absorbing knowledge, remembering, forgetting, encountering situations that may or may not become transformative events on the personal and political stages of our lives. Individual and collective directionality may foster either adherence to what a given moment has to offer as its inherent, immediate truthfulness, or to potentially "unending" Evil that has nothing to do with mythical fire and brimstone but whose vast, earthly spectrum ranges from the bigoted, nationalistic atrocities of Nazism to the mediocrity of everyday self-absorption that prohibits access to ethical "processes of truth."

Who determines the validity of an event's "truth-process?" The obvious answer is the individual at the center of that process. The human being alone is responsible for establishing a truth, be its process one of medical ethics (does a doctor throw bureaucratic caution to the wind and apply the necessary treatment regardless of a person's inability to pay?), as in Badiou's example, any given social exchange whereby judgment, power, desire, respect, or love may be at issue, or common identity formation, the "truth" or fallaciousness of being. "The important thing," Badiou argues, "is that the power of a truth, directed at [generally unreliable] opinions, forces the pragmatic namings (the language of the objective situation) to bend and change shape upon contact with the subject-language" (82), the subjective language that informs the objective situation. The individual maintains some power of decision, of language, to construe the position of that line between mere opinion, so often at the behest of "publicness," and the integrity of a situation that calls for specific discourse or action. In the validation of a Deleuzean becoming of "subject-language," "they," as a self-ascription forcing the pragmatism (or grammaticality) of the word into a context that is best suited to one's internal experience of non-binary gender, for example, executes an essential "truth-process." On the other hand, "every attempt to impose the *total* power of a truth ruins the truth's very foundation" (our italics 84). When someone asks a stranger about preferred pronouns, there emerges an opportunity to foster authentic, conscientious reciprocity, one that honors the rich diversity of our lives by honoring alterity and further legitimizing one's innate sense of Being, perhaps enlarging another's range of thinking on the ontology of gender. It also runs the risk of compromising the exchange, its "truth's very foundation," by foregrounding a display of less-than-pragmatic identification over the immediate fact of two distinct individuals, one of whom may have no relationship to non-binary gender and thus no frame of reference for the direction of the exchange. "This is who I am" by way of introduction can operate as a mechanism of self-empowerment *or* power over discourse and thus over the other. Of course, the "total power" of an exchange and its "truth" reveals whatever it needs to reveal in our communications, the loss, gain, or radicalization of reciprocity. Terror arises when one invents a damning name *for another*, that reduces and essentializes, that sows seeds of domination. If there is terror to be found in the social comportment of the individual seeking merely to remain faithful to a performed alterity over and above the empathy and capacity for listening essential to generating or discovering affinity (which is obviously what we all desire in our interlocutors), however psychologically and somatically integral that alterity may be, it is probably more akin to the gradual loss of authenticity and the horrific realization that "subject-language" will not ultimately fill the void (or overcome death, for that matter). For better and for worse, the horror of extinction that pierces the body, that gets inside and haunts, as opposed to terror whose sole purpose is to humiliate or destroy in a flash, does not discriminate according to identity.[9]

Badiou's alternative to "ethical ideology" entails a radical reformulation of ethics that merges "the imperative to 'Keep Going!' [i.e., Lacan's advocacy for remaining faithful to the Real], resources of discernment (do not fall for simulacra), of courage, (do not give up), and of moderation (do not get carried away to the extremes of Totality)" (91). It may be said that most people have the aptitude for qualities such as discernment, courage, and moderation given the fact that super-egoic civilization would crumble without them, though this claim obscures the massive challenge of exercising the most basic conditions for their full realization. In our utter dependence on technology and its countless screens that, one way or another, reify identity, our desperate efforts to constitute ourselves – in language, in yoga poses, in the relentless pursuit of recognition and the first-to-the-top mountaineering often required in corporate or academic lifestyles, in roles as individualized participants in unapologetically homogenous pop culture, and in the confines of "safe spaces" that, in their regulated physicality, serve the crucial function of eliminating or containing prejudice, while in the context of interpersonal encounters may inoculate us against the real and healthy abjection – in all of our performativity, how capable, really, are we of evading the seductions of simulacra, practicing fidelity to "truth-processes" and the eventual expressions of our lives? The encounter between Julia Craye and Fanny Wilmont is at once safe and sublimely dangerous.

It is relatively easy to target inauthenticity. Inaugurating a program for the development and nurture of authenticity, however, strikes at the core of the modern self and must tease out uncomfortable questions that have a way of burrowing into prickly spaces of the comfortable existence, the cocksure or diffident self-absorption of a person. Assuming the reality of isolated "events" in our lives, those moments of being stirred to passion by a fascination, a devotion to some phenomenon, Badiou locates himself, and by extension his reader, in distinctive relation to an inspired "there:" "I am altogether present there, linking my component elements via that *excess beyond myself* induced by the passing through me of a truth. But as a result, I am also suspended, broken, annulled; dis-interested. For I cannot, within the fidelity to fidelity that defines ethical consistency, take an interest in myself, and thus pursue my own interests" (49-50). There is life – grand, horrifying, stimulating, soothing, hazardous, artful – happening beyond the multitude of likes and dislikes, the dramas of personhood, that unfolds into immediate, ephemeral truths. The irony that is so very difficult to grasp in lived experience is that fidelity to this richly disorganized choreography essentially translates into selflessness, or at least the absence of a dogmatically insistent self. The "truth" or depth of *jouissance*, of pleasure or personal or cultural revolution, is only accessible via self-effacement. It is here where Badiou stands apart from Heidegger, Deleuze, and indeed, most representatives of 20th century French post-structuralism, to the degree that he collapses pure being into the set theory of mathematics. Badiou's sense of "Being," according to Peter Hallward, "cannot be intuited (Bergson), phrased (Lyotard), or actualized (Deleuze). At most, being can be inscribed, subtractively, without presence, in the formal presentation of mathematical writing" (*Badiou* 61). For Badiou, Being is best characterized as a complete neutrality, a "'nothing' or absence of positivity that is the medium of pure thought," as opposed to "unadulterated" affirmation (60). While we are inclined to take the road relatively more traveled, that endless stretch of highway on which one may feel and intuit – "clear," "let be" – one's way toward the immediacy of truthfulness, there is clearly no truth of being without nothingness, a fact of which subversive literature, and horror in particular, is acutely aware. Badiou's wariness concerning Heideggerian affirmation and Sartrean "anguish" notwithstanding, he still arrives at an invaluable ethics of selflessness.

This relinquishment of self, however, does not equate to disempowerment or de-legitimization. It is not a matter of silencing what one holds dear as the rudiments that make me *me* in some kind of wrestling match with oppressive interiority, or at the hands of others who would rob one's voice, though silence doubtless plays a significant role in what we are identifying as authenticity. As Mahon O'Brien explains, Heidegger "alludes to the possibility of a less debased existence" that "involves the interplay between humans and what calls to humans" (*Heidegger* 110). It is easy to understand why some interpreters of *Being and Time* locate a nod, or perhaps an ebullient arm wave, to mysticism in terms of the "what" that calls, a perspective that is not entirely out of line with our own project but one that may nevertheless be bracketed in light of Heidegger's clarification, however obscure it might remain. The "what" for Heidegger is "conscience" that "has the character of an appeal to *Dasein* by calling it to its ownmost potentiality-for-Being-its-Self" (*Being* 314). In Badiou's terms, this potential is for immersion in a subversive or otherwise transformative "event," as opposed to quotidian wandering in "publicness." For Heidegger, the call is equally radical to the degree that it operates "against our expectations and even against our will. On the other hand, the call does not come from someone else who is with me in the world. The call comes *from* me and yet *from beyond me and over me*" (320). The latter claim has the paradoxical quality of a Lovecraft story or a horror film by legendary director Lucio Fulci, whom we will have occasion to reference again later; but of note here is the notion that the "beyond' is not necessarily metaphysical but an aspect of the self that is less confined by the "they," at once nascent and, like the Freudian unconscious, ever present. O'Brien understands this beyond as an "uncanniness" (*Heidegger* 39) that "ultimately lurks in the shape of a silent summons behind all of our activities waiting to be listened to. It is that silent unease that seems to track us incessantly but which we in turn drown out with myriad diversions, losing ourselves in the everyday world of publicness" (40). Outside the harrowing presence of grotesque zombies or other creatures, we are not too far removed from the horror genre here. Unease appears when diversions fail, when inauthenticity becomes apparent in crevices of the mind and body, as though we are being watched through internal windows of our own construction when the noise of culture and manufactured identity can no longer drown out the "silence." It is in such a state, it may be fair to presume, that the "call" is loudest.

This is not to say that there is no work to be done. The "call" in fact requires active (or actualized) "listening" on the part of *Dasein*, which, under ordinary circumstances, "[loses] itself in the publicness and idle talk of the 'they,'" and thus "fails to hear its own Self in listening to the they-self" (*Being* 315). This normative, compromised version of *Dasein*, of course, is hardly limited to individuals in perpetual search of recognition and a dubiously individualized persona to match, or to right wing tribal fantasies, or to the fundamentalist Christian awkwardly attempting to square an infantile notion of love with rabid support of an infantile president. On the contrary, it rears its head in the faculty meeting or dinner party when a professor holds forth with no regard for conversational decorum, espousing opinions, however elevated, that Badiou might call "representations without truth, the anarchic debris of circulating knowledge" (*Ethics* 50), or when the actor continues performing off-stage and off-screen, or in the case of the average human being whose vocabulary (and by extension, the capacity for critical thought) becomes increasingly limited to pop jargon, all of which coalesces around the incessant, cavernous conjunction "like," or its equivalent in non-English languages. Habits of speech, self-representation, and ideological affiliation are hard to break. Doing so necessitates the cultivation of what Heidegger calls "resoluteness [that] brings the Self right into its current concernful Being-alongside what is ready-to-hand, and pushes it into solicitous Being with Others" (*Being* 344). So while the call to conscience does not emanate directly from other persons, it *regards* them, from what Silverman refers to as a productive, conscientious, active form of idealization, when one exercises the will for authenticity and recognizes the capacities of others to exercise the same will.[10] While Badiou's being-neutrality may have a productive kinship to *Dasein* as tabula rasa or Schopenhauer's "blissful repose of nothing" (*Essential* 10), here we find ourselves more aligned with the Deluzian potential for actualization of the immediate space of *Dasein*, for intentionality, resolution, and active compassion, or love.

To be clear, then, this will is inverse to domination; Heidegger's sense of will as a mode of "letting" the latter unfold (rather than enforcing or subjecting it) in *Introduction to Metaphysics*, in tandem with his claim that "the primordial Being of *Dasein* itself [is] care" (*Being* 169), suggests a relationality that reverberates with both Silverman's ideality and, tangentially, Badiou's "truth-process." That said, care must first be given to the conditionality of being a social being, much as a parent is instructed to don the airplane oxygen mask before placing it on a child so as to increase the chances of their mutual survival. In other words, until one becomes relatively free of the simulacra that populate the socialization process of "enframing," events precipitating fidelity to circumstantial truths will quickly deteriorate into mere situations dominated by the larger, abstract willfulness of "publicness." Heidegger's project is finally the advancement of a philosophical and, invariably, a psychological practice that emerges in concert with the "world." In acknowledging this practice, "we are thereupon summoned to hope in the growing light of the saving power. How can this happen? Here and now in the little things, that we may foster the saving power in its increase. This includes holding always before our eyes the extreme danger" (*Basic* 338). The danger, of course, issues from what O'Brien observes as the "impending triumph of Enframing [that] threatens to seclude us completely from the locus of originary truth" (*Heidegger* 112). If read through Badiou, the "originary" nature of a truth is the starting point for non-ideological ethics, the source or ground upon which the truth may be brought to bear on Being both "beyond and over me;" it is the quotidian material of a life, the "little things" (other people, situations) that hold out the promise of empowerment for one willing to shut out, or at least muffle the noise, in order to listen with care.

But the "little things" can be tenacious in their volume and urgency. They can either anchor us in authenticity, by virtue of our acute attention to their machinations in the larger field of awareness, and to the potential events in which they become manifest, or they can slowly chip away at Being to the point of there being no "there" in the statue of the person, neither the Hegelian presence of *Dasein* nor Heidegger's aptitude for care. O'Brien's contention that "at any given moment and *at our most authentic* we are an attempt to synthesize and fuse these myriad disparate elements into a coherent, authentic whole" (44) harkens, we suspect unknowingly, to the foundational, psychological structure of humanity according to G.I. Gurdjieff, for whom the self is a predominately uncontrolled amalgamation of "I's." "Every thought, every feeling, every sensation, every desire, every like and every dislike is an 'I,'" claims Gurdjieff's most prominent student, P.D. Ouspensky, who continues: "These 'I's' are not connected and are not co- ordinated in any way. Each of them depends on the change in external circumstances, and on the change of impressions" (*Psychology* 14). Each "I," generally provoked rather than exerted or consciously wielded, *reacts* rather than *responds* to the world (that in turn informs thought, feeling, sensation, etc.), a key distinction signifying immersion in "publicness" or the Heideggerian "Being-in-the-world" of care and coherence, respectively. From Gurdjieff/Ouspensky's perspective, every "little thing" is deceitful so long as its illusory contribution to a more or less static identity or personality is not seen through. Along with the advocacy of Nissargadatta, theirs is not a world-hating psychology; rather, it attempts to "synthesize and fuse these myriad, disparate elements into a coherent, authentic" person who is not constantly at the mercy of the fallacious, "levelling down" tendencies "of Being for the 'they,'" the self-serving demands of the world against which Heidegger warns. Achieving said synthesis, we would argue, amounts not only to authentic selfhood but to genuine, dissident alterity in the context of (Western) culture that so often promotes highly spurious, prepackaged brands of ultimately self-promoting "otherness."

If this sounds excessively harsh or too generalized, we might consider the degree to which basic actualities of situations have become hollowed out. Donald Trump's hard-to-forget "alternative facts" and the cultural abortion of far right fantasies they have promulgated are surely the quintessential example of current, inauthentic alterity that reacts rather than responds to situational conflict on the basis of a strident "Don't Tread On Me" affectation that is itself centered around the strangely victimized, isolated sensibility of predominantly white, lower to middle-class America.[11] Such brazen absurdity is doubtless the symptom of a broader sophistry in the cultural landscape of discourse and visual self-representation that has paradoxically manifested anarchic relationships to being centered around ideological monoliths of "Truth" in every crevice of the political spectrum. The real threat of this free play with *ethical truths* is, of course, to genuine alterity. For example, as the befuddled, literalist proclivities of fundamentalism give the larger category of Christianity (including its mystical and other subversive orientations) a truly pathological name, a *reactionary* galvanization of social justice (as opposed to a powerful, modern, all-inclusive, *responsive* mode) born of the current milieu wherein relativity of truth or facts marries the "ethical ideology" of simulacra arguably risks corrupting the immense importance, truthfulness, and potentiality of various progressive movements. In other words, in the particular "events" of social justice, it behooves us to consider the degree to which the "Me" of Don't Tread On Me may permeate *any* collective effort to combat oppression and violence. To what extent is the "me" capable of pushing against the grain of reaction by recognizing and remaining faithful to a "truth-process," thereby honoring the immediacy and thoughtfulness of ethical response bereft of raw greed or castigating, puritanical moralism? Practicing such recognition and fidelity as an ethics is a form of productive alterity in its eschewal of populist identity-politics. It is a genuinely alternative, ethical practice that repudiates the "ideology of insularity" at the same time that it acts (to question government power beyond self-serving, adolescent patriotism, to foster integrity in race relations, or to call out the grotesque male who forces a woman, in the words of the Fugazi lyric, to "suffer [his] interpretation of what it is to be a man" ["Suggestion"]) according to a truth that "forces" knowledge and thus "breaks" with compromised, totalizing tendencies that Badiou calls evil.

The distance between the force and violence of patriarchy and the "forcing" of knowledge in a truth-process is vast. This chasm, as it happens, is actually crucial to understanding the flexibility of language in adapting to an ethic of truths and, indeed, in responding to a call of conscience the aim of which is authenticity. Even in light of discursive (and its correlate of physical) violence, concession might be made to the power of aggressive, traditionally "male" language to undermine instances of terror and evil. Is addiction – to screens, to "self-strutting," to the Lacanian *moi* – breakable without force, the kind that, in the wrong hands or mouths, dehumanizes? Is such concession not indicative of fertile, benevolent sacrifice in the face of pervasive inauthenticity? Is the suffering inherent to sacrifice not inevitable in an age of – to be only slightly melodramatic – cultural and mental enslavement? Gurdjieff is an important figure here to the extent that his psychological framework aligns in certain crucial ways with Heidegger and Badiou but operates as indispensable actualization, or *practice*, beyond thought processes, however valuable these may be. [12] For Gurdjieff, consciousness is not merely the ego that navigates and interprets the world – often erroneously, through the many filters of that world – it is that which cultivates access to "truth-processes" via its depth of attention to a multitude of phenomena internal and external to the person. The Gurdjieffian system demands tremendous sacrifice in the sense of movement (the practices are physical as well as psychological) but more importantly, in terms of what it refers to as personality (as opposed to "essence" that requires Herculean maintenance), or identity, that field of being that is largely bereft of Heideggerian self-analysis due to its potential for artificiality and reliance on preconceived ideas that may have little or nothing to do with the "truth" of a situation. The "forcing" of essence over personality, in challenging, liminal moments, then, is the forging of "events" that arise at the cost of the fantasies one entertains about one's self.

Gurdjieff refers to his teaching and its body of practices as "esoteric Christianity" by virtue of its focus on such seemingly mundane qualities as attention and manners of emotional, intellectual, and physical expenditure as these relate to divine Otherness. Terry Eagleton's *Radical Sacrifice*, though ultimately concerned with the cultural treatment of disenfranchised others from a Marxist perspective, is also deeply interested in what Gurdjieff would call self-development by way of sacrifice. Their visions are different, to be sure, in so far as the philosopher proper is far more invested in material conditions, i.e., the world and its soap operatic politics, than the spiritual teacher for whom self-sacrifice attends to a larger scope of the human condition. However, both attempt to hack away at the "false consciousness" of an individual whose illusory self-knowledge severely limits his or her capacity for authenticity and thus access to "events" that coalesce around blossoming truths. Strangely, despite his apparent appreciation for Badiou, Eagleton claims that the former's ethics "have no truck with anything as distastefully mundane as pleasure, virtue, interests, happiness or self-realization" (*Radical* 94). In addition to the obvious fact of Badiou's 2009 publication *In Praise of Love*, we might point to his situational focal points of politics, science, art, and love (*Ethics* 45) as examples of Badiou's awareness of material circumstances beyond abstract philosophy. That said, this glaring oversight highlights Eagleton's distaste for theory (particularly that of the postmodern variety) bereft of social consequence, an orientation that further obliges him to political commitment. Subversive, liminal experience, yes, as long as it serves the betterment of pervasive, lived, *cultural* experience in the real. By extension, he is also at odds with Heidegger's "prerogative of the spiritually patrician few, not a condition of which *Das Man* – his contemptuous term for the deluded masses – is remotely capable" (*Radical* 100). We're not convinced that this "ordinary Nazi" deemed himself the arbiter of the elect, so to speak, though Eagleton's argument once again indicates an eschewal of transformational insight or practice without a clearly designated social function. Moreover, it elides a key aspect of the contemporary real: cultivation of and addiction to personality/identity traits by dint of technology and social media are inherently inclined toward states of delusion. An online profile, for example, is obviously and fundamentally delusional to the degree that it conceals, more or less unconsciously, those aspects of lived experience that one fails to advertise. Contemporary *Das Man* is in part a collective of serial, compulsive, self-promotional advertisers, and in this lived reality it is crucial not to overlook Ouspensky's contention that the "injustice" of a Heideggerian prerogative, for example, has as much to do with the fact that many people are too distracted and simply have no desire to prepare for and engage in the work of authenticity or Being as it does with the undeniably oppressive cultural factors of class, race, gender, sexual orientation, etc.

Where Eagleton dovetails with the project at hand is in his observation that "those who are already camped out on the far edge of history, taking their cue from the future and living in imminent expectation of death," exercise "self-dispossession [that] takes the form of giving to others, not of some solitary existential self-expenditure" (*Radical* 105). As we have argued, solitude is surely a requirement for the kind of self-examination necessary to authentic relationality – precisely to the extent that such subjective space is where a process of coming to terms with death must ultimately unfold.[13] Needless to say, death eradicates personal identity. To reach the far edge of both contemplation and a truthful, ethical generosity without the baggage of "self-*possession*," however, demands that one make the rigorous journey to this exotic destination. What does it look like? How does one get there? It is unlikely that Google Maps will reveal the trajectory. How rigorous it might be probably depends on the magnitude of one's identification with a persona, begun between the ages of six to eighteen months while struggling before the mirror reflection, if Lacan is on point, and possibly earlier.[14]

Awareness of mortality would seem instrumental to diminishing the power of the mask-like, Jungian persona, the literal, inevitable disintegration of which happens figuratively when priorities of attention and value are shifted away from "publicness." As Eagleton puts it, "death and monstrosity are akin in exposing the provisional nature of social forms" (164), an unveiling that may distance one from those Heidegger refers to as "the pressing throng of beings unthought in their essence" (*Basic* 235) – hence the invaluable monstrosity – as much as this unveiling produces the ground from which one may foster relatively authentic relations. The result of such disintegration ideally assumes "a positive form of de-differentiation, one that acknowledges that individuals are alike in their being-towards-death and political vulnerability" while being "[distinguished] from a murderous disregard for individual difference" (Eagleton, *Radical* 157). To what degree is one (the professor who holds forth for a living, the non-binary gender activist, the politician, for example) what Eagleton might call a necessary cultural scapegoat who generates societal disorder and thus transforms the conventional order of society in a manner that is reflective of an ethical "truth-process?" In so far as one is monstrous rather than murderous, a vocal without screaming champion of being "on the far edge of history," a conscious subject of death and consequently a proponent of multiplicity in life, one is capable of sacrificing the superfluous (the chatter, argumentative and otherwise, the opinions, the brute egotism whose face is a mere guise), for the "call of conscience."

Genuine, productive alterity is neither fashionable nor impervious to the ravages of time, time whose future it knows is death. It listens, intuitively, to ephemeral but momentous, immediate truths and grounds itself in events that demand respect and alertness to Otherness. It is highly unpopular in its authenticity that nevertheless yields respectful, compassionate, ethical relations. It has absolutely nothing to do with Nazism or that peculiar, ideological theater where right and left proclivities merge in (virtual) public bouts of ecstatic Puritanism, what

Schopenhauer might call the "burlesque distortion" (*Essential* 12) of what is potentially authentic in the individual and the community. It is spiritual in its manner of self-divestment and awareness of more than meets the eye without falling prey to the literalism of fundamentalist religiosity. Dissident alterity is artful in the sense not of contrivance but of disciplined attention devoted to the furnishing of a life whose being-towards-death inspires creative, aesthetic impulses. It acknowledges the merit of "tragic art for which one has to be hauled through this desert of the Real in order to recognize the arbitrariness of one's precious scale of values, and so to emerge with some more authentic view of what is to be prized" (Eagleton, *Radical* 166). Though Eagleton is prone to criticize the liminal as yet another spurious product of postmodern theory, his evocation of distant locations, remote edges, vast deserts, suggests an imperative around the threshold or in-between spaces of *real* life, the quotidian, sometimes tragic milieus or "little things" through which, paradoxically, one may tap into modes of being outside, or on the border of both the "they" and the "they-self." His figurative language is also indicative of poiesis, the at once simple and tremendously complex act of making something that may very well have no utilitarian use and thus automatically situates the maker in a position of alterity against the grain of (certainly American) garden-variety pragmatism. The creation and consumption of art, of course, is the example *par excellence* of a tipping point, perhaps a liminal space between what Eagleton observes as "the imagination [as] a form of self-dispossession, seizing selflessly on its object" (20), and the identity of an artist whose self-regard may tower above the actual quality or thoughtfulness of the maker's productions.

In her *The Threshold of the Visible World*, Silverman foregrounds the centrality of representation, be it visual or discursive, that informs subjectivity and power relations. Consequently, she argues, "it can only be through the creation and circulation of alternative images and words that [one] can be given access to new identificatory coordinates" (81). The driving force of her revolutionary project, then, is the implementation of "ceaseless textual intervention" (ibid.).[15] There is a curious parallel here (that would have been far less apparent in 1997 when Silverman's book appeared) with the efforts of non-binary gender activists to shift language with the intent of reconstituting the personal and cultural parameters of identity. In both cases, the projects are revolutionary in their efforts to strike with Badiouian force at the very nexus of individual and collective thought and behavior. A key difference, however, may lie in the quality or sophistication of the intervening "text" and the intentionality of its promulgation. Is it feeding insular or collective narcissism as a kind of power-grabbing, Althusserian interpolation ("hey you – don't tread on me!") or, less cynically, is its circulation attempting to cultivate a truthful ethics that neither repudiates nor subsumes the other, that endeavors to contact shared humanity – our common mortality – while appreciating and advocating for difference? Silverman examines works such as Marcel Duchamp's *Étant donnés,* Cindy Sherman's *Untitled Film Stills*, and Isaac Julien's *Looking for Langston* as examples of radical, interventionist texts seeking to re-orient ideological perspective, all of which are necessarily avant-garde in orientation and require critical engagement. This aesthetically transgressive sensibility is a compelling model for any "textual intervention" to the extent that it is grounded in an aim beyond the self, however much said self may benefit. The visibly and incontestably self-absorbed "alt-right" is a recent, radicalized "text," as are "alt facts," though neither of these phenomena exhibit the informed unorthodoxy of an avant-garde mode of Being. Even INCEL, the disparate community of males blaming women for their "involuntary celibacy" in an astoundingly violent, collective performance of stunted adolescence and 21st century misogyny, has its own terminology to designate self *and other*. In each instance, people are struggling, in the larger cultural context, to foster an identity, to institute a self whose condition of lack may be perceived as originating in the public's disavowal or abandonment more so, it would appear, than in an inherent nothingness or impermanence, acknowledgement of which cultivates the possibility of Being over seeming. Hence the domineering interpolation, the incessant naming and categorizing of contemporary identity-inscribed discourse. The underlying premise of gender designations (this is what I am, naturally, constitutionally), among other substantial traits, obviously distinguishes it from neo-Nazism and childish, toxic male theatrics – as long as it is resolutely, productively attuned to figurative death.

That said, Silverman's Lacanian approach to Being "underscores the reluctance of the subject to arrive at a conscious acceptance of his or her "being-for-death" – his or her unwillingness, that is, to confront the nothingness or *manqué-à-être* out of which desire issues. The ego represents the primary vehicle of this denial, that through which the subject procures for him or herself an illusory plenitude" (62). The struggle to fill a primal gap with delusional coherence (what Gurdjieff calls "personality") is common to every person, from the privileged, white, heterosexual male to the Black person who identifies somewhere on the overlapping LGBTQIA+ spectrum and confronts as much bigotry in the 21st century as a civil rights activist in 1960s America. Any demographic, we would argue, may benefit from the proclamation of another avant-gardist for whom nothingness is central to both Being and art: "I have nothing to say/ and I am saying it (Cage, *Silence* 109). Composer John Cage's comment doubtless asserts the aesthetic act of creating and circulating alternative texts (in his case, transgressive music and poetry) but does so without a self, or to be more specific, without the need to decree an identity.[16] It is this capacity that is especially apposite for one navigating the balance between giving voice, standing firm for social justice, and extracting the power and perspicacity of non-Being from Being, discerning the existential nothingness that is in need of no plenitude beyond attention to a "truth-process." From the standpoint of nothingness as a figurative blank canvas, or an Eagletonian, distant landscape, it is the central precondition to what we would characterize as sincere alterity that is acutely aware of humanity's mutual ground in mortality and, equally important, the fact that the severe limits death places on life must finally be incorporated into the many situations and events of that life in solitary confrontation and contemplative practice. The deceptive surrogate for such authenticity, of course, is any form of populist, tribal alterity, the subversiveness of which quickly becomes subsumed, in "ethico-ideological" fashion, by the mechanisms of egocentric, dysfunctional groupthink.

Giorgio Agamben's notion of the "Muselmann," a person essentially bereft of cultural status or dignity, is a genuine form of alterity. Such a one is "least human, because culture is constitutive of our humanity; most human, because those plundered of their cultural identities have no claim on their fellows but a human or universal one" (Eagleton 156). The homeless, the exceedingly off-kilter, the exceptionally marginal that inhabit rural and urban environments alike, function at the base level of survival, with or without help from others. More commonly, individuals of low-grade status or otherwise socially compromised identities (often for reasons beyond their immediate control) remind others of our mutual animality in death, if not in the vulnerability and hazardous desire of life, as can subversive texts that direct one's attention to abjection.

Marc Augé's *No Fixed Abode*, for example, follows a homeless man through his journaling practice in a manner that allows the reader to celebrate, perhaps, his final commitment to alterity despite the option to return to a relatively bourgeois and semi-conjugal existence after having found love. The protagonist of Dominique Fabre's *The Waitress Was New*, a lonely, middle-aged barman living and working in a peripheral suburb of Paris, is surrounded by the lives and mini-dramas of others but lives predominantly in his daily, quotidian observations and anxieties around aging and death. Nothing particularly novel occurs in this text outside the ordinary life of a man contemplating death and belonging.[17] Heidegger's insistence on the import of "little things" seizing our attention for the sake of being-awareness comes into focus when an "event" of literature, for example, interjects the real into our daily routines of what he considers "dangerously" automated preoccupations and behaviors. "Might not an adequate look into what enframing is," he asks, "bring the upsurgence of the saving power into appearance" (Heidegger, *Basic* 334)? In this sense, the value of "ceaseless textual intervention" lies in its revealing of both compromised, sometimes toxic modes of being, and the potential remedy – through example in form or content – for a less than enriching life. Whether the subversion is horrifying, as it must be on some level, like Kafka's "axe for the frozen sea inside us," or quietly, slyly hermeneutic with regard to the "little things" that glitch and perturb in the everyday, it exercises a kind of homeopathy, poisoning the artificial tranquility of a surface with insight essential to health, well-being, and depth. The quality or adequacy of one's "look" depends, of course, on authentic, resolute, aesthetic engagement, a "letting" the "upsurgence" unfurl with minimal obstruction by personality. Art requires sacrifice.

It also necessitates questioning. Heidegger's fundamental question in *Introduction to Metaphysics* is concerned with the basic fact of existence, of beings rather than a void. One obvious response as to why we exist at all places the philosophical and psychological revelation of Being at the center of this existence. From an ethical, and less abstract standpoint, we might marry Being and belonging, a marriage not unlike that of Kristeva and Sollers in which alterity is allowed to co-exist with civil structure and union. To return to Etchison, the skeptical son, witness to his father's aging decline, will feed his father's obsession with the supernatural in a narrative turn that is at once deceptive and poignant, though not before sacrificing that skepticism for the sake of sincere inquiry ("maybe there is a key to some kind of truth in the asking, in the very questioning itself") and familial intimacy. Despite protestations of his morbidity, there is something in Heidegger's prerogative that is clearly attuned to human potential, including its flair for fraternity. With regards to the humanism that both Heidegger and Badiou interrogate, the former asserts that it "is opposed because it does not set the *humanitas* of the human being high enough (233-34). We are not limited to the human prostrate before identity-politics, trendy presentations of self, and the technological media that stand above and within that self. Heidegger foresees, in the late 1940s and 50s, a point when "the frenziedness of technology may entrench itself everywhere to such an extent that someday, throughout everything technological, the essence of technology may unfold essentially in the propriative event of truth" (340). Essence may be understood here as that aspect of a phenomenon that exceeds its human abuse. There is in technology, then, as in countless modern or postmodern preoccupations (civil rights, gender identity, equitable political relations, conscientious governance, to name a few), what Heidegger calls a "revealing" of truth, that which is naturally malleable and adaptive to a given situation or event. We may be loath to concede the philosopher's hierarchy of truth, though even a cursory glance at contemporary Western culture exposes the ominous, stultifying "frenziedness" identified in his prediction and warrants consideration of a "higher" mode of being.

So we use the means we have at our disposal to address our mutual impediments. This study will continue in the tradition of Silverman and others in its proposal of imperative textual intervention. Perhaps the core of such an enterprise, however, is significantly larger – and more intimate – than aesthetics. Etchison's story exemplifies the slow-burning danger of insularity, blinkered thought and conduct, along with humanity's aptitude for transcending its isolationism and its borders, be they pointedly misanthropic or unrealistically, neurotically "social" in digital ether. What finally emerges from the horror story is a feeling and an act of love that requires, in addition to myriad gestures and reflections in an ongoing truth-process, a pronounced degree of what we have spotlighted as selflessness. Badiou goes so far as to say, not without a sense of humor, that love is a form of "minimal communism" (*In Praise* 90) in so far as it prioritizes a collective over self-interest and thus provokes "thinking that is created against all order, against the powerful order of the law" (79). The latter is indeed powerful in a culture of addicts and sycophants, among other, far more pleasant qualities. And yet the range of Being may come into sharp visibility when countering such inauthenticity with a state of being in love beyond the self, wherein, as Slavoj Žižek illustrates, "I am nothing, but as it were a Nothing aware of itself, a Nothing paradoxically made rich through the very awareness of its lack" (quoted, Eagleton, *Radical* 177). It is such wealth that this study seeks to examine and enable.

Chapter 2

– The Spiritual Life of Trees and Beyond: On Algernon Blackwood and Charles L. Grant

The Arboretum of Algernon Blackwood

Sex and death occupy similar positions in Western – and particularly American – culture. They both commandeer, in equal parts, the collective space of mass entertainment despite (and probably as a reaction to) the fact that they remain essentially taboo. We see them, representationally, on multiple screens on what is for many a daily basis, and we may hear about them in popular music, but contextualizing them in casual or even intellectual discourse, where there exists an expectation of more or less taking them seriously, can result in what Erving Goffman calls a "definitional disruption" (*Presentation* 7) in the social exchange. To correct the unwelcome intrusion, one may employ a diversionary or buffering "protective practice" (ibid.) in order to restore order and comfort. One laughs, changes the subject, or demurs. When confronted in explicit, non-romanticized terms, the public, discursive spaces of sex and death tend not to be deemed safe. Introducing a novel with explicit sexuality or extended passages that dwell on the gore or pathos of death in a low-level, university literature course in the US, at least, can bear this condition out, revealing the distinctly American conservatism at the core of many lives. Death is not merely enshrouded by desire and temptation as the fundamentalist markers of sin that might haunt a classroom; in its literal form it is a definitive end to shopping, tweeting, and the vicarious pleasures of performing an identity. There are as many ways to circumvent the prohibitions around sexuality as there are people who desire intimacy, while death is that tacitly, if not unconsciously acknowledged but repulsive inevitability that is best left to an indeterminate future.

It is no surprise, then, that the centrality of "Being-toward-death" in Heidegger's philosophy strikes some readers as excessively morbid. Nevertheless, "in this darkening" that is Western culture's feverish embargo on incorporating mortality – and thus sacrifice – into its lived, collective life for the sake of bringing depth and dignity to that experience, we may lose something that is precious beyond our identities in abnegating Heidegger's approach to Being and time. O'Brien states that "far ... from an oppressively bleak picture, Heidegger is depicting a transformation that has little or nothing to do with the coffin-ripe, macabre preoccupations of some individual *Dasein* close to death but everything to do with liberation from paltry preoccupations and insignificant worries" (*Heidegger* 59). Eagleton makes a comparable claim: "Genuine enjoyment must involve a certain consciousness of itself, as mindless immersion does not. It is the mindlessly immersed who will find death a terror, not those self-aware enough to keep one steady eye on it in the midst of their pleasures" (*Radical* 87). Mr. Sanderson, painter and lover of trees in Algernon Blackwood's "The Man Whom the Trees Loved," receives a reaction in line with that which Heidegger provokes regarding the artist's adoration and wisdom concerning all things arborescent. "His sensitiveness" is deemed "morbid" by another who, heretically, cannot tell the difference between one tree and another (Blackwood 213). As the story unfolds, it becomes clear that the legitimate heir to the macabre belongs to this "heretic," making Blackwood's story a cautionary tale that in fact utilizes a "coffin-ripe" existence immersed in the "publicness" of puritanical ideology to illustrate the power of "genuine enjoyment."

Phillips has written elsewhere about what he calls literary and filmic "critical horror" that "is aligned, overtly, or more commonly, peripherally, with critical theory as a philosophical and exploratory approach to culture, as well as with the notion of 'imperative' in one meaning of 'critical'" (*T.E.D. Klein* 2). Increasingly, the latter definition would seem to shift the focus of O'Brien's statement above in terms of the need to foreground the macabre in a homeopathic manner for the sake of cultural diagnosis. Hence Phillips's study that posits a certain exigency around horror as filtered through Frankfurt School Marxism, horror that "manifests its seemingly malign, critical vision as an urgent response to aspects of human experience in desperate need of the kind of interrogation that can meet its subject matter with comparable or exceeding phantasmagoria, with spectral absurdity even, that horror alone can provide" (ibid.). From this perspective, critical horror is aligned with Eagleton's vision of authenticity and is distinct from that of "the cynic or nihilist ... who folds death back into life, allowing the prospect of the end of value to sabotage the current reality of it" (*Radical* 166). The critical horror text looks squarely into death (and sometimes sex) in a way that mirrors our often shoddy handling of its reality and, indeed, of the real in general, but does so with a conscience, as though attempting to fold life back into death. In this sense, horror is intrinsically subversive.

"The Man Whom the Trees Loved" is especially adroit at achieving this delicate balance of menace, cultural critique, and life-affirmation. It is also united with Heidegger's environmentalism to the extent that both writers value natural resources according not only to their surface beauty but to a complicated essence that exists beyond this surface. As O'Brien observes, "the essence of something, Heidegger insists, is not the same as the thing itself. In thinking of the essence of a tree 'that which pervades every tree, as tree, is not itself a tree that can be encountered among all other trees'" (*Heidegger* 94). Hence Sanderson's caustic response to a secondary character who mistakenly presumes that all trees are the same: he comments on the predictably generic nature of the character's husband, as one among many bourgeois husbands. Her attitude is indicative of a mode of Being removed from Being, and specifically from the time and essence of nature, that is responsible for what Blackwood calls, in relation to the natural world, the "terror of devastating Man" (216), that produces "woodcutters ... those who take the life of trees ... you see, a race of haunted men" (231). Though Blackwood's central critique targets another woman, the wife of a man slowly coming into his own sense of authenticity after having met Sanderson, whose paintings of trees not surprisingly manage to capture their essence. Over the course of the story, Mrs. Bittacy becomes haunted. Hardly a logger, her crime is simply having no relationship with the forest behind their home. She is completely neutral on the subject that begins to captivate her husband, David, to the point of his ultimately paying little attention to her. This is not to say that Sophia Bittacy is without her own ingrained preoccupations; as the "daughter of an evangelical clergyman," her central vice is a "religious mania" that she has yet to "outgrow" (217-218). Consequently, she perceives something deeply unsettling in the forest, and in those whose kinship to its trees she cannot fathom or incorporate into her religious ideology that draws a clear distinction between humanity and an anthropomorphic deity. By the time she ventures into the wooded density behind their home to locate her husband, she resembles Hawthorne's Young Goodman Brown, a puritan whose own forest adventure motivated by unambiguous dualism finally transforms his piety into profound neurosis and alienation. During visits from the painter, whose conversation David finds increasingly illuminating, she is always "on her guard" (222), partly out of fear of the incomprehensible vocabulary used by the two men: "Beelzebub lay hid among too many syllables" (228), she thinks. She even sneers at the mention of a socialist, leaving the contemporary reader to ponder where she might have stood on the subject of Bernie Sanders relative to the unabashed monstrosity that assumed command of the US presidency in 2016. In fact, Mrs. Bittacy, like many a zealot, is haunted long before a man whom the trees love enters their lives.

Sanderson finds value in the darkness of the forest by night, when the trees reveal their livingness. Such is his Heideggerian "morbidity." And his Badiouian love. In his painting, "he kept to trees, wisely following an instinct that was guided by love" (211), an intuition that makes itself known to David in the form of "the 'something' trees possess that make them know I'm there when I stand close and watch. I suppose," he continues, "I felt it then [when he and his wife were courting] because I was in love, and love reveals life everywhere" (214). Sanderson will go on to observe how the trees' "love for you, their 'awareness' of your personality and your presence involves the idea of winning you – across the border – into themselves – into their world of living" (227). Crucially, the revelatory endearment only occurs in the context of a corresponding "consciousness" to the forest's dynamism, one that has developed through its understanding of complex ideas and its willingness to literally and figuratively cross borders into a greater sense of Being. And yet, Blackwood does not categorically limit love to a hierarchical structure. His narrator praises Mrs. Bittacy who, "in spite of much surface foolishness that many might have read as weakness … had balance, sanity, and a fine deep faith. She was greater than she knew. Her love for her husband and her God were somehow one, an achievement only possible to a single-hearted nobility of soul" (240). Nonetheless, her "surface foolishness" that prohibits her from joining David in his expansive *Dasein* eventually lands her in an "atrocious loneliness" and "gradual mental disruption and collapse" (266). Like Hawthorne's doomed protagonist, her mind, "preying upon itself, and fed by constant dread, went lost in disproportion" (271). One wonders the degree to which her clergyman father resembled Goodman Brown's own semblance of the devil he meets in the wilderness and thus instilled in his daughter not the wisdom of her name, but a disproportionate paranoia that allows the surface to burrow into the interior, thus stunting the possibility of her "greatness" to flourish.

In direct contrast to Sophia's downfall is David's burgeoning consciousness of self and other, of love as an outgrowth of contemplative practice and presence. Of course, his estrangement from his wife and the world on the margins of the forest would suggest that this love is compromised, even selfish, though David's experience of love is ultimately closer to *agape* than to the romantic or familial *eros* or *storge*. It is also indicative of what this study is calling dissident alterity. "Her husband had somehow altered these last days … a change had come over him" (221), she observes. By the time David begins to forgo household duties, in addition to his slow movement away from emotional and other obligations in matrimony, "deeply submerged in him there ran this tide of other thoughts, desires, hopes" (242). This is not the otherness of a costume, a potentially fleeting ideological stance, or even a common subject-position. Rather, it is inside, even more than Sophia's evangelicalism, as a "tide" that at once waxes or wanes with the undulation of time and weather (determining the needs of warmth or sleep) and becomes invariable, immanent. Toward the story's conclusion, "the hidden thing blazed out without disguise" (251); David has transitioned from admiring the aesthetic, textual representation of a painting purchased

from Sanderson to embodying its essence. In other words, he has entered
the real, the "injustice" of which with regards to Sophia has less to do with
the husband mistreating his wife (when home, he behaves as normal with
her, though she perceives a distance in his manner, as though his thoughts
and desires are elsewhere, as they assuredly are) and more to do with
Ouspensky's notion of justice. Much like libraries and websites, the
majesty of the forest is literally in her backyard, but without interest in the
"love" it has to offer, it remains inaccessible to her, if not dangerous. She
does not want it. The horror of the story lies in her failed efforts to retrieve
David from its grasp, particularly when she enters its domain and, in
similar fashion to Shirley Jackson's Hill House, her horror "steadies and
locates" (*Haunting* 58) her while David strolls quietly among friends: "the
entire mass of what Sanderson had called the Collective Consciousness of
the Forest strove to eject this human atom that stood across the path of its
desire" (Blackwood 263).

The "hidden thing" that emerges gloriously from David provides the
basis for his pantheistic knowledge and experience. The forest produces a
malevolent veneer only to those who bring too much of themselves into
its vicinity; David has listened to its call and emptied himself of
presuppositions. Among the trees he inhabits a persistent, evolving
variation of Eliot's "still point of the turning world," the forest a liminal
axis mundi where he is most aware of a far more amorphous, substantial
God than that of his wife. The trees induce a meditative way of being for
one who opens oneself to their aliveness. Fearing that David may be
pathologically alone, Sophia asks if God is with him, to which he responds,
"magnificently" (265). There is nothing aberrant about being a Christian
in the West. Being a mystic, on the other hand, having access to the "still
point" where no intermediary holds sway to dictate how one is to think
and occupy time, is another matter entirely. The "thing" "blazes" forth in
a paradoxical quietude, having recognized and stripped the person of the
personality that accedes to artificial ways of being. We might say, then,
that David comes to embody the most radical, authentic alterity
imaginable, that which dispenses with the self.

But David is not necessarily the protagonist of this story, despite
Blackwood's title. He is often referred to as "her husband;" he is thus the

pivot on which revolves *her* quandary and *her* dread. At one point that approaches stillness, we learn that "hitherto she had divided the beyond-world into two sharp halves – spirits good or spirits evil. But thoughts came to her now, on soft and very tentative feet, like the footsteps of the gods which are on wool, that besides these definite classes, there might be other Powers as well, belonging definitely to neither one nor the other. Her thought stopped dead at that. But the big idea found lodgment in her little mind, and, owing to the largeness of her heart, remained there unejected. It even brought a certain solace with it" (264-65). This is prior to her cognitive and emotional collapse, though it speaks once again to Blackwood's sensitivity to her potential, her large heart and her access to the consolation of "largeness" well beyond the simplistically divided "beyond-world." Is a productive, mystical, self-effacing alterity available to Sophia? Of course! The "other Powers" reach out before they reject her, at the comparatively neurotic point where her own radical thoughts die to their fulfillment. When David claims with great enthusiasm that God is "everywhere" (ibid.), she covers her ears so as not to have her anthropomorphism challenged, the hallmark, Blackwood suggests, of a "little mind."

So a line is drawn between the man who eventually merges with another class of being and a woman who cannot quite get there, who will end her days in solitary oblivion, between the unforgiving walls of a home misrecognized as "God's house." Badiou and Cassin comment on the disparity between the "great and the little" in the life and work of Heidegger (*Heidegger* XIX). He commonly referred to his wife Elfride in letters as "little soul," a woman who clearly sacrificed herself for the sake of her husband's "great" philosophical genius. They see this disparity as central to the inherent tension of Heidegger's various allegiances – to philosophy, National Socialism, his marriage, extramarital affairs, running a Nazi-affiliated school, and all the "little" responsibilities of everyday life that can impede progress in the "greater" areas. In service of the "great," he was able to rationalize the diminution of the "little." We assume that everyone does this on some level, though both Heidegger and Blackwood (born twenty years before the philosopher in 1869) were surely products of their cultural environments in terms of the women, real or fictional, in their lives; as is a contemporary male who manages to have his way while a woman may aspire without reaching or even fully conceiving of her path into what Badiou calls the "void" that "allows a genuine event to be at the origin of a truth" (*Ethics* 73). But we nevertheless return to the fact of Sophia's options. David invites her, on multiple occasions, into both discussion and ambulatory exploration of the forest. She declines, refuses to engage thoughtfully with the "devil's" exceptional vocabulary or wander the forest with an open mind that would compliment her heart. Ultimately, she is incapable of the one sacrificial act that would escort her into genuine alterity, namely, the sacrifice of her identity as an evangelical, even in the face of definite awareness and "solace." Emmanuel Levinas's notion of the face as being "naked," as "what cannot become content, which your thought would embrace [or repudiate]," as the "uncontainable" that "leads you beyond" (*Ethics* 86-87), is precisely what Sophia is invited to behold in all of its denuded, *natural* authenticity. It is that which would lead her beyond her "little" thoughts that can see only the familiar context of her surface perception, to what Levinas identifies as "signification without context" (ibid.). That she is yet another woman born of early twentieth century patriarchy is most unfortunate. That she is finally incapable of offering her self on the altar of Being is the importunate condition of humankind, or at least those for whom literalism is a guiding darkness brashly mistaken for light.

Despite Mr. Bittacy's continued efforts to maintain the status quo of their marriage, Mrs. Bittacy detects the alterity beneath the surface. "The ceilings and closed windows [of their home] confined him," she thinks. "Yet, in it, no suggestion that he found *her* irksome. Her presence seemed of no account at all; indeed, he hardly noticed her. For whole long periods he lost her, did not know that she was there. He had no need of her. He lived alone. Each lived alone" (Blackwood 264). It is the alienation between them that in the end completes the horror for the wife but does not adhere to the husband's sense of self. On the contrary, David is anything but alone. Only Sophia, like Goodman Brown, whose lonely, "dying hour was gloom" (Hawthorne 354), has chosen to remain tethered to her opinions over and against visceral experience, her struggle that slowly morphs into a daily nightmare of smallness and insignificance.

Ironically, it is the plight of her husband, this aloneness, but with the important caveat of his shift constituting a productive diminishment of ego, as opposed to the painful chipping away at her lingering, determined adherence to the surface "thing" instilled by an evangelical clergyman for whom alterity was most likely the literalist's isolating vision, that spits gently into the face of everything deserving the designation of humanist ethics.

The Beyond of Charles L. Grant

Nevertheless, one could argue that religious fundamentalism is unabashedly nihilistic. In contrast to secularism, it takes mythical evil and the Hell from which it spawns literally, at the same time that it employs a form of metonymy in its attribution of evil to situations, ideas, and people it deems abject, thus condemning itself to both corruption (of "truth-processes") and bigotry. Metal music and horror may utilize satanic imagery for the sake of exploring the Luciferianism of certain cultural imbalances, or for the raw shock value inherent in such images, though it is rare to find a studied, spiritually-refined musician, writer, or filmmaker for whom the Devil is a literal entity. Even one of the most prominent, current satanic organizations, The Satanic Temple, maintains an essentially progressive political agenda and denies any investment in superstitious religious belief. A recent film such as *The Blackcoat's Daughter* (2015) depicts a shadowy Horned One while ultimately highlighting the lengths to which one may go to assuage the immense suffering of loss and the need to belong. Other filmic examples, however, including *The Witch* (2015) and *Hereditary* (2018), locate conventional human narratives (confronting a self-righteously religious parent, the death of a loved one, respectively) amidst the force of an overtly satanic figure whose merger with the protagonist yields a triumph of heresy. Despite these distinctions, in each case a metaphorical, aesthetic nihilism that runs counter to biblical inerrancy instigates the homeopathic methodology in an effort to foster textual intervention via the real. Christian fundamentalism is nihilistic in its intent to deprive alterity of its value and richness. Critical horror escalates alterity, often provoking a variety of nihilism whose purpose, ironically, is quite other than stripping individuals of dignity.

In his marvelously extensive book on the films of Lucio Fulci, *Beyond Terror*, Stephen Thrower asserts that the seminal *The Texas Chainsaw Massacre* (1974) "is horrific because it refuses to respect anyone – neither its victim characters, its ridiculously domesticated maniacs, and certainly not the delicate sensibilities of its 'readers.' The film is an absurdist nightmare. Nothing matters – human beings are merely so much prattling, perambulating meat" (217). It is difficult to imagine a film as grittily brutal and misanthropic as *The Texas Chainsaw Massacre* being very popular with contemporary viewers who have absorbed a milieu of "delicate" "publicness" in which all varieties of possible triggering must be preemptively admonished. The *Saw* series is fine – as long as its violence unfolds according to the rules, however perverse, of a *game* and there is a particular gloss over the film to remind one that it is all in excess of the real, no problem.[18] *The Texas Chainsaw Massacre* rips its spinning, metal teeth, along with its abstract sound design, innovative close-up cinematography, and relentlessly bombastic screaming through any sense of viewer safety in a 16mm visual and sonic storm. The remarkable aesthetic of its nihilism is unparalleled. And yet, for Levinas, literary – or filmic – nihilism is "the precondition for the ethical relation" (quoted, Weller, *Beckett* 14) in so far as it "saves us from that real nihilism which lies in canonization, sacralization, Messianism, soteriology – in short, the nihilism of any final solution, of any final and absolute integration, of that identity-thinking which would abolish all difference and is, according to Adorno, radically evil" (46). Critical horror is a mechanism of the "saving power" of being aesthetically qualified by productive, forceful non-Being in the familiar but destructive face of venomous ideology, religious and otherwise.

Contemporary of Stephen King and himself a prodigious horror writer, Charles L. Grant presents, not unlike Blackwood, the quiet side of horror that creeps rather than saws its way into one's psyche. His novels and stories tend to focus on drifting protagonists, often female and toeing the line between resilient independence and fragility against the odds of some supernatural phenomenon. They drift in the sense of life direction rather than geographical variance or displacement and often end up, or return to, Oxrun Station, Grant's quaint but invariably haunted, fictional Connecticut town. The first more or less stand-alone part of his *Dialing the Wind* (of the same title) offers a gripping example of Grant's aesthetic and thematic preoccupations. Caroline has lost her husband, Harry, to cancer and has settled in Oxrun, in a medium size home that feels larger than it is and in a job at a florist where she excels with her affinity for arrangements. She remains haunted by her loss, a condition that is amplified by building tension around recent murders of young women in the general vicinity. One of her co-workers, the twenty-something, love-torn Stacey in the process of being abandoned by her boyfriend, is set up to be another victim, as is, expectedly, the more mature Caroline. When not working, the latter sometimes stands outside her home at a fence, in the night, clandestinely listening to live mandolin music from a nearby porch, or she loiters in her kitchen and finds unexpected consolation in a bizarre, ecumenical radio preacher whom Stacey has recommended. Her radio fails periodically; it produces a wind sound that Caroline finds equally mesmerizing.

There is a pervasive assemblage of forces operating in Grant's story that will come to a head by its conclusion, as is the case with most of his work that takes the reader far beyond a simple binary of good and evil. Central to "Dialing the Wind" is Caroline's need for control – over her environment, the daily fluctuations of her life, and the husband-stealer that is death. With its slow pace relative to Hartford, charming shops, its park, its two main restaurants, and familiar faces, Oxrun Station is precisely the type of town where one might expect to exert such control, thus making it the perfect location for unexpected horror to bloom. The tendency of horror to attack where it's least expected, those suburban landscapes that maintain a façade of safety and coherence, certainly reflects not only Grant's commitment to the real, but a general need for the incursion of the liminal.[19] *Dialing the Wind* was published in 1989, at the border between 1980s excess and the impeachment of a president over a sexual affair that would both resurface in the context of 21st century "Me Too" gender politics and be completely eclipsed by another president whose unparalleled misogyny has been embraced by middle America, including its evangelical base. In the current milieu of 2023, the two sides of that border have caved in, in equal measure, on the liminal space, though it is possible that aesthetic horror, along with other texts that seek to disrupt normative inauthenticity, is nevertheless one of the few remaining arenas where genuine alterity can intervene by way of a particular "force," despite 21st century versions of enacting control. For her part, Caroline also exercises newfound agency by way of expertly arranging flowers.

Early in the story, Caroline awakens from an especially nasty dream, whereupon she remembers "nothing but a vague notion there was dying to be done. The tears [over her deceased husband] were supposed to have stopped months ago. Years. Control she should have had, and couldn't find, and it was wrong" (Grant 18). She goes on to call herself a "jackass" (ibid.) for having such thoughts, which may or may not be accurate, though she is correct in her nocturnal intuition that death is both pervasive and imminent. It takes the lives of young women as well as environmental occurrences ("a wet breeze swept through the woods and died on the lawn" [23]), displaying the subtlety of Grant's literary style. He is also entirely capable of sober realism, as when Caroline contemplates Stacey's heartbreak, "wanting to tell her that losing a man this way was infinitely better than sitting alone at his bedside, watching the skin grow flaccid as what beneath it dissolved. Shrinking him. Discoloring him. Reducing him to a mockery while nameless men and women in white walked past him without seeing, stopping only long enough to take a pulse, a blood pressure, make a note, and move on" (36). There is a correlation between Caroline and Blackwood's David that speaks to two forms of death: the physical, dehumanizing demise and the figurative disappearance into authentic alterity, respectively. Blackwood's interest in mysticism and Golden Dawn occultism made him more amenable to the latter form, while Grant, poetic as he can be, is invariably more hard-boiled, more invested in mortality as horror, an orientation that applies, in this story at least, to his view of traditional Christianity.

The radio preacher, albeit with greater clarity, is not too far removed from Etchison's paranormal radio voices in "It Will Be Here Soon." Is it salvation or death at stake in absorbing said voices? Or are they ultimately the same phenomenon? When Caroline first hears the sermonizing, she says aloud, "Swell. I'm about to be saved" (19), with no small degree of cynicism. If it is salvation to be had, she is not interested. On the other hand, Caroline is in need of something given that control is not quite working out, which makes her become more amenable to the preacher, as to "hillbilly" music emanating from a nearby house. "The wind faded, and the preacher was there," in her kitchen following difficult thoughts of Harry, speaking in garbled phrases: "'... put your hands on,' he said, voice still hoarse, still gentle. 'The saving power of...'" (25). She finds him "grotesque" (ibid.), and yet soon thereafter, when the voice begins to fade, she laments his disappearance, with the poignant statement, "'Damnit, if you die on me, too,' she [threatens]" (26), the real threat being to her sense of belonging and hope. In Grant's brand of horror, of course, the preacher's "saving power" is diametrically opposed to that of Heidegger's, which prompts the "revealing" of authenticity or "truth-processes" over and against the they-centered machinations of ideological "enframing." The evangelical salvation can end only in harrowing death rather than a truth, but not before it plays its part, however significantly or insignificantly, in framing Caroline's reaction to her blossoming carnality and the guilt it provokes, as aligned with its pervasive cultural power. She summarizes her current predicament, in the privacy of her thoughts, as "Harry's dead, you miss him, and now the mourning's over, and you hate yourself for it" (42). Surely she feels conflicted over her desire for another (specifically, police officer Glenn Rowan, with whom she flirts at the florist's) who is not her late husband, though the psychological and somatic truth of her "evental" situation necessitates her reemergence into desire and intimacy. The preacher's continuously interrupted sermons may speak of the need to "feel" but their salvatory power will foster neither love nor radical sacrifice. By the time Stacey, sorely missing her own intimacy, becomes the third woman to die inexplicably (her "body rippled from neck to knee, the breasts sagging further, the stomach sinking more, her ribs stark and her hipbones sharp and her face abruptly old while her hair turned white and feathered to the floor"), Caroline's radio blinks on and the preacher instructs, "Feel the power, daughter" (55), and the radio dies. Popular religion, here, is another uncanny factor in grisly, untimely death.

Caroline will perish in the same manner. By the story's conclusion, on what is presumably her final night of life, she is left with "one hand on the radio, the other dialing for the wind, weeping and laughing, and *feeling* the power bring her husband back home, while the preacher said heal and the mandolin [from the neighboring house] said *love* and the hair on her head turned white and trembled, and feathered to the floor" (57). Earlier in the story, when she first encounters the live music, her initial reaction is just that, reactionary and disgruntled, until she listens more closely and realizes that "the mandolin knew how lonely she was" (16). Such can be the force of art, of texts. As she begins the dying process – already foreshadowed by her sense of having aged relative to the younger Stacey – the single, non-phantasmagoric aspect of the surrounding and internal environment is the "speech" of the mandolin. We know this because the scene has been immediately preceded by Caroline's rather sophisticated ideas around authentic love. "The difference," she asserts in her imperiled but clear thoughts, "between true love and truly loving – the first is an affliction on the young by the young, and the second is the way love really was, was really meant. Stacey loved, but she was selfish" (56) Stacey is also, she reminds us, deceased, along with, she continues, "all the other young lovers who only believed in their own loneliness, not their love" (57). These "true lovers" are alienated from Being by virtue of their insular self-absorption and thus lack the selflessness intrinsic to an act or practice of love. Caroline's tragedy, then, following Harry's death, is her recognition of Badiou's love as existential project that comes too late. Her physical death precedes a figurative, recalibrating death and the horror reaches its apotheosis.

Grant leaves us with the morbidity of incessant fatality; Caroline's hair, like Stacey's in the instantaneity of premature death, grays and "feathers to the floor," as though this scene will repeat *ad infinitum*, and of course, with infinite variation, it does. Heideggerian "morbidity" is nothing if not acutely aware that the fact of mortality lends a certain value and immediacy to life, to the evolution of *Dasein*. O'Brien grants "such an extraordinary transformation requires something rather sobering, then again, are not such life-changing events always somewhat unsettling? Don't we need something profound and perhaps disturbing to jar us out of our desultory lives?" (*Heidegger* 59). Critical horror sobers us to the weight of ontology hanging heavy on quotidian, and often the most comfortable representations of, existence. A "weird" science fiction writer such as Pamela Zoline in her story "The Heat Death of the Universe," for example, quickly lets the reader know that though its human protagonist is an ordinary, well-educated, bourgeois woman by the name of Sarah Boyle, the real star of the show is ontology and the text will ultimately be concerned with "the problems of the nature of existence or being" (13). As in the horror text, attention will be given not simply to universal questions but to "problems" as they unfold in the lives and deaths of people who might otherwise appear impervious to the otherness of being.

Sarah's life is replete with chaos despite a comfortable home, her "fine Eastern college" (21) education, and her love of Bach. Her role as a homemaker and mother (if there is a father, his breadwinning probably inoculates him to the domestic sphere – he is not mentioned) both "makes" this chaos by virtue of her particular disposition and observes it, horrifyingly, in the forms of wild, seemingly feral children, unremitting chores, and the quiet assault of products necessary to an illusion of fulfillment. At the center of this everyday bedlam is the fact of entropy playing out on both universal and domestic scales. Zoline numbers each of her paragraphs, another attempt at Sarah's much-needed order, and periodically inserts philosophical or scientific passages that address the fatal decrease in energy. Like the impact of cereal sugar on her children's teeth, everything is in a state of decay, which is at one point transferred to "the metastasis of Western Culture" (15). By the story's end, Sarah is weeping alone in her kitchen, not listening to the wind or a dubious preacher on the radio but throwing eggs "through the fine clear air" (28) in a manner that mimics Dada as an art form "intended to outrage and scandalize" (20). "The Heat Death of the Universe," like some horror, is Dadaistic in its open, abstract challenge to literary and bourgeois conventions. It utilizes the deep-rooted chaos of life to both revel in its aesthetic possibilities and to expose its real beneath the surface of power structures whose opportunistic intentions are to mask and buffer those realities that otherwise wreak havoc on comfortable, capitalistic designs. For Sarah Boyle, even love is another product, another futile attempt at

order. The only hope of something better, or "something profound," as
O'Brien puts it, lies in what Sarah recognizes as scientist J. Willard Gibb's
notion of "local enclaves whose direction seems opposed to that of the
Universe at large and in which there is a limited and temporary tendency
for organization to increase. Life finds its home in some of these enclaves"
(26). For the artist who seeks to intervene in "publicness," home is rarely
where or what one thinks.

By the conclusion of Blackwood's story, "the man whom the trees
loved" has merged with his beloved, gone gently into the animate night of
his true home, the forest that bellows, reaching Sophia's ears to inform her
that "her husband's voice was in it" (274). The horror films for which
Lucio Fulci is most known never allow a protagonist, however likable, to
escape as peacefully as David into an enclave where needs are fulfilled
and authenticity fully achieved. Rather, as in Fulci's *The Beyond* (1981),
in which Liza inherits an old New Orleans hotel, quickly encounters the
deaths of hired help, a ghostly, prophetic blind woman with white, serpent-
like eyes, a book that foretells the arising of the dead, and the company of
a handsome doctor, the "beyond" that eventually subsumes Liza and John,
MD, is "a fatefully magnetic destination – out of reach but paradoxically
inescapable – visible in the malefic geometry of the Seven Door Hotel"
(Thrower 169). The hotel's name, of course, references the seven gates of
Hell, one of which is located in the basement of Liza's bequest. After
numerous, horrific trials with the walking dead, Liza and John are left
stranded in the bowels of this "beyond" to inaugurate a denouement
resembling both Caroline's and Sarah's predicaments in its unrelenting
abjection, questionable ambiguity, and incalculable alterity. Unlike Gibb's
enclaves, these spaces are anything but hopeful, though, with Fulci, the
viewer has nevertheless been taken to a liminal wasteland between life and
death where she is left to contemplate the value of a "beyond" relative to
what Zoline calls the everyday "simulacra of a complete listing and
ordering" (17) that informs – if not dictates – the borders dividing genuine
alterity and inauthenticity. As Thrower observes, "Fulci's insistence on
depicting victims who are devoid of opposition to their dissolution finds
its analogue in the receptive face of the horror fan, strangely immobile
also, before a repulsive spectacle of attack on the sense organs" (171).

Fulci guides his viewer into this uncanny terrain with unstoppable force, offering not a neat resolution but a new, somatic beginning beyond terror, an immersion into something called horror that seeps into the body/mind, beguiling and permeating the false consciousness of exteriority.[20]

The Beyond is very much about sight and representation. The film's prologue finds an artist/warlock, Schweik, finishing a painting (in the hotel, in 1927, before a group of men abduct and torture him) that is essentially the beyond in which Liza and John will eventually find themselves, a desolate, desert-like topography lined with bodies and open stretches of an endless, hellish (though not fiery) landscape. So attention is drawn to the re-presentation of the beyond from the beginning, allowing it not only to immobilize Thrower's "horror fan" but to reveal its presence as forebodingly symbolic. We are always already submerged in its depths, though we lack the eyes to see. Like the doctor and Liza before him, the viewer may believe solely in science, pragmatism, in the proud, American "they" of popular tastes and manners to whom one lives in unconscious obedience, but Fulci gouges, or highlights in close-up, multiple eyes as though signaling an imperative of true sight. By the time Liza and John are imprisoned in the beyond, pragmatism is gutted as they behold their new home that is Hell only to gain the sight of horror's blindness and, like the iconic blind woman, to potentially reappear among the living for the sake of warning others, if it is not too late, as it sometimes appears to be in Donald Trump's willfully corruptible 21st century America.[21]

Badiou's version of evil is the simulation of a "truth-process" that corrupts the only viable, sensible ethics as radical as Eagleton's notion of sacrifice and as dark as Heidegger's "darkening" of "mediocre" modernity. The warlock's initial, representational painting is *The Beyond*'s first warning regarding the opening of the gates to Hell, a truth that Fulci will protract until the beyond becomes the grotesque, existential real that it is. Schweik lives and dies in genuine alterity, in that marginal area between heretical practice and ethical obligation. Both the painting and the film reflect an extension of the darkness of ignorance and inauthenticity into a realm, for the viewer at least, of homeopathic insight. This is not to say that horror writers or filmmakers necessarily set out to make an overt attempt to heal anything or anyone. And yet, as horror scholar Gina Wisker explains, "in the recognition of the representational nature of horror, the significance, the symbolism, the conceptual, meaningful element underlying and informing it, lies the crucial element of both intentionality and reading practice" (*Horror* 7). Horror texts intend to frighten, to remove one from the sense of everyday safety the scaffolding of which is typically erected on buffering, often alienating presumptions of immortality, while readers/viewers make a pact, however temporary, with themselves and the representation to "practice" what it has to preach. In this sense, *The Beyond's Eibon* is perhaps the ultimate example of "textual intervention" that fails, though Fulci's film, like countless other horror texts, cinematic, literary or otherwise, excels in exposing evil in magnificently seductive ways, and thus in prompting us to heed its voiceover narrative that "calls" to us as Liza and John transition to their novel mode of "seeing" in the beyond: "And you will face the sea of darkness, and all therein that may be explored." Likewise, Grant's Caroline dials the wind and in shattering disintegration locates the quiet horror of another broken, lonely person.

Chapter 3

– The Alterity of Haunting: On Shirley Jackson, Thomas Ligotti, Dennis Etchison, and David Seltzer

The "Maniac Juxtapositions" of Shirley Jackson's House

If the accusations concerning Heidegger's morbidity are in need of philosophical qualification, no such qualifying is necessary with horror. It revels in its morbid preoccupations and dramas for the sake not only of disemboweling egotism but to celebrate the distinct pleasures of liminality. And to frighten us. That said, the horror fan need be no more nihilistic than one who engages in the many forms of religious sacrifice, in compulsions or intuitions that feel authentic and therefore perversely pleasurable as they run screamingly or meditatively counter to the presumptive, restrictive "ethics" of humanist compulsions. Unless, of course, one is in fact nihilistic – and it is this possibility, this potential warfare between damaged, ego-maniacal fanaticism and truthful, curious, critical devotion that precipitates the friction that in turn fuels and validates alterity. Horror is the skull on the 17th century scholar's desk as a healthy reminder of mortality and the imperative of action, be it contemplative or otherwise. It is the menstruation that awakens the woman (if indeed she needs such awakening) to her body and the flow of blood. Horror suffuses the childhood neighborhood aged over many years as a fog moving over dilapidation and compromising memory. It is the graveyard and, naturally, the old house on the hill, or by the cemetery, that neither screams nor meditates, only broods and stares back.

As she travels, surreptitiously, rebelliously, to the eighty-year-old house that will simultaneously save and destroy her, Shirley Jackson's protagonist in *The Haunting of Hill House*, Eleanor, will misread a sign. What in actuality says "Daredevil," she interprets as "DARE EVIL" (19). On one hand, Eleanor is in the process of daring the evil of her sheltered existence, as well as that of a presumably haunted house. She is entering, necessarily and compulsively, liminal spaces (a car that only half belongs to her, the open road, an unfriendly town, a diabolical home) on a number of levels and for a variety of reasons, some of which are common to human experience (especially to teenagers, which this thirty-two year old woman may as well be) while others remain specific to Eleanor's predicament of having spent her adult life so far taking care of her mother, now dead, and living an essentially asocial life with her sister's family. On the other hand, Jackson's novel is arguably intent on daring evil as Badiouian simulacra, re-presentation, so easily misread when the interpreter reads from the site of her egotism, his neurosis, their self-absorption. Specifically, Jackson is daring the inauthenticity of ordinary human relations as unconsciously (but commonly and sometimes horrifically) enacted in the misreading of situations through the insularity of one's egoic proclivities. From this perspective, *The Haunting of Hill House* is tremendously morbid. It takes no prisoners, as "they" say, in its staunch evisceration of faux belonging, always aware of the underlying alienation slowly or swiftly eroding the human capacity for fellowship.

But there is another, related but less obvious and more pleasant entry point into this renowned horror novel. Eleanor arrives at Hill house to join three others: Theodora, Luke (both approximately Eleanor's age), and the curator of the event, Dr. Montague. As the four dine and bond during their first night at Hill House, the young participants beg the researcher (whose doctorate is in anthropology) to tell them more about the house and the nature of his experiment. "You are a mutinous group of assistants," he exclaims playfully. "After dinner, then … Now, however, let us talk about music, or painting, or even politics" (Jackson 68). Mutiny will assume a variety of forms in *The Haunting of Hill House*, as it does from its first page on, imputing a kind of elegance, an arresting quality to Montague's otherwise casual remark. He attempts to raise the bar of the conversation to include the intervention of texts, even the day's political discourse sufficing. As Silverman implies, texts, certain texts, have a way of cutting through or exposing the layers of cultural and psychological misrecognition and revealing the immediate nature of "truth-processes." Though Montague will use Samuel Richardson's novel *Pamela* to induce sleep in the night, he is not unaware of the *pleasure* afforded by texts and their contribution to elevating both thought and communion. Of course, both Silverman and Badiou are clear about the potential challenge of a "truth" to conventional, bourgeois sensibilities, which implies that a genre such as critical horror is amply appropriate to ethics, or to culturally rich discussion and solitary individuation.

Which raises Jackson's novel to the level of an evental "truth-process" in its own right. But what are its truths? Most scholarship around the novel points to an overarching theme of alienation, one that is impossible to deny. Characters approach and ricochet off one another quickly or slowly, over a period of false starts and knowing, increasingly malign comments, expressions. Behind these not uncommon developments, however, there lurks the monster of inauthentic *Dasein* that negates, to put it mildly, the possibility of genuine intimacy, mutual understanding, or more broadly, love. The opening paragraph begins with the claim that "no live organism can continue for long to exist sanely under conditions of absolute reality; even larks and katydids are supposed, by some, to dream" (3). "Absolute reality" may ultimately equate to a form of insanity, at least without the assistance of textual involvement or some other avenue toward enacted self-knowledge, though dreaming or fantasizing is clearly a dubious sanity. However informative a dream may be, when it transforms into the waking unconsciousness of mere fantasy (as it does for Eleanor, at least, day and night), it becomes a mutiny (of countless delusions and the various "I's" that spawn every chimera or nightmare) against the real. The real, of course, no matter its primal or universal dimensions, can be transformed *within* the perceiving, developing self. This is not the same cultural or psychological dynamic as self-serving "alternative facts." From a Gurdjieffian perspective, the more singular a person, the fewer "I's" generating the everyday deficit of attention (disorder), the more authenticity of Being available for Badiou's "fidelity" to a "truth-process," the more "resolute," to use Heidegger's term, one can be in grappling with the real, staring into its face regardless of its abjection or unknowability. The central characters of Jackson's novel, who assume the traits of a family (and are labeled as such by the narrator), are constantly struggling, in their own unique ways and situations, against the absolute real and the seduction of dreams, though some will fare far better than others.

Luke is a character in every sense of the word. He will inherit Hill House and is there as a family representative by order of his aunt, as well as by Jackson to assume the role of comic relief and verified skeptic. Theo, as she prefers to be called, is a poised, elegant psychic and lesbian (a fact that Jackson was compelled to veil in the late 1950s) who will become Eleanor's foil. Dr. Montague is working toward both scholarly relevance and prestige, making his experiment a matter of professional as much as personal importance. His wife, who eventually turns up with a friend and fellow paranormal enthusiast, is thoroughly obnoxious and judgmental. The caretakers of Hill House, Mr. and Mrs. Dudley, appear, at the beginning, utterly destitute of humanity, or perhaps they are all too human. Eleanor is not psychic but has been included in the study due to rocks having mysteriously fallen on her family's home for three days when she was a child. She is at the center of this novel's drama, a woman whose immense desire for companionship and purpose is boundless, contained only by the prison of her life prior to Hill House and her excessive propriety. The latter will become increasingly porous as she immerses herself in the "family" dynamic, and indeed, in the house itself. Built by Hugh Crane eighty years prior, it stands as a gothic mansion replete with seemingly incongruous angles and perplexing spaces, an anthropomorphic character that Eleanor intuits as "vile" and "diseased" (33) when she first slams on her car breaks and digests its overwhelming presence. It embodies a "maniac juxtaposition" and its "face" appears "awake" (34); the narrator deems it "arrogant and hating, never off guard, can only be evil" (35). It is the essence of what Jackson's characters and her novel as a whole seek to dare.

Hill House is clearly the space and atmosphere of "absolute reality," though this real is ultimately unlimited in scope, extending well beyond its walls. Eleanor's immediate family is arrogant and disrespectful. As she walks a city street to retrieve the car, she collides with an older woman who "damns" her five times for knocking her groceries to the ground. When Eleanor offers her taxi fare, the woman relents and claims she will pray for Eleanor, an offer that comes across as hardly genuine or ameliorative (though the affection-starved Eleanor accepts it with relief). At Hillsdale, a small town near Hill House that Dr. Montague has urged them not to visit on their way, she stops nonetheless only to discover a "tangled, disorderly mess of dirty houses and crooked streets" (23) and soon wonders if the coffee she has ordered at a dreary, alienating diner, is poisoned. Theo has fled a compromised relationship, while Luke will eventually steal off to Paris. Dr. Montague's career is likely in jeopardy, if not altogether ruined after Eleanor eventually dies (whether by the house's or her own hands remains unclear), in addition to his being stuck with Mrs. Montague. "In the night … in the dark," Mrs. Dudley explains robotically, "there won't be anyone around if you need help" (39). The novel is constantly unfolding layers of distance between people, always unfurling a quality of being "far away," as the four primary characters are thrice described when the house attacks them, collectively, for the last time (203). Hence the "disorder" and "crookedness" that applies equally to Hill House and to any location where people are engaging with other people, or with the turmoil of singular isolationism.

Kristeva and Sollers draw a distinction between an evolving or becoming love, by virtue of its increasing selflessness and sensitivity to the other, and egoic "love" that is always already vulnerable to love's opposite. The reference is to Lacan's notion of "*hainamoration*" ("hatelove") as a common form of ambivalence between love and hate (Kristeva, *Marriage* 90). It is exactly this mode of Being that pummels the family dynamic of Hill House, be it that of the original owners or the strikingly familiar "theater" of Dr. Montague's curated domestic environment with all of its familial aspirations, desires, and spite. It does not take long for the novel's conflict to escalate once all inhabitants are settled and more or less comfortable. Following the house's first "attack," punctuated by banging, creaking, grunting sounds and childlike murmuring, Eleanor grows annoyed by Theo's repeating its name, as though the house might track and assault them once again. Theo reads her thoughts: "'Hill House, Hill House, Hill House,' Theodora said softly, and

smiled across at Eleanor" (Jackson 123). Later, Eleanor thinks that she has
"never felt such uncontrollable loathing for any person before" (157),
referring to Theo, and continues, glancing at the latter's head, "I would
like to hit her with a stick … I would like to batter her with rocks" (158),
to do, in other words, what some malevolent force has done to her home
years prior. "I would like to watch her dying" (159), she thinks. Luke
receives Eleanor's scrutiny when she determines that he won't listen to her
(much less, love her), caught in his own isolation as he is, and will
eventually become chummy with Theo, leaving Eleanor to feel excluded.
Dr. Montague has only to contend with his wife who inquires, rhetorically,
"how many hours – how many, *many* hours – have I sat in purest love and
understanding, alone in a room and yet never alone" (196) when
confronted about her ill-advised wish to sleep in the most psychically
dangerous room of the house. The irony, of course, is that she is incapable
of extending that "purest love" to *living* beings. Outside the paranormal,
each conflict is quite ordinary in terms of needling, family tensions and,
specifically, the sense of one's feeling singled out in a negative manner.
"'Everything is worse,'" Dr. Montague explains to Eleanor, "'if you think
something is looking at you'" (120). He is referring to the house's
particularly nasty and threatening demeanor, and yet the implication of
this statement for humanity is profound. The gaze, male or otherwise, has
the power to dehumanize the human experience. Of course, it also has the
ability to dignify it, lovingly, though Eleanor, as the doomed protagonist
to whom one grows accustomed in horror, will crumble under its weight,
the weight of both human and architectural eyes, and succumb to death.
      Eleanor dissolves into Hill House. Once her predicament worsens, she
confides to her surrogate family that she is "always afraid of being alone
…but I know I'm not really going to be hurt and yet time is so long and
even a second goes on and on and I could stand any of it if I could only
surrender –" (160), at which point the others become understandably,
deeply suspicious. She can "feel them all looking at her" (ibid.) after they
interrogate her meaning of the word "surrender." Being and time: for
Eleanor, the severely compromised quality of one conditions her mode of
inhabiting the other, respectively. Her only option, as she understands it,
is to commit her Being to the all-embracing power of the house, which she

does in the final, fatal drama of her life, speeding her car away from the others and into a tree on the Hill House property. Not surprisingly, she questions her action just before the collision, the implication being that it is not of her own volition. And in a sense – even without necessarily relying on a supernatural explanation – she is right. Despite the alterity of her extreme social awkwardness, Eleanor is the quintessential "they-self" that is so desperate for recognition it will give its life – its being and its conscious, truthful use of time – over to the most powerful force within its orbit. At first this is Theo, until the house exerts its malevolence on both of them together, reducing the stronger of the two to a state of primal fear. Theo will bounce back, while Eleanor remains distinctly other, though only in relation to those whose navigation skills in the realms of "publicness" allow them to withstand or temper its inevitable impact (and in relation, of course, to the living).

The protagonist dissolves as the fundamentalist "surrenders" not to what J.D. Salinger, among others, calls "Christ consciousness," but to insularity bereft of both consciousness and conscientiousness. As creator of Hill House and staunchly pious Christian, Hugh Crane has inadvertently designed an Eden-like prototype of "absolute reality," a place of solace from the wicked ways of the world but one whose dimensions and atmospheres unknowingly generate confusion, "sin," and death for those who are vulnerable to its own compromised sanctity. Luke finds a book that Crane has assembled for his daughter out of cut and pasted images, his own writing, and, psychotically, his own blood, the inverse of *Eibon's* occult admonitions. Luke reads for the group: "Daughter, could you but hear for a moment the agony, the screaming, the dreadful crying out and repentance, of those poor souls condemned to everlasting flame! Could thine eyes be seared, but for an instant, with the red glare of wasteland burning always! Alas, wretched beings in undying pain! Daughter, your father has this minute touched the corner of this page to his candle, and seen the frail paper shrivel and curl in the flame; consider, Daughter, that the heat of this candle is to the everlasting fires of Hell as a grain of sand to the reaching desert, and, as this paper burns in its slight flame so shall your soul burn forever, in fire a thousandfold more keen" (169). Hell may be other people but the Being of a given person determines in part the nature of one's effect on the other. In Crane's case, we presume there have been no stellar parent awards offered, and in fact, his family members die in either violent circumstances or reclusive unhappiness. "Absolute reality" equates to an ultimate solitude, the truth of occupying one's somatic psychology and traversing the inevitable extinction of that body/mind alone, though it also, and more unnervingly, connotes the tension inherent in Lacan's "hatelove" that emerges from a fundamental propensity for misrecognition. When Dr. Montague refers to Hill House as "a masterpiece of architectural misdirection" (106), he is referring to the house's disjointedness that applies to cultural and individual architectures as well, particularly those, like Eleanor's, that are highly susceptible to misrecognizing both their inherent *preciousness* and their tremendous value and potential for Being.

Kristeva speaks specifically about terrorist fundamentalism when she contends "these fanatics, patching up their crumbling psyches with odds and ends of religion taken to extremes, these gangster fundamentalists who have lost all sense of right and wrong, of self and other, of inside and outside, embody a real anthropological disintegration and thus a radical phase of the nihilism that threatens all globalized cultures" (*Marriage* 92-93). Sollers, however, makes the broader claim that "one is exiled in humanity" (55). Somewhere between the critique and the general admission, between the deadly or merely hackneyed exhibitionism of self-absorption and the healthy relationship to exile and genuine alterity, may lie an antidote to Hill House, of which we are all inhabitants. Another way of framing this is to repeat, with Heidegger, that we are susceptible to "homelessness" as a "symptom of the oblivion of being" (*Basic* 242), or the illusion of a stable, "sane" "home" where, as Eleanor puts it, "I can dream and tell myself sweet stories" (Jackson 195). Dr. Montague and Luke, on the other hand, though certainly "homeless" in terms of human intimacy and fraternity, reveal their relative lack of oblivion in the claim that "we are only afraid of ourselves," which Luke amends by adding "of seeing ourselves clearly and without disguise" (159). Crane has told himself less than sweet stories about his daughter's eternal damnation in a literal Hell, while Eleanor fabricates literally every communicated vision of herself. Their mutual homelessness, in spite of attachment to Hill

House, derives from an inability to manifest the clarity of authenticity, what we might identify as a balm for our common plight of exile *and* a precondition for love.

"Journeys end in lovers meeting" goes the refrain that culminates in the lead up to Eleanor's "surrender" to death as "go forth and meet your lover" (226) in the voice of child, a voice that only Eleanor, much to her satisfaction, can hear. A misdirection or misrecognition if there ever was one, and a tragic foil to Sollers's assertion that "the love encounter between two [or more…] people is the rapport between their childhoods" (*Marriage* 17). There is the quality of that childhood to contend with on the part of the other, but more crucially, the manner in which the adult has processed her formative years, his desires, resentments, triumphs, and rejections, etc. Eleanor is a failure in both regards, a "lover" and, like Crane, a "property owner" in death after having never known neither the selflessness of love nor the value that death portends for life beyond mere escape. Nevertheless, this sad irony is not the whole story of love with its many entanglements and perils. There are still musical, painterly, even political texts and ideas as healthy, critical insurrections into the culture, the self, maps to authentic ways of being. *The Haunting of Hill House* is another revolt that cares about its fated protagonist as much as it serves to "unmask" the reader. When Jackson writes of the foursome gathered in Theo's room in the middle of the night, a family who "spoke lightly, quickly, and gave one another fast, hidden, little curious glances, each of them wondering what secret terror had been trapped in the others, what changes might show in face or gesture, what unguarded weakness might have opened the way to ruin" (133), she is digging deep into the killing psychology of interpersonal relations, the impossible odds against knowing another definitively amidst whatever strife or pleasure, thus offering the gift of insight, arguably a truly loving gesture that wages battle against any and all self-centered orientation.[22]

While it is possible that the 1999 feature film version of Jackson's novel by Dutch filmmaker Jan de Bont, *The Haunting*, presents a case study in virtually everything that is wrong with late 20th/early 21st century cinematic horror and, not ironically, capitalist America, Robert Wise's 1963 adaptation (also *The Haunting*) is a very different beast that warrants attention here. In addition to its superlative cast and screenwriting, the film ensures that its viewer is brought intimately into both Eleanor's crumbling interiority and the "maniac juxtaposition" of supernatural events through cinematography that relies on close-up, rapid tracking, and wide-angle shots. Its sound design (punctuated by loud banging and breathy grunting that seem as though the voice is at the very front of the mix, for example) relies on unnerving silence as much as environmental sounds and music. Though abandoning key scenes from the novel (including Eleanor's run-in with the older woman who damns her, her awkward experience in Hillsdale), the film stays true to Jackson's text, utilizing some of its dialogue and certainly capturing the novel's disturbingly atmospheric qualities. Eliminating particular scenes keeps the menace mostly confined to Hill House, thereby foregrounding the horror as paranormal threat over cultural critique. Nevertheless, the film's horror is tremendously successful at merging interiority and exteriority by way of its paradoxical stillness relative to contemporary American films (in any genre or non-genre) that tend to cater to a general desire for faster pacing.

Aesthetically, we might say that Wise's *The Haunting* "dares evil" by bringing a powerful sense of immediacy to what is very much a human dynamic given that no inhuman entity is ever witnessed. It resembles George's Romero's 1968 *Night of the Living Dead* in this regard – zombies running amuck in the countryside, terrorizing people whose collective dysfunction ultimately remains the focus of the film – but with no exteriorized presence and a far more sophisticated artistry. It takes the viewer to "the beyond," that "fatefully magnetic destination," as Thrower puts it, of alienated *Dasein* and its occasionally pathological attempts to *be* in relation to others. The "evil" of relationality is not merely the profound impossibility of fully knowing another (or oneself, for that matter), but its compulsive quality that precipitates an excess of what Gurdjieff targets as the personality in all of its performativity and inauthenticity. Both the novel and the film succeed in compelling one to look squarely at what is "vile" and "diseased" and to either confront the evil by daring it to reveal itself at the risk of death or to flee, to "get away from here at once" (33), as Eleanor instructs herself upon beholding Hill House for the first time, to return to a life of subservience and mere dreaming wherein "sweet stories" can turn to absolute "loathing" and hatred in the time it takes for a child's healthy heart to beat.

The Shadows of Thomas Ligotti

Despite our reservations about contemporary horror film, David Mareau and Xavier Palud's film *Ills* (*Them* 2006), similar to Brian Bertino's *The Strangers* (2008), depicts an essentially bourgeois couple being terrorized by vicious killers because, as the perpetrators more or less contend, they can, in a deeply unsettling, effective unmasking of the real. The violence, the chaos, is random and thus functions as its own unstable *Dasein* amidst French or American complacency and privileged comfort, an entity in its own right for which the murderers, mostly in their teens and twenties, appear as mere vessels, predominantly anonymous in hoodies and masks. The two films stand as texts in which the horror replaces Heidegger's "they" with a "them" of another order. Its knowledge is of the "truth" of violence – the knife, the machete, the stalking, predatory impulse – and, of course, the truth of death. It is arguably such knowledge, foisted upon the viewer in creeping, graphic detail, that accounts for the films' popularity, the tension-laden immediacy of human vulnerability – evil "respects no one" – like Freud's notion of horror that emerges as much from within as without. [23] Daring evil is potentially destructive, both psychologically and physically, a dare that assumes a particularly invasive quality when enacted, consciously or unconsciously, in the home.

The stories of Thomas Ligotti are known for their bleakness, their cosmic pessimism, and, in the case of "In the Shadow of Another World," a Lovecraftian alterity that is more likely to augment than to assuage human folly. Here the "them" assumes a form not of weapon-wielding psychopaths but of "spectral ontogeny," an ever-developing "marriage of insanity and metaphysics" (Ligotti, "In the Shadow" 375). It is an "other realm" (366), profoundly other to a rational world in which civil and natural order are generally taken for granted, any phantasmal incursions being merely the stuff of fantasy and impossibility, until the impossible becomes entirely and menacingly real, as it does in Jackson's novel, at least in terms of Eleanor's inner life. At the beginning, however, this realm is relegated to a particular house owned by Raymond Spare, a man whose surname is taken from the previous owner who has earlier endowed the house with supernatural qualities, as a kind of kaleidoscopic portal to "another world." We encounter the narrator on his way to meet Spare and tour the residence that will instill its visitor and owner alike with a potent sense of "nightmare." The word is repeated four times in the story; it is the sort of fact that digital humanities scholars like to propose as deeply meaningful beyond its surface observation, one that in this case at least attempts to evoke a comparable experience for the reader. There is an "irreducible certainty of nightmare" (377) at play in the house, a "pageant of nightmares" (375) assuming a full spectrum of colors and sounds, voices, though Spare's reading of a text by the original Spare, a practitioner of the "science of nightmares" (371) – identity here being both static and fluid – reveals the notion that "nightmares are born from the impress of ourselves on the life of things unknown" (372). As in Jackson's novel, paranormal alterity is such in relation to the human and, more importantly, *by virtue of* human qualities that make us susceptible to mystical insight, psychological perforation, or damnable ruin, especially in so far as one is inclined toward "hopelessly dreaming" (ibid.).

The narrator will echo the story's title when he claims that "we truly live in the shadow of another world" (372-73), a "beyond" that reveals itself as closer than breathing, or what in ordinary life we may consider home, when circumstances are ripe and our usual buffers are more porous than usual. That we live in the shadow of this otherness implies a hierarchy of value or power, that the other world is somehow superior to our own, a revelation that unfurls slowly, then wildly in Spare's residence, not unlike the ontogeny of Hill House. The two homes differ, however, in that the former first appears to the narrator as "sterile," "safe," and, in the words of the inhabitant, "spiritually antiseptic" (369), as though its interior face is concealing a secret, which, of course, it is. Eventually, the narrator senses a "shift in atmospherics" that will soon lead to "the visible [giving] way to the transcendental" (370). What might this mean? Is "the transcendental" comparable to genuine alterity, radical self-effacement? Quite possibly. What is clear is that it has little to do with a romantic, Emersonian ideal. As the house transforms, with window shutters opening to expose signs and colors, it does so "toward an eclipse of this world's vision" (371). If living in the shadows is not enough, the house obscures not only the "world" but its collective, materialist perception to bring about a nightmare of the real. It presents a version of Lovecraft's own prismatic "From Beyond" and "The Colour Out of Space" in which rationality gives way to metaphysical insanity, to paraphrase the narrator. Ontology is at once evolved and eroded in this "other realm" that becomes "dominant and [pushes] through *the cover of masks*, the concealment of stones, [spreads] its moldy growths at will, generating apparitions of the most feverish properties and intentions, erecting formations that [enshadows] all familiar order" (our italics, 376).

Lovecraft's fiction tends to leave little room for ambiguity in terms of the Other's malevolence, at least from the perspective of terrorized or dying humans. That which creates shadows in Ligotti's story, on the other hand, however "feverish" its intervention into "natural" order and sanctity, is diametrically opposed to Badiou's notion of evil as simulacrum of truth, as it is to Hill House. Rather, the house, as the narrator observes, is "possibly the only place on earth, perhaps in the entire universe, that [has] been cured of the plague of phantoms that [rages] everywhere" (375-76). Spare's home is a paradoxical place of healing through exposure and rendition of truths. It is an authentic "safe space" to the extent that it overcomes the disease of mere simulations of life and death and the animalistic anger that these can provoke in a world of common (mis)perception. But it is not without horror. It recognizes what Deleuze calls "the world" as "the set of symptoms whose illness merges with man," compelling "literature" to function "as an enterprise of health" (*Essays* 3). People outside are the horror in need of cure; Hell is other people. While Spare and his guest become increasingly immersed in the swirling, spectral alterity of the house, the world on the margins continues in the ways of its sickness, likely perceiving the house's exterior as Augé's anthropological "non-place," an environment that fails to meet the standard criteria of place due to its fleeting purpose – in this case, the home of an eccentric whose contribution to community is negligible. "Ethical ideology," Badiou maintains, as opposed to an ethics based in "truth-processes," "is simply the final imperative of a conquering civilization: Become like me and I will respect your difference" (*Ethics* 24-25). Spare is unlike anyone, save his namesake; his ethics lies in the fact that he will not be conquered by self-sameness, neither the repudiation of nor the subsumption into "publicness," while he is psychologically and spiritually aligned with the house as an authentic place of insight and becoming-"thereness," like a forest of knowing trees.

The "plague" of the garden-variety world is its dismissive or violently averse positions against genuine alterity and its facile attempts to cultivate scurrilous individualism. Ligotti's narrator will eventually leave the house with his life intact, while Spare is last heard "screaming – *the windows …pulling me into the stars and shadows*" (Ligotti, "In the Shadow" 378), whereupon he vanishes. Death, yes, but the implication is that he lives on in another state, that the man, the personality called Spare, has given way to a far more radical mode of Being. He has knowingly sacrificed, been divested of self for the sake of accessing that which eclipses the world in all of its disingenuousness – a minimalist orientation despite the baroque machinations of the house. As the guest views the place of Spare's metamorphosis from outside, it becomes clear to him that the windows with their many revelations are "for looking *in* as well as out" (378). The ostensible evil of this text is finally the challenging disclosure and rewards of interiority. A man has been transformed into something that exists on the periphery of mundane self-concern and cultural submission. The actual evil assumes the form of delusion as, years later, the narrator learns of the house's poor reputation from the standpoint of locals who deem it unhallowed. "They cannot see," he claims, "nor even wish to see, that world of shadows with which they consort every moment of their brief and innocent lives. But often, perhaps during the visionary time of twilight, I am sure they have sensed it" (379). Heidegger's "they" remains operational as it always is and shall be. Nevertheless, the "them" of "other realms," ever-ready to hack away at illusions of immortality, or to envelop the scene of a banal moment in the lived life, make themselves known to the senses, the slow blunting of which, ironically, exposes one even more to the hazards rather than to the triumphs of rebirth.

Lovecraft, for whom the particular atmosphere of horror is everything, according to his classic essay *Supernatural Horror in Literature*, charges those fictions that recoil from the immersive menace of the genre with proffering a contrary "smirking optimism" that "deprecates the aesthetic motive" via heartening didacticism (12). Reading contemporary, popular American fiction driven by the combination of cute allusiveness and clever pathos goes a long way to substantiate this perspective. In his essay collection, *The Conspiracy Against the Human Race*, Ligotti is more methodical, more late twentieth century cultural dyspepsia in his aversion to sanguinity. He is by far the furthest removed from the philosophical project of this study by virtue of his absolutist pessimism, a stance that culminates in the notion that being and consciousness (as "the parent of all horrors") are "MALIGNANTLY USELESS" (Ligotti, *Conspiracy* 133). Life, then, is discerned as "that which *should not be*" (ibid.). Between the all caps and the italics, the message is not lost. Where this argument succeeds is in its acknowledgement that the waking unconsciousness of daily life generates problems that horror is especially proficient in spotlighting. There are certainly things (situations, behaviors, staunch, ideological positions) that are better left to the dung piles of history, that perpetrate malignant acts outside of time, so "natural" as to seem persistently intrinsic to a totalizing force of history whereby time is collapsed into a perpetually grotesque present. Ligotti's sense of horror's atmosphere evokes the dour, Schopenhauerian urgency around the "something pernicious that makes a nightmare of our world" (185), a world beset by environmental and other devastations.

On the other hand, the obstinacy with which he promotes the worthlessness of humanity cuts all too close to Freud's identification of "horror" as "fascinated dread in the presence of an immaterial cause" (qtd. *Hartwell* 4). "Something" material – and quite possibly immaterial – is doubtless awry in the world, constituting a series of ongoing nightmares, to be sure, though "dread," particularly that which exults in its *difference* beyond the pale of survival and simple – or complex – pleasures, runs the risk of limiting *Dasein* to what we might call identification-alterity. Horror is fascinating, as are the lengths to which people will go to affirm themselves amid the unknown and familiar, dehumanizing ruin. Genuine alterity, however, identifies neither with absolute dread nor superficial wellbeing in so far as these cannot account for the truth of a given process. These conditions are, rather, in their prerogative stances, lost in an atmosphere of septic disavowal or trivial privilege and self-aggrandizement. Consciousness can indeed give birth to monstrosity, though there are degrees of both basic cognizance and self-awareness, at one end of which spectrum lies authenticity. As an extension of Lovecraft's self-evident claim that "the spectral macabre" requires "a capacity for detachment from everyday life" (*Supernatural* 3), developing consciousness necessitates detachment not from the macabre but from dread-as-identity. The "they," be it spectral or the universal cessation of life, can be inevitable without determining identity. Viktor Frankl, among others, has a few things to say about this.[24]

Ligotti ultimately eschews any attempt to cultivate consciousness that does not fall under the umbrella of pessimism. He offers, for example, a superficial, sleight of hand critique of Buddhism's "three-ring circus" (*Conspiracy* 132) that aligns it with pessimism while making no distinction between its "dogmatic authorities" and "those of Christianity" (133) (or, in fact, those of pessimism). There may be much to critique in any religious tradition, though without attention to nuance, especially in so broad and psychologically rich a practice as Buddhism, one's assessment is doomed to mediocrity in the service of a self. Like the condemnation of postmodernism by professor turned YouTube performer Jordan Peterson, much is overlooked. In some respects, Peterson and Ligotti comprise two sides of a coin, though the latter's position can clearly be linked to the horror of "absolute reality" that diminishes egotism, while Peterson and his followers have a tendency to engage in the sophistry of mere power schemes to further provoke the ill-fated selfhood implicit in Don't Tread on Me. What is missed in both examples is the value of intuitiveness that, according to common knowledge, may be inborn or, less understood, nurtured. The fashionable category of "philosophical disenchantment" is much too devoted to establishing its antithesis to life to care about the psychological and somatic amelioration of intuitive consciousness. Likewise, the blanket dismissal of postmodernism (be it at the hands of Peterson or the far more compelling Eagleton) neglects, intentionally or otherwise, the subtleties of Being and belonging that emerge in the lived life from foregrounding play, process, indeterminacy, or rhizome over purpose, complete object/idea, determinacy, or root.[25] In other words, each rendition of Buddhism and postmodernism, respectively, finally privileges Truth over truth.[26] And yet, with Ligotti, we can wholeheartedly agree that there are doubtless "other worlds" of which most of us perceive only the shadows, if that. Shadows as inviting signifiers without a cultic, dominating, transcendental signified – only wisps of intuition and the possibility of dark, or discreetly illuminated, other worlds.

Dennis Etchison's "Horrorthon"

In Wise's *The Haunting*, Eleanor elaborates on why she sleeps on her left side: because, she thinks, it wears the heart out quicker. This poignant confession tells us much about the character's sensibility and the extent of her personal nihilism. Sometimes the film version adds to rather than detracts from the original literary form. In the case of Jack Martin's (a.k.a. Dennis Etchison, to whom the novel is dedicated with tongue securely in cheek) novelization of 1982's *Halloween III: Season of the Witch* (the third sequel to John Carpenter's seminal *Halloween* [1978]), we find a literary reboot that absolutely adds to the film's cult-status legacy through the craft of Etchison's fiction. Though Carpenter did not direct the film, he did compose the soundtrack, which, like the house in *The Haunting of Hill House*, as well as in its original cinematic interpretation, is very much its own forbidding character in *Halloween III*. Etchison follows with the language and literary style indicative of a comparable atmosphere as he faithfully details the film's key scenes and contributes flare and nuance to an already absorbing narrative. Of course, the term novelization has a tawdriness about it. The notion of moving *from* film (the medium that Adorno famously eschews on the grounds of its ideological reflections of mass culture) *to* a novel attempting to emulate such a popular medium tends to smack of vulgar commercialization. As with Diane Keaton's intellectual in Woody Allen's *Manhattan* who the male protagonist berates for wasting her talent, the novelization is thought to be a fast buck and little more. The comic and occasionally quite serious director, of course, was attempting to bring an Ingmar Bergmanesque quality to his comedy with *Manhattan* at what was perhaps the height of American cinema's unabashed depth (the 1970's); this and other films stamped their mark on the culture with brazen wit, intelligence, and grittiness that are arguably unmatched by 21st century American films.[27] Though Etchison's novel certainly has its current rivals, it manages, circa 1982, to push beyond doing justice to the film and ultimately captures the spirit of both its antecedent and an age that was not too far removed from the relatively permissive zeitgeist of the prior decade; and it does so with what philosophers of radical ethics and sacrifice might call a conscience.

There are different, competing forces at work in *Halloween III*, the first one being communicated before the novel even begins to unfold, in its tagline, "The night no one comes home," a reference (one of several) to that of Carpenter's original *Halloween*: "The night he came home." In the initial film of the franchise, Michael Myers returns to Haddonfield, Illinois to terrorize suburbanites after having spent the previous fifteen years in an institution for murdering his sister. You can go home again, as it turns out. Myers's homecoming brings him to the house of his childhood and his crime while his doctor braces himself and a skeptical sheriff for mayhem. If *Halloween* speaks to the violent destabilization of home via one of its own, *Halloween III* (which has nothing to do with the former and takes place in Northern California) is more interested in the haunting of "homelessness," which assumes numerous forms in the novel/film. One way to read the third installment's slogan is that there will be no boogeyman, no literal Return of the Represssed, just a corruption that emerges from within and thus de-centers, to put it mildly, the home. A more obvious explanation is to interpret it through the example of protagonist Dr. Dan Challis, a middle-aged man separated from his wife and children, a drinker, and an underpaid medical doctor whose life is complicated by a murder that takes place at the hospital during his shift and the victim's daughter who is convinced of foul play. Dan's general attitude is that of a blue-collar worker forever trying to make ends meet. He lives alone in an apartment, loathes his ex-wife, misses his kids, laments not making enough money, and drinks to forget. Ellie Grimbridge, now without a father, is also adrift, devastated by her loss but intent on solving the mystery. Outside of what comes to be their mutual investigative project, together they constitute what Dan observes as the everyday "tired, the desperate, the walking mad" (Etchison, *Halloween III*

22) who suffer under the weight of the American class system.

So together they follow a trail of deadly masks; specifically, those Halloween masks designed by the Silver Shamrock company from which Ellie's father, we know, has recently fled for his life. They travel to Santa Mira, a small, ghostly town, meet a suspiciously, exceedingly hospitable Irish hotel owner, a few shockingly middle-class guests, and eventually take a tour of the factory only to discover that the father's car is hidden there, whereupon Ellie is soon abducted and Dan is left to battle the CEO, the elegant, devious Mr. Cochran, and what turn out to be his android workers. In the process, Dan meets a genuinely homeless man, a local who has not succumbed to Cochran's literal infiltration of the town and its people and who complains of being denied a livelihood, forcing him to live in a makeshift shack where he, too, drinks his life away (before being killed by the well-tailored robots in bloody, grisly fashion). But it is the masks and the technology that fuels their unholy function that will be the focal point of the narrative's late 20th century cultural and cosmic homelessness. What it will identify as "the tyranny of the machine" (156) will manifest most malevolently in Cochran's androids that are indistinguishable from humans except for their static dispositions. On the other hand, early in the novel Dan will think "that's what they want to be these days: as much like machines as they can possibly make themselves," regarding the average person. "It's an old story. It goes back to goose-steppers and the whole military mystique. No. It goes back further than that. A lot further" (19-20). It goes back to primitive expressions of "publicness," as well as to the machinations of Heidegger's favorite dictator. It speaks to "ordinary" fascism that reaches the citizen of 1982's America via television to create "televised psyches" that cannot resist absorbing "reels of the same relentless stalking of the heart of the American dream" (218). But technology also transcends the banality of mass conformity in Etchison's novel. It commandeers the "season" that Dan sees as "a state of mind. It's always here. Only the true ugliness of their money-grubbing doesn't show through so blatantly the rest of the time" (21). We will come back to the phenomenon of Halloween. Crucial to grasping Dan's observation – aside from the consumerism of shopping and trick-or-treating – is the fact that the Silver Shamrock masks come equipped with an electronic chip that, when worn during a particular airing of the incessant Silver Shamrock commercial on Halloween night, kills the wearer and, most likely, those around him or her. The "state of mind" – television addiction and mass consumerism – will be manipulated by Cochran to wipe out the population.

"Man against machine," thinks Dan as he sits in a bar watching a children's cartoon. "That's the new battleground" (65). The machine "sets upon nature" by attempting to extract its resources to transform them into commodities, in Heidegger's view, which in Etchison's bleak universe equates to technology dehumanizing humanity. And yet, he will also wrest the notion of "man" from any romanticized essentialism. Dan and Ellie meet the Kupfers – Buddy, Betty, and Little Buddy – at the hotel, a middle-American family whose business works with and idolizes the Silver Shamrock company. They arrive in Santa Mira in their Winnebago to pick up an order just before Halloween. The ineffectual patriarch is excessively nice, the wife tackily demure, and the son a repository of distracted energy and covetousness. Etchison writes "Challis was being set upon by a family of overweight Mousketeers … together they were an unstoppable force of nature, like kudzu and income taxes" (97). Caught in the machinery of American culture, the Kupfers are doubtless the stereotype that nevertheless has its basis in (absolute) reality. Today, they might want to "make America great again" and embrace the online/blogosphere fascism that has galvanized tribes in desperate need of community over and against the many strains of progressivism such collectives reject, and quite possibly, misrecognize. Etchison continues: "He's a low-potential achiever with high blood pressure and a tendency toward ulcers; his wife's hypoglycemic and undoubtedly a nag, and his kid is badly in need of a prescription for Ritalin. A workaholic prone to fits of depression, not above a shady deal now and then to keep them in doubleknit polyester" (98). It is this creepily familiar terrain that "sets upon" the protagonist who is clearly navigating his own depressions and workaholism, though he does so with a savvy knowingness that sets him apart from the Kupfers. Dan may be an outcast to his family, but he is not "extracted" from his humanity, he is not "homeless" in the sense of being dehumanized by

Disneyland ideology, a fact that is highlighted by his heroic efforts to defeat the truly monstrous force of the story.

The horror novel pits evil against evil when it comes to the Kupfers and all that they represent, however stereotypically. On the morning of Halloween, the family is brought to a room at the factory under the auspices of offering feedback on a new commercial. The room is outfitted in typical middle-class furniture and design, the "typical mail-order catalogue of home furnishings in America" (182), including, naturally, a television. The usual commercial suddenly appears, much to the disappointment of Buddy, and instructs children to don their masks. What follows is a brutal slaughter in which Little Buddy's head is turned to mush, along with the pumpkin mask, only to excrete a cauldron of spiders and snakes that soon take out the parents, Betty first, in an outlandish gnashing of fangs in the picture perfect American living room. Buddy is "pulled down with the rest of his family … as the defiled head of his son [opens] like the doorway to another dimension and [spews] forth darkness and decay" (189). He is accosted in Lovecraftian feverishness by "the unspeakable malformations of nature's underside" as "his physical body and the family he had created, the substance of his life and the world of his choice, all he had lived and worked for and the only dream he had ever known disintegrated before his eyes into a churning, formless mass of unleashed chaos" (ibid.). As the typical head of the family, or at least the breadwinner, Buddy has chosen his world of devotion to capitalism, to Mr. Cochran, as has Betty, a world of unthinking worship and death they have bequeathed to their son. Dan, having been captured, is forced to watch their ghastly demise and will respond with genuine anguish.

In terms of its cultural critique around technology and middle-class American values, *Halloween III* is all the more relevant in the 21st century. In other ways, the novel reveals its age, or more specifically, its milieu, but does so with a nod towards the integrity of its critique. Though marriage, for example, is forever a battleground between some lost, rampaging psyches tethered to wedlock, the frequency of Dan's/the novel's verbal, vitriolic jabs at his nagging ex-wife would appear to communicate a broader claim about the institution that borders, to put it mildly, on misogyny. At one point, the narrator – not Dan – refers to her as "the dark woman" (34) who has regressed to a kind of primitive childishness. Dan criticizes her parenting skills when he complains "with her help [their children will] turn into petty fascists, all intolerance and kangaroo court judgments and inhumanly rigid verdicts. Like machines" (16). Such comments accumulate. On the other hand, some parents are especially effective at producing fascism, intolerance, and general automatism in offspring. Dan's nurse and friend, Agnes, plays along with his manner at the hospital when he jokes "'I think I should have married you, Agnes'" and proceeds to pat her "bottom" to which she responds 'Watch it, buster! I play for keeps!' and receives a 'That's what they all say' in return (48-49). In the current epoch, a friendly "bottom pat" in the workplace is obviously anachronistic, along with its literary representation, despite the fact that it doubtless still occurs where it is clearly unwanted. And yet, the relationship between Dan and Agnes, hierarchical and thus inherently reliant on a power structure though it is, is also genuinely affectionate. They like each other. However, Dan will eventually find companionship with the considerably younger Ellie, who, as it happens, is the one to initiate sex under the auspices of husband and wife at the hotel in Santa Mira, a carnal surprise (for protagonist and reader alike) that finds some justification in her grief and in Dan's compromised self-esteem, not to mention the fact that people have sex on occasion.

Agnes, a Black woman who is at least Dan's age, is a unique character in *Halloween III*, a woman who knows how to joke with the relatively cynical doctor but is utterly committed to her faith and to her work. Dan reflects on her great value as a human being: "Good, kind Agnes, who believed with a faith she had never seen verified by empirical evidence, who had ignored her own discomfort for so long she had ceased to be conscious of it until it no longer mattered…. She did it to save lives. Which was another way of saying she did it for her soul. For her own kind. For all of them" (200). The "them" here refers to "us," as opposed to a Heideggerian "they." He goes on to consider the inter-relational and inter-dependent qualities of existence that determine her reason for being: "the circle of self-perpetuating life continued. Hardly powered by the stone relics of a doomed past. But a living energy that dwells in all that breathes" (201). It is this recognition and esteem, the notion of a life force, a "living energy," that certainly plays a role in Dan's own ethics, and thus his conscience, when he repeats a statement that Agnes makes about him in the privacy of her own thoughts: "this man matters. He can make a difference" (12). Later, when another chattering guest at the hotel, Marge Guttman, is brutally silenced by a mishap with the chip of a Silver Shamrock mask and who Cochran's people will dispose of discretely and quickly, Dan thinks "but it's important.... It matters. This woman matters" (125). Agnes's "adequate look," as Heidegger puts it, into people and situations – events – suddenly emerges as the "saving power into appearance" of the narrative. It is a remarkable moment in the horror text that positions conscience or the "call of care" as a force to combat the "homelessness" and "fallenness" of inauthenticity. It calls to mind Primo Levi's 1947 memoir *If This is a Man* detailing his experience in Auschwitz. What is a human being amidst such incomprehensible inhumanity? It is perhaps impossible to say, particularly for those who are fortunate enough not to have encountered such experience, though the cultivation of authentic *Dasein* would ideally lead to an acknowledgment that any given life matters by virtue of one's increasing aversion to frivolous self-regard, especially those lives that are under immediate attack at the hands of those who are supposed to protect.

But alas, the "saving power" will not be adequate to defeat the evil of *Halloween III*. Nature's "malformed" underside, as Buddy Kupfer learns, oozing from the macerated head of his son only to strike the father repeatedly, to kill the father, is a considerable force. This is especially the case when it is driven by a long-standing coven of witches who have learned how to harness this underside via the technology of 1982. Cochran may be quite high in the echelons of his coven, though it is clear that he himself matters very little relative to the comprehensive aim of global domination. To this end, he and his androids have stolen one of the stones of Stonehenge (for its supernatural properties) to fuel the mask chips that will destroy millions, a "primitive gravemarker for an entire nation" (177-78). This ludicrous plot point assumes gravity as the story develops and "too much of the chaos [breaks] through" (57) the straightforward cause and effect scenarios of Dan's rational – and ultimately ethical – universe. The male hero escapes his bonds and saves the woman. Together, they rain boxes of chips on the factory's control room containing the monolith, which kills all androids and eventually – with a devious, complementary smile – Mr. Cochran. But Ellie, as it turns out, is dead and has been replaced by a surviving android that makes a final attempt on Dan's life. He escapes death once again, rushes to a phone to call the three major television networks of the era in hopes of preventing the commercial from being aired, and succeeds with all but one. The novel concludes with Dan yelling "STOP IT!" repeatedly, whereupon "there was only the sound of rain outside in the endless blackness of the long night and, presently, the rising tones of a pitiful wailing within and without, spreading across the nation, the town, and the land without end" (228).

This viral hellishness supports Dan's earlier thought that evil "plays no favorites. And it respects no one" (204). Rich and poor alike buy into the capitalist self, with whatever means they have available. We purchase our way into dreams that become nightmares upon realization of consumerism's fault line to that abyssal chasm that products and identity formations can never fill. "Children" may don the masks that implode the child and release dreaded creatures into the living room, the suburb, the nation – the home – but adults create the skeleton of the dream and know with greater clarity what is at stake when fantasy gives way to absolute realities, those moments when non-being asserts its right to exist in consciousness, however briefly and incrementally. The narrator avows that "variations of figures like Cochran had come again and again to towns like this all across the country and the world, and would continue to come in endless variety and profusion whenever the days grew short and the true horror of an unburied past returned to haunt the long night of the human soul" (218). The "long night" is the inevitable fissure in excess self or personality, vulnerable to the hauntology of a walking dead past absorbing the present and formulating a future equally susceptible to death. The "true horror" lies in the abrupt, axe-wielding night-stalker or the ghostly slow-drift forms infusing being with a profound sense of cognitive and cultural dissonance. As Arthur Machen's Ambrose asserts in "The White People," "true evil has nothing to do with social life or social laws, or if it has, only incidentally and accidentally. It is a lonely passion of the soul – or a passion of the lonely soul" (116). In Etchison's novel, evil emerges from an elegant, Irish witch whose life in America is spent in the presence of mechanical humans with no capacity for emotional response, much less love, and it is perpetrated upon living people whose family units and contributions to an economy are actually far less efficient than the artifice of the androids. In his great passion, Cochran brings the horror of true evil to everyone whose authenticity has been compromised by a dream that is as universally and destructively unconscious as it is uniquely American.

The original film version of *Halloween III* was initially intended by Carpenter to be the first of a series unrelated to the previous films but associated one way or another with All Hallows' Eve. It marked a radical divergence from the 1978 slasher not only by bypassing the Michael Myers narrative, but in its assault on a nation, and ultimately the world, rather than a neighborhood. It positions the celebration as a threshold whereby, as Cochran explains, "barriers [come] down, you see, between the real and the unreal. The dead might look in, sit by our bit of fire ... our glorious festival of Samhain" (Etchison, *Halloween III* 191). On one hand, it is a night of masking the everyday masks of the school face, the work face, church face, domestic, power-relational faces, the face of mundane desire. From another perspective, it does more than mask these surfaces; it elides them, like a sound omitted, and joins the person to a quality of being that is potentially more authentic to the individual's sensibility. The Halloween mask, like Levinas's notion of the "the face," can communicate a "nudity;" it may be "destitute" of excessive Being, and therefore contains an "essential poverty" that "offers access to the face [that] is straightaway ethical" (*Ethics* 85-86). This is not to discount the playfulness of dressing up, receiving candy, and partying as though it is just another weekend but with a different costume, though the sanctioning of being *other* than the self one parades on a daily basis may, for some, produce a sense of alterity that is strangely immanent, that has a flavor of the real. One could argue then that Halloween stands as the symbolic but enacted nexus of authenticity and alterity wherein costumes reflect not only fantasy but a potentially taboo or otherwise unpopular aspect of the "ethical" face.

Like the film's singular soundtrack that eschews the typical string and piano arrangements and the crashing, sonic jump scares of horror so quick to relegate its impact to the safety of expectations, the Halloween mask can signify a kind of minimalist, "nude" alterity. Carpenter's eerie, repetitive, or floating drones never release tension despite their relative quietude. Comparable to the static androids who stand guard at the Silver Shamrock factory in doorways, on roofs, completely still but ever alert, or like Hill House, the music watches, negates convention, and immerses the viewer in very real trouble indeed. However, this *real* need not be confined to the trouble of blackened witchcraft or even quotidian dreams; on Halloween, it may simply be a matter of reducing the prefabricated self in favor of an otherness whose trials, should this alterity be realized beyond the margins of the season, would be the necessary venture into ethical Being. The season of witchery is thus a medium of exposure. That Halloween is also an example of operational, culturally approved generosity adds fuel to the fire of its provocative, exultant otherness.

David Seltzer's Secret

The Omen is another novelization of a film, both the novel and the screenplay of which were written by David Seltzer, whose diverse work spans *The Omen's* franchise and, strangely, writing/directing such films as the tender, coming-of-age *Lucas* (1986) and the Tom Hanks/Sally Field dramedy *Punchline* (1988). The novel is also intent on exposing the shortcomings of humanity, diverging from *Halloween III* only in the scale of its subversiveness. Rather than witches deploying deadly masks, *The Omen* famously charts the coming of Satan's son in a quest for world domination, thus harkening to the source of all evil, at least from the perspective of fundamentalist Christian cosmology. Damien is born of a jackal and substituted for the murdered-at-birth infant of a powerful couple, the Thorns, with the cosmic aim of his ultimate maturing into supreme power.[28] Over the course of the narrative, the parents come to the individual and collective realizations that something is awry. By the end, the wife is dead, pushed out a window by a minion of the Devil, and the husband is killed by a police officer in his effort to destroy the boy whose identity is finally apparent to him. Evil triumphs with Damien's adoption and inevitable rise to dominance.

Early in the novel, a working-class servant notes that Damien "is like a little man from Mars ... like he was sent here to study the human race" given that the child appears exceptionally perceptive and "rarely used his voice" (13). Damien studies humanity, and alongside him, the reader shares in these observations that assume the form of an omniscient narrator. What he/we perceive is precisely, in the universe of the novel, the fallible core of humanity's many excesses and misrecognitions. These are initially revealed with the tragic fact of Katherine Thorn's third pregnancy following two miscarriages, in which "one lonely cell found another" (5) to complete fertilization. We are born of alienation. Like the servant, Katherine is eventually attuned to certain peculiarities and events surrounding her son, and yet her secondary role in both her marriage and in the larger cultural sphere of patriarchy condemns this awareness to dismissal until it is entirely too late. When she complains to her husband (known throughout the novel as "Thorn") regarding expectations around his trip to Saudi Arabia and women offered as prostitutes in such business arrangements, he discounts her concerns, to which she responds, "I guess we're all whores, Jeremy" (29), which speaks to a common proposition in the novel: the degree to which humanity is subservient to its base impulses of survival and egotism. Consequently, marginalized groups (women, the working class, etc.) are ultimately not alone in suffering the travails of being human.

For his part, Jeremy Thorn is prone to over-thinking, to "speculation … to keep his mind off reality" (55). This tendency will finally haunt and end his life, as reality, the real, is never far from the surface in *The Omen*. When he gives a public speech touting progressive virtues and economic policies, a young communist begins questioning his motivation and demands action rather than pleasing bromides. Soon the audience is cheering for the activist rather than the dignitary: "The assault was impassioned. The boy clearly scored" (85). The implication, of course, is that Marxist views that highlight the truthfulness of material circumstances over democratic platitudes and capitalist privilege carry more weight, though what is really at stake is Thorn's identity and the lifestyle it affords him being compromised. Likewise, Katherine's psychologist determines that her suspicion regarding Damien not being her child has to do with "desire" rather than fear. "She subconsciously wishes she were *childless*. This is a way of accomplishing that. At least on that emotional level" (116), he explains, or explains away what the reader knows is Katherine's acute, and accurate, intuition about Damien's aberrancy. Even one trained in psychological insight misconstrues the real, which is both operative in and beyond the mind. The Cartesian self in Seltzer's novel, particularly that which thinks highly of itself and most benefits from social hierarchy, is wildly compromised as it confronts the unknown, even when it does not realize its oversights.

Desire, of course, is a powerful feature of the real that asserts its obstinacy against attempts to deny or sublimate its potency. This is especially the case in terms of the novel's critique of religious certitude. Edgardo Emilio Tassone is horrifically involved in the original exchange of one baby for another after having "the fear of God literally beaten into him" (95). By the time he assumes the mantle of missionary he is perpetrating the same violence on those he aims to convert: "He beat them as he was beaten and came to realize that in the heat of religious ecstasy he took sexual pleasure in their pain" (ibid.). As his violent escapades continue, he is subsumed into a satanic cult, *the* satanic cult that intends to assure conditions for the arrival of the diabolical son. How easily religious fervor becomes something else in the mind and body of one pulverized into an ideological framework and its accompanying identity, bereft of compassion, dignity, or critical thinking skills. As the narrator explains, "the Satanists provided sanctuary where the judgement of God did not exist" (96). Here there is at once an allowance for the real and a distortion of its value in light of the final intentions of the cult to insure their dominion. Jackson's Eleanor desires intimacy, belonging, and she, too, finds it in the "sanctuary" of Hill House at the cost of her seemingly eternal subservience.

The most damning condemnation of humanity, however, comes from a holy man, a guardian, as it turns out, of "the heart of Christianity" (178), an underground city of tunnels where the stories of the Bible were originally recorded, a guardian in a long line of such figures. Bugenhagen explains to Thorn and the dubious but realistic photographer with whom he has travelled to Israel that "most of the [passages are] passable except for recent cave-ins. They [archaeologists] keep digging up there, creating cave-ins down here. By the time they get here, it will all be rubble.... But that's the way of man, isn't it....? Assume that everything to be seen is visible on top" (179)? The way of humanity, then, is to engage in what we have already observed from Badiou: a "process of simulation of truth." In context, this simulation amounts to superficial perception, of the world, self, other, and of the Bible, skating as the fundamentalist (or in this case, the archaeologist) does on thin surfaces of excavation or literalist interpretation that serve to both reduce truth to "rubble, or "beat" fear into the adherent, and corroborate a delusional sense of Being among the elect. Moreover, this process is, it is important to recall, for Badiou the definition of evil. Evil is a procedure of Lacan's *meconnaissance*, misrecognition, and by extension, a travesty of authenticity.

The primary simulation of the novel is obviously the son of Satan masquerading as the birth child of Katherine and Jeremy Thorn. But Thorn shoulders the burden of his own intentional, counterfeit truth that colors most of the novel's drama. Given Katherine's struggle with childbirth over the course of two pregnancies, he secretly acknowledges the "failure" of the third and accepts the substitute infant in order to please and ameliorate her. And yet, as events escalate, he finds that "the secret [is] still there.... When things were going well, it was easy to hold it down, keep it dormant. But now it was somehow becoming important, and he felt it bourgeoning in him as though it would clog his throat" (47). The "secret" is the real, the human contribution to a cosmic shift the target of which is the downfall and subservience of humanity. Thorn is slave to his concealment of truth; Katherine to her failure to embody her perceived, societal role; Tassone to his guilt; while every other character that has an inkling of trouble is subject to fear. Curiously, the only character to reach the novel's conclusion with his integrity and his authentic sense of truth intact is Damien.

As Thorn completes the arduous journey back home, his companion having been decapitated, as is foretold by one of his own photographs that always tell the truth about death in *The Omen's* universe, he finds himself immersed in fog, not uncommon in London. His limousine arrives at the airport, though the drive is slow, "the inability to see anything passing by creating the sensation that they were not moving at all. It was as though the car were merely hanging in space, and it helped Thorn to resist the temptation to think about anything that lay ahead. The past was gone, the future unforeseeable. There was only this moment, lasting an eternity until

Pereford [his estate] finally came into view" (186-87). This "space" is thoroughly liminal, outside of time, in a fog that so often haunts the horror narrative. Prior to its discombobulation, Thorn is approaching the real conceptually but has yet to act on the enormity of its implications. In the fog, the present is rife with implication, consequence, though he remains a neutral figure not unlike Bugenhagen sequestered in his underground fortress. On the other side, however, lies the real in all of its violence and self-abnegation, where he will attempt to kill Damien and save humanity. He fails, of course, and the film (1976) cannot help but add a slight, fiendish smile to young Damien being escorted in his own limousine following the funeral of his surrogate parents.

What does it say that evil triumphs in this exceedingly popular novel/film in light of Badiou's and, indeed, Seltzer's commentary on the antithesis of truth and goodness? While the real is not inherently evil, it is subversive insofar as it necessarily cripples notions of *simulated* Being. Subversive literature is liminal by nature, a waystation, the posterior margin of the text operating as lived alterity *in potentia* by virtue of insight gained at the critical point between modes of Being. From this perspective, Katherine fails as a Deleuzian character in the sense that her obsession with motherhood is socially designated. Alternatively, however, she represents an act, that of giving birth, that functions as an event, a becoming-person, and thus the possibility of what Deleuze and Guattari recognize as "becoming-woman."[29] Damien is born, or rather, reborn, from an animal with the potential of "becoming-animal," though his rebirth occurs concurrently with "a movement in the galaxies ... the splintering of three constellations that produced the dark, glowing star ... with magnetic certainty, melding into a pulsating galactic ember" (1). The rebirth, the coming-into-being of Lucifer's offspring, is in some way cosmically fated, the number of the beast signifying the evil of raw humanity, its legion of base instincts and power-wielding, as well as the most radical rebellion possible in a world that is increasingly certain of its delusional, constipated certainties. As with the "there" in Jackson's profound claim regarding Hill House ("whatever walked there, walked alone" (*Haunting*, 3), the "there" of Damien's likely ascension to diabolical power is everywhere.

Chapter 4

– Rituals, Reproductions, and Rebirths: On Richard Matheson and Robert Eggers

The Blood of Richard Matheson's Son

Rebirth can never be easy. Nor is "born again" a phrase that necessarily conjures auspicious beginnings, or Deleuzian becomings for that matter. It is too mired, for the critical thinker, in the horrors of possession, the kind that assumes a benevolent veneer only to unleash quiet vitriol, bigoted attitudes, ignorant belief systems on unsuspecting others, unlike the demonic inhabitance that is ironically easier to dispel, if its representative films are to be believed. A second birth connoting an ascension to greater heights of human experience – healthier morals, more selflessness, healthier living – all too often (and straight out of the womb, so to speak) produces a decline into cultish ideology, its morality predicated on intolerance, its self-sacrifice merely a reorientation of egoic identity bolstered by emotionally-charged communal settings, and its life much closer to death in terms of a self that may be pushed even further into the mire and unconsciousness of embittered preoccupations. Typically, "rebirth" is not a "becoming," a salutary broadening of horizons or exploration or acceptance of alternate truth processes, but the reinstitution of a different Being, a nihilistic rejection of one's past. But with a dose of the very literalism upon which fundamentalists base their religion, the phrase also suggests a rebirth into authenticity. I was lost in myself, in my limited conception of myself, and then I was found by a developed sense of genuine selflessness born of interiority, as the famous hymn might be altered. For being born again to hold any value, it must entail a profound level of self-expulsion, leaving only the immediate intelligence of a body, a mind, a critical, creative spirit bereft of the *moi* that Lacan observes as succumbing to the "vertigo of the domination of space" (*Écrits* 28). Selfless interiority dominates nothing, neither politics nor the countless subjects of political power, including oneself. Rather, it unfolds time out of the space in which it finds itself by adhering to a "truth-process" that is of the moment, as conscious equilibrium, as opposed to vertiginous preponderancy. The hope for the anomalous, enquiring fundamentalist (or the culturally traumatized right winger, for that matter) lies not in some delusional martyrdom, but in the evocation of Heidegger's "little things" that go into forming a capacity to love authentically and "resolutely."

Richard Matheson's "Blood Son" complicates the above claims with considerable force. Following the trajectory of "In the Shadow of Another World," in which Spare is utterly transformed, his otherness driven to the point of death, "Blood Son" examines the move toward self-disavowal as self-realization – fully realized alterity – in a manner that strips selflessness of its productive, mystical contexts. The mystic embarks on a course of exchanging old wineskins for new to allow for the receipt of new "wine" that won't be spoiled or corrupted by old ideas/ideology – egoic proclivities, frivolities. Mysticism minimizes personality, in Gurdjieff's sense of the term, to make room for essence, and it does so, ostensibly, for the benefit of all, its "rebirth" a matter of exemplifying the sacred amidst the profane. Matheson's protagonist, Jules, exhibits a wildly apparent alterity from his childhood on, one that will evolve over the course of his pre-teens to assume a form that is anything but benevolent, in true horror fashion. And yet, until the story's shocking conclusion, his condition compels one to question not simply the sincerity of his desires, his Being, but the extent of his pathology. From early on, the narrator explains, "He made people shiver with his blank stare. His coarse guttural tongue sounded unnatural in his frail body. The paleness of his skin upset many children. It seemed to hang loose around his flesh. He hated sunlight" (Matheson 44). A doctor suggests that the empty gaze, contrary to his parent's concerns, is not blindness, "just a vacuous stare" (ibid.). Moreover, we learn, "He never spoke a word until he was five. Then, one night coming up to supper, he sat down at the table and said 'Death'" (ibid.). But it is not only his physical presence that unsettles others: "his

ideas were a little out of place for the people who lived on the block"
(ibid.). The accusations regarding Heidegger's morbidity, or indeed, that
of the horror genre itself, have drawn comparable suspicion on the parts
of "people who [live] on the block" of scholasticism and other institutions.
This critique has been shown to be misguided by virtue of the
philosopher's *affirmation* of life via the necessary engagement with
mortality and cultural inhibitors of authenticity, while the relatively overt
morbidity of critical horror, though certainly prone to perversely
pleasurable excess, may be understood in comparable terms. For his part,
Jules is fixated on death because he wants nothing more than "to be a
vampire" (ibid.).

He is especially attracted to the idea of draining the blood of females,
which places the reader in the compromised position of feeling for the
plight of his abjection and being critical of what seems a rabid misogyny
beyond the typical vampire romance (that he has yet to encounter). At one
point he is caught "undressing Olivia Jones in an alley" and later,
"dissecting a kitten on his bed" (45), leaving one to surmise his desire to
do to the former what he will do to the latter, to "dominate" females.
Jules's obsession with drinking girls' blood has an erotic resonance,
especially when one considers menstruation. To a morbid boy in the midst
of puberty, menses likely represents an excess of blood and perhaps shows
the vagina as the source of women's blood. Following this line of thinking,
drinking girls' blood offers a kind of closeness to the female reproductive
organs, a means of participating in sexuality, of controlling the
(heteronormative) site of male desire. Jules's violent actions hardly endear
him to other people, including the reader, so one may continue to follow
his narrative for the sake of learning how far his pathology (for this is what
it is, one likely decides) will go. How many girls will he traumatize? Will
he actually drink blood? Will his fixation develop into insight and
wisdom? Will he become an eccentric but productive, upstanding citizen?
Literature has a tendency to lead us, up to a point at least, where we expect
it to go. It traumatizes, then it ameliorates, or shocks us with unsettling
ambiguity; either way, we get what we want. We excoriate the monster,
lament the loss or suffering of decent human beings, shiver at unhappy or
outrageous endings, and smile in the face of a protagonist's triumph to the

extent that we ourselves become fleshed out, so to speak, like a character. We relate to incidents and emotions, even when the literary style is especially innovative or challenging.[30] We locate the familiar rooms and corridors of our "being there" enough to enjoy or denounce the text and move comfortably back into the flow of habitual routines. "Blood Son" fulfills such expectations with two crucial exceptions: it submits a profound, Badiouian "event" predicated upon "textual intervention" and it repositions Jules's "pathology," which may come close to provoking sympathy, even in the wake of his socially unacceptable behaviors, to a point of alterity so authentic that the horror is nearly overshadowed by the former's realization.

At the age of twelve, Jules sees what is presumably the Bela Lugosi version of *Dracula* (1931). He leaves the theater and walks, "a throbbing nerve mass, through the little girl and boy ranks" (ibid.). The film inspires him to cut himself, to draw blood, after which point he steals a copy of Bram Stoker's novel from the library and reads and rereads it incessantly, "ceaselessly," as Silverman might put it. He has already begun to devise his own vocabulary ("nighttouch," "killove" [ibid.]), and eventually changes his name to "Jules Dracula." He stops going to school and social services eventually stops inquiring. From a twenty-first century perspective, he becomes aligned, in a mode of Comic-Con theatricality, with both the well-intentioned gender pronouns and chosen names on the part of LGBTQIA+ activists and, more importantly, with the INCEL insistence on naming self and other, its physical alienation, and fetishistic, misogynistic, boy's club internet addiction. And yet, Jules is stranger and more interesting than the next century's outsider communities, including, perhaps, the cabal of scholars who present papers on vampires and psychoanalytic desire at academic conferences. He is utterly alone, that is, until he makes a friend at the zoo in the form of a living bat whom he christens "the Count" and feels "in his heart was really a man who had changed" (49). Like Blackwood's protagonist who cannot imagine a day without occupying the forest of his beloved trees, Jules's discovery takes him to the zoo every day while his peers attend school and become the social beings they are destined to be. Jules expedites his "truth-process" of becoming-vampire at this particular point where he is struck by "a rebirth of culture" (ibid.). It is an "event" *par excellence*, a moment of self-aware re-orientation, of "truth" not unlike, perhaps, the experience of clearly acknowledging one's gender or other fluidity. But for Jules, the event has been preceded not only by the intervention of filmic and literary texts, but by his own written testimony, referenced in the story's opening sentence: "The people on the block decided definitely that Jules was crazy when they heard about his composition" (44). Matheson takes his time to return to this instrumental creative effort, definitively entitled "My Ambition by Jules Dracula" (47), that stands as a forerunner to his ultimate ambition to "reproduce" himself.

According to Gurdjieff, any major project, particularly that of self-development, has to commence with an aim, without which one tends to begin, then waver as the effort becomes difficult or boring, whereupon different "I's" (those with other agendas, largely unconscious but magnetically powerful) interfere, come to dominate the field of subjective desire, and eventually one gives up the enterprise entirely, with or without a vague sense of guilt coloring the next endeavor. Jules is no such conventional person. He memorizes large sections of Stoker's novel before determining he has learned all he needs to know from it, which amounts to the necessary rudiments to fulfill his identity. The recognition of the bat and his devotion to its observation signifies an "event" to the extent that "*a subject*, which goes beyond the animal (although the animal remains its sole foundation [*support*]) needs something to have happened, something that cannot be reduced to its ordinary inscription in 'what there is'" (Badiou, *Ethics* 41). Jules exceeds the normative "given" by virtue of remaining scandalously faithful (as aligned with Badiou's notion of "fidelity") to the truth of his process – his ambition – of becoming-vampire. The procedure includes such developments as "'[living] forever and [getting] even with everybody and [making] all the girls vampires. I want to smell of death,'" along with having "'a foul breath that stinks of dead earth and crypts and coffins'" (Matheson 47). His goals grow increasingly violent as he reads his composition to his classmates, much to the horror of their teacher: "'I want them [his teeth] to slide like razors in the flesh and into the veins … I want to drink girls' blood!'" (48). Like most misogynistic tendencies, Jules's puberty-ensconced desires appear to be rooted in unfulfilled intimacy or simply a lack of positive recognition, though such a diagnosis, as we eventually discover, shortchanges the evental quality of his trajectory. His ambition is to complete (and control) his rebirth by any means necessary, a transformation that has been informed by textual "culture" and taken to the point, the "event," of becoming-animal/bat, in the sense of Deleuze and Guattari's program.[31] Jules is in process of composing himself not according to conventional, cultural mandates but radically, absolutely, in league with culture that is at once popular (which may signal suspicions concerning "truthfulness") and thoroughly infused with abjection.

"Month after month," the narrator states, "Jules stared at the bat and talked to it. It became the one comfort in his life. The one symbol of dreams come true" (49). The protagonist is certainly close to Jacksonian dreams here, the kind that buffer "absolute reality" and allow a character such as Eleanor to enjoy a few gratifying but isolated experiences before the real comes crashing in. This prospect surfaces for Jules when the central event of his life thus far gives way to a new stage, a liberation of the bat from its cage and their escape to a dark, dingy shed where the two, boy and animal, can merge, as Jules understands it. He releases the bat, slices open his finger and pleads with the creature to drink his blood. After failing to attract his accomplice, and accidentally cutting himself on the open lid of a tin can, he finally succeeds on pulling the bat to his neck at which point his ambition is nearly fulfilled – until he begins to sense his life slipping away, and "suddenly his mind was filled with terrible clarity" (51). Here the reader is led to sympathize with Jules at the same moment one may encounter that familiar satisfaction in the triumph of the real over some feeble, self-involved or otherwise pathological attempt to achieve a problematic selfhood, satisfaction toward which Matheson directs us in numerous ways. It is a peculiarly human tendency that emerges most dramatically in conservative denials of legitimate difference (homosexuality, non-binary gender orientation, for example), but also becomes hazardous in relatively neutral or progressive forums, this text being no exception. It inevitably raises the question as to who decides what is or is not authentic. In the current context, a marriage of philosophy and literature – specifically Badiou's ethical process and the example of a twelve-year-old boy – culminates in an answer to this question. His name is Jules Dracula.

He becomes acutely aware, there in the decrepit shed, that he is "lying half naked on garbage and letting a flying bat drink his blood" (52). He manages to crawl out of the shed and attempts to call for help, though "no sounds save a bubbling mockery of words [come] from his lips" (ibid.). If Jules is not pathologically unhinged, he is most certainly pathetic and, in this instance, cut off from reproduction. But horror is prone to baiting human egotism and presumptuousness before alerting us to the fact that the real is both beyond our limited knowledge and, in some cases, far more unsettling. The sound of the bat's wings on air suddenly disappears and "strong fingers [lift] him gently. Through dying eyes Jules saw the tall dark man whose eye shone like rubies. 'My son,' the man said" (ibid.). Jules realizes the full implications of his ambition, his identity, as he is reborn into what he is meant to become, gloriously aware that "the Count" is real, that he will feed and his alterity will be immortalized. At which point, the savvy, progressive reader smiles with his, her, or their recalibrated sense of satisfaction while, curiously, the reactionary does the same with perhaps only a dim awareness that Jules is emblematic of lived realities all too often thoughtlessly and selfishly denied outside the relatively safe world of fiction.

Yet Jules' victory–his rebirth–is also a state of victimization, one that reveals the symbolic violence of men's desire for women. His single-minded pursuit of becoming a vampire figures as a neurotic fixation on female sexuality. During his reading of *Dracula*, Jules pays particular attention to suggestively erotic passages, underlining quotes "Like: 'The lips were crimson with fresh blood and the stream had trickled over her chin and stained the purity of her own death robe.' Or: 'When the blood began to spurt out, he took my hands in one of his, holding them tight and, with the other seized my neck and pressed my mouth to the wound'" (46). In stating his goal of becoming a vampire and preying on women – "I want to drink girls' blood!" – Jules forges an identity that offers him erotic intimacy with women, a possibility denied to his alienated boyhood self and that thus must be created by an alternative, stronger Jules (48). When Jules forces his own conversion by trapping "the Count" in a shed after breaking the bat's cage, luring him by offering his own blood via a cut in his finger. Interestingly, Jules' (violent) vampiric conversion also suggests an erotic encounter. After cutting himself – creating bloody openings in his body, perhaps makeshift vaginas – and offering up his blood, "He started to moan and clutch at his chest" (51). Though Jules seeks to control the scene, control his own becoming-vampire, his life ebbs away from him as "the Count" consumes his blood, his desire. Through this symbolic creation of gashes, vagina analogues, and experience of vulnerability, of being subject to someone else's desire and control, Jules's becoming-vampire also figures as a becoming-woman.

What would it mean for Jules to transform "all the girls into vampires"? If we consider Jules's own transformation, at the end of which "the Count" acknowledges Jules as his son, Jules' conversion of girls into vampires would enable him to relate to them as their "father." If patriarchy, some engagement with family and reproduction of genetics or culture, were Jules' primary aim, why not seek to convert "boys" as well? In becoming a vampire, Jules converts thwarted desire into predation, sustenance. Fixating on transforming only "girls" only implies a desire for women to exhibit and depend upon the desire as he does. But do women experience desire the same way as men do? And do women seek to control their objects of desire as men do? In her song "Female Vampire," Jenny Hval offers a paradigm of female vampirism that completely subverts the male hunt. Whereas Jules imprisons the predator and inaugurates his own conversion, possibly dying in the process, and thus acts as a hunter himself, taking even while prey, Hval's unnamed female vampire hunts by posturing as prey. Hval describes how a woman hunts: "But if I'm coming I must be hollow enough / I follow the body, I mustn't rest / When I'm near you become someone else / I'm so tired of subjectivity / I must justify my presence by losing it" (Hval). Thus, she suggests that women hunters ensnare prey by appealing to it, and even in taking, are giving. Jules, in his obsession with consuming and converting girls into monsters, is himself trapped by his singular devotion to his "ambition." Considered together, "Blood Son" and "Female Vampire" illuminate gender socialization and their attendant pathologies.

Matheson's "Blood Son" functions as a disavowal of reproduction, both birth and the family structure, and enculturation through texts and stories, the means of reproducing a culture's values. Jules, whose first word is spoken at age five, is clearly not the son his parents want. His insistence on becoming a vampire is a journey towards belonging, towards being embraced as a parent's blood son. Jules is fascinated by and gifted in composition: "In some subjects like reading and writing he was almost brilliant" (Matheson 45). His neologisms, such as *"killove,"* evince his efforts to communicate his feelings, his vision, with other people: "They said things Jules felt but couldn't explain with other words" (45). That Jules reads "My Ambition by Jules Dracula" to his class reveals a desire to be understood and that Jules's self-conception, even his newly constituted identity of Jules Dracula, is a social being. In giving voice to his dreams and feelings and making words to express them, Jules enables people to identify with him and searches for connection, possibly even people who share his ambition. His composition and neologisms figure as attempts at cultural reproduction. When Jules seizes on *Dracula* as the narrative off of which to pattern his life, he "[sticks] the book down his pants" to sneak it out of the library (Matheson 46). Next to Jules's reproduction organs, the text is spatially and symbolically aligned with reproduction. When Jules recognizes a father figure in the zoo's vampire bat, he experiences his "rebirth of culture" (49). When Jules accomplishes his ambitions of becoming a vampire and finding a father-figure who embraces him, a conversion analogous to copulation and thus reproduction, he loses speech, succeeding only at making sounds, not words. In realizing his becoming-vampire, wilfully rebirthing himself, he is severed from the possibility of "normal" reproduction, either sexually or culturally, though he gains exceptional alterity.

The delicious living of Robert Eggers

There is another reality with which to come to terms, namely, that fiction – textual intervention – is not entirely safe, especially in so far as it eschews or problematizes the conventional happy ending. In representing alterity, a departure from the safe and normal, "Blood Son" thwarts the "reproduction" of dominant culture. The boy, whose fantasies include haematophiliac aggressions and the transformations of "girls" into monsters," is going to be a vampire after all; shadows envelop the world and even the average person has a flicker of ominous recognition on occasion; the witch may lose the battle, but the greater war will leave the failing doctor screaming; the everyperson that is more or less Eleanor has always been part of Hill House and will always "walk alone;" well-meaning women die or lose their sanity in their efforts to navigate desire and home; the man, too, will disappear into the forest, leaving his humanity behind, or perhaps elevating it. Horror and other texts are unsafe to the degree that they expose the nerves of core alienation, or at least the frailty of our efforts to prop ourselves up on an identity that is finally as collapsible as it is disingenuous. They scoff at and, in some cases, disembowel the personal sense of singularity, particularly that which masquerades as a kind of precious abjection, martyred alterity. Of course, every individual has something to contribute to life and death, embryonic though it may be, perhaps destined by some spectral fate to remain nascent. An ethics that is able to bypass reactionary ideology would seem to be quite interested in shifting such fate. In any "event," the text levels the field by implicating one and all in the very difficult search for "home" that may be undertaken with intelligence and sincerity or with desperate, clownish fever, much to our detriment.

Such texts can also uplift, though they do so by modifying the grounds and perspectives of fidelity to a given process. Sometimes the witch is victorious in every way. Robert Eggers's 2015 film *The Witch* offers a forceful upgrade of *Halloween III* and, more strikingly, Matheson's "Blood Son." In short, the witch wins everything, including her salvation. But not before her family is excommunicated from a Puritan settlement over the father's extremism and rigid, divergent biblical exegesis. As their isolated subsistence on the edge of a forest becomes increasingly compromised by failing crops and the loss of a newborn, familial fear, paranoia, and violence begin to erupt, uniting them in their shared humanity but separating them in a battle of false equivalents: the "good," the "holy" Puritanism versus what emerges as "evil," "unholy" witchcraft or possibly Satanism that is in fact being practiced in the forest near their home (and is responsible for the disappearance and ritual consumption of the infant). Though child murder is far from ideal, *The Witch* illustrates the genuine evil of self-righteousness and self-imposed estrangement as inimical to the ongoing "truth-process" of a self/other dynamic, not to mention of the difficulty of coming to terms with general, human fallibility. The family is reduced to three children after the baby disappears and the eldest, preteen son, Caleb, is lured into the hands of a witch and transformed before eventually dying an agonizing death, at which point, the youngest two (twins) accuse the eldest daughter and protagonist, Thomasin, of being a witch.

Thomasin becomes-aberrant in the context of her puritanical family dynamic, initially as a sexual object for the innocent but sexually curious Caleb, and later as a supposed apostate, despite the fact that it is the twins who are revealed as having been communicating with the family's sinister goat, Black Phillip. Two key events cement her transition into occult otherness, along with its refreshing, primal beauty. Once Black Phillip eliminates the father, in strikingly brutal fashion, and Thomasin kills her demented mother in self-defense near the film's conclusion, she follows Black Phillip into a shed and demands he speak to her. He speaks. He asks, "Wouldst thou like to live deliciously? Wouldst thou like to see the world?" – questions that might seem suspiciously tempting were it not for the utter deprivation and fear in which she has been living with her family. Her answer is a quietly resounding affirmative, at which point she is asked to sign her name in a book and encounters a man in black, "a tall dark man" (Black Phillip become human incarnation of Satan, in all of his elegance and quiet strength, rather than a vampire) who will escort her to the forest (now back in goat form). This journey finds Thomasin in long shot walking toward a tree that would not be out of place at the edge of Blackwood's wooded landscape and that will parallel the film's final shot. In the forest, she encounters a coven of witches moving spasmodically, ritualistically, around a fire. As the women begin to levitate, so too does Thomasin, whose surprise, then laughter and ecstatic victory complete her transition into absolute alterity, as depicted, again in long shot, floating near the tip of a fire-illuminated tree. Evil wins, unapologetically, though the cost of such triumph is finally the mere egotism of dictatorial forces, be they at the hands of Puritans or simply other "people on the block." *The*

Witch showcases the power of alterity, illustrating how Hval's female vampire could find prey at all, not in spite of, but because of the ability to "justify my presence by losing it." Thomasin, though a full-fledged witch by the end of the film, is innocent. Labelled a witch, blamed by her family, she is not their scourge, but their desires. She is able to live the life that her family merely desired, and in their desire, feared and rejected. Sometimes horror is as intent on advocating for authenticity and truthful, productive alterity as it is committed to unraveling every stitch that threads through the arrogantly cohesive self born of dubious entitlement.

Part II

The "Call of Conscience" and Authentic Alterity

Chapter 5

– The Being Here of Strangers: On Marie Darrieussecq, Jean Toomer, and Emmanuel Bove

Darrieussecq's Life of Paula

How strange, to transition from horror to what some might consider peculiar but genuinely *literary* fiction, from an awkward boy vampire, a series of haunted houses, a witch, to a thoughtful, sensitive German painter as represented by contemporary French writer Marie Darrieussecq and a beguiling young Black woman in Jean Toomer's lyrical but gritty "Fern," and a man who will likely have to lose everything to realize what he has in Emmanuel Bove's *Armand*, only to follow these texts with the likes of James Baldwin, Philippe Sollers, Virginia Woolf, among others equally thoughtful and sensitive to nuance, critical observation. While the French writers under consideration here certainly occupy their own stylistic milieus apart from a Baldwin or a Woolf, collectively they all have a great deal to say about authenticity and genuine alterity, and by extension, subversive Being. They fulfill Warren Motte's characterization of what he calls the "critical novel" that is "aware of the tradition that it has inherited, and it positions itself with regard to that tradition in a variety of manners; it puts its own "literariness" into play for the benefit of readers who are attuned to that discursive gesture. It is also mildly avant-gardist in nature. It questions (either implicitly or more explicitly) prevailing literary norms; it puts commonplaces on trial through irony or parody; it seeks to adumbrate fresh possibilities; it asks us to rethink what the novel may be as a cultural norm" (*Fiction* 11). Though this particular collection of texts will rely less on the kind of levity (via irony and parody) that is delightfully abundant in the works Motte tends to examine, and more on other, "fresh possibilities," it certainly distinguishes itself from current, non-genre American fiction, for example, that runs the gamut from various forms of earnestness (the experimentally hybrid; the poetically grave; the agonized self-expression) to a quality that is acutely aware of its lack of "literariness" (adorable, allusive, or commonly anecdotal humor; "street" realism), all of which are vulnerable to treading suspiciously close to Kristeva's category of the "selfie memoir." This claim is not without harshness and cynicism, and yet it is precisely such a critical mode that informs the *horror*, and thus the subversiveness inherent in the broader "critical novel" – the horror of no definitive self around which literary expectations would otherwise be met and celebrated, or lamented, wept over by a reader eagerly awaiting the Hollywood or independent film version. The "critical novel" is so in part by virtue of its form being as significant as its content. It is this critical balance that has a way of minimizing the authorial persona in the reading process and that allows John Cage to "have nothing to say" and to say it with considerable, cultural impact.

Darrieussecq's first novel, *Pig Tales*, is too brazenly comical to fall under the horror genre though it is doubtless replete with horrific imagery and hyperbolic but no less relatable predicaments. In a similar gesture, her *Being Here is Everything: The Life of Paula Modersohn-Becker* is neither comedic nor genre specific while its historical protagonist's painterly *life*, as such, can hardly escape what Darrieussecq identifies as "the slaughterhouse of the twentieth century" (*Being Here* 29). Nor can anyone's, really, neither before nor after the century that gave us Nazism given the culminations of violence that seem to presage one another and, as of the time of this writing, are looking very much like comparatively dumber but dangerously techno-frenzied explosions of fascism. There is also, of course, the relatively simple matter of death. Darrieussecq's book, episodic and tastefully poetic as it is, is not a biography in the traditional sense of this term, though it treats a life and the lives around it, once living individuals who found one another, fulfilled desire, and left their marks, or failed to do so, depending on the degree to which cultural constraints infected their trajectories prior to death. "Their marriages consummated or not, all these people are dead," she states categorically, and continues: "when I hear the word 'consummated,' I think of soup, of globules of fat floating on stock. I'd rather look at Paula's paintings. Bodies turned to dust, disappeared. The nub of their desire, the essence of their ardor, pulverized" (66). *Being Here is Everything* neither shrinks from nor makes sport of death. It laments its violence at the same time that it returns death to its rightful position as a prime motivator of effort and authenticity. "Let us not forget the *horror*," she reminds us, "that accompanies the wonder; the horror of this story, if a life is a story: to die at thirty-one with her work still ahead, and an eighteen-day-old baby" (our italics, 12).

There is a constant tension between authenticity and inauthenticity in Darrieussecq's account, such tension that any woman living in the world between centuries (1876-1907) might have encountered, but especially one with ambitions, intentionality beyond the cultural pillars constituting a woman's place. To chart the course of this tension invariably means beginning with religious strictures despite Paula's disinterest in theology. The artist is ultimately too busy painting and thinking to be bothered with religion, and yet it will mark her in death, on her gravestone: "a verse from the Bible, Romans, 8:28: 'And we know that in all things God works for the good of those who love Him.' For someone who never mentioned God, except when she read Nietzsche" (13). Inauthenticity is inscribed into the granite of her resting place, but at whose hands? Perhaps it is too easy to dismiss this act as that of a nefarious, or simply unthinking, Heideggerian "they;" on the other hand, what Darrieussecq recognizes as "the German program for women" of the time, and that would eventually be taken up by the Third Reich, the mantra of "children, kitchen, church" (77), certainly speaks to the propaganda of a "they." It is the meeting point of religion and patriarchy *par excellence*, a state of Being that is much closer to the darkness of essentialism, or Eagelton's notion of excessive being, than to, ironically, the philosopher's advanced, exultant *Dasein*. A woman's place is in the home – being there is everything.

There is an ethereal quality to Darrieussecq's book, a reveling in the beauty and humble tenacity of Paula's story. Patriarchy nevertheless situates itself in this life and is arguably responsible for her premature death (she died soon after childbirth from massive pulmonary embolism, the consequence of having remained bed-ridden, at her doctor's advice, for too long). From Paula's final aesthetic expression (she described her desired grave in a paragraph of detail, including location, the type of surrounding trees, "and in the center, a black wooden tablet with just my name, no dates, no other words" [13]), to her initial foray into the professional life of an artist, her first exhibition that a male critic, made "sick" by its innovation, dismissed as "most regrettable" (18), she is faced with the challenges of operating as a committed artist in a world governed by men. Darrieussecq foregrounds even the conundrum of writing her subject's name, that intersection of public and intimate identity that will require another seventy years to escape the reach of patriarchy. "Women do not have a surname," she explains. "They have a first name. Their surname is ephemeral, a temporary loan, an unreliable indicator. They find their bearings elsewhere and this is what determines their affirmation in the world, their 'being there,' their creative work, their signature. They invent themselves in a man's world, by breaking and entering" (45). To be an assertive, ambitious woman beyond occupying the few acceptable spaces and situations of the "program," to forge "events" in Badiou's sense of the term, then, is to be a criminal. Darrieussecq calls Paula Paula. It is, at least, to the satisfaction of past, present, and future patriarchs, her Christian name.

Of course, it is difficult, nearly impossible, to escape the allure of desirous others. There is a truthfulness to the rich complexities of desire. "Journeys end in lovers meeting," no matter the productive or sublimely deleterious nature of a given coupling, the promise of a new becoming that pulls at our bodily sensation and transforms our thoughts, creates ancient emotions. Paula Becker eventually marries fellow painter Otto Modersohn, a sensitive man who will eventually let her travel alone to Paris on multiple occasions and even pay her way (as a male, after all, he is the more successful artist of the two), a contract that will nevertheless come with advice from her father: "she will have to submit to the wishes of her husband, and learn to forget about herself, because it is up to the wife to maintain the harmony of the couple. She will have to relinquish any egotism…" (62-63). From the grave to the first, modest surge into public art, and into the very coils and rivulets of a lived psychology in the everyday between life and death, patriarchal "advice" would color the entirety of the woman. By the late 1920's, Virginia Woolf, who makes more than one appearance in Darrieussecq's book, is emboldened enough to reframe Carl's (Paula's father) argument "that girls' education consists in getting them used to the idea of putting aside their egos to look after someone more egotistical. Whether that 'someone more egotistical' is an infant or a husband makes no difference" (71). In revealing the paltriness of male power – along with a realist perspective on motherhood – and thus the great paradox of the patriarchal power dynamic, Woolf reshapes the span of the woman's everyday and makes possible the transformation of mere situations into "events" of her own conception.[32] Prior to Woolf, however, there is simply Paula and her struggle for solitude (a word that appears throughout the text as a bastion of relief, revelation, and rejuvenation) to paint, to think, even in the throes of love and marriage.

Darrieussecq notes how Paula "marvels at finding herself 'happy almost every time Otto and I are apart ....' It's when she becomes Paula Becker again. And that is pure joy. 'Half of me is still Paula Becker,'" the artist claims, "'and the other half is acting as if it were'" (88) in the context of her relatively exceptional marriage. Bohemian or not, the Modersohns are not quite the example of "marriage as a fine art." There is no "minimal communism" here in so far as the power structure remains essentially intact in Darrieussecq's representation as a consequence of, among other things, the economic imbalance. But Paula must also contend with her particular priorities that determine both the focal and the vanishing points of her perspective. She draws from her own experience in establishing that "marriage does not make one happier. It takes away the illusion that had a deep belief in the possibility of a kindred soul. In marriage one feels doubly misunderstood. For one's whole life up to marriage has been devoted to finding another understanding being. And is it perhaps not better without this illusion, better to be eye to eye with one great and lonely truth?" (75). It is rewarding to know that Kristeva and Sollers (two powerfully independent names) have been capable of aestheticizing their marriage (in contrast to Lacan's claim regarding the severe limits of sexual affinity between men and women that makes a strangely conspicuous appearance in the pages of Paula's narrative), though Paula is left only with calling out inauthenticity and extolling the virtue of integrity. Toward the unexpected end of her life, she will also kindly but adamantly request that her sister, in anticipation of Paula's child, refrain from including the words "nappies" and "blessed event" on her postcards (139). Obviously, women play their own roles in reifying illusion and inscribing potential "events" with grotesque, prefabricated romanticism, a fact of which Pamela Zoline will be acutely aware in 1967.

The larger cultural manifestations and calcifications of inauthenticity are abundant in Paula's life, such phenomena that she and her companions, including a young poet by the name of Rainer Maria Rilke, will critique with more and often less success. Ironically, however, Paula's observations concerning spurious behavior tend to focus on artists and other cosmopolitans. In her journals and letters, she speaks of their "small-minded feelings" (28), "all the powder, all this vanity" (58), of Rilke having "become a sychophantic socialite" and his wife – and Paula's closest friend – Clara being "in love with herself" (85), not to mention "a Polish girl [in Paris] who dresses and behaves like a man. And others who are too coquettish and insufferable" (96) in the "huge personality of Paris" (25). There is a remarkable timelessness to these accusations. Whether or not Paula is justified in her claims, narrow-mindedness and self-love would seem to be eternal properties of certain expressions of subjectivity. And yet, significantly, she is not without the self-awareness that makes self-scrutiny not only possible but essential. When she gives Rilke a collection of her drawings and sketches, she qualifies them by lamenting that some are "not me at all" while others are "too much me" (59). She struggles on the psychological and creative line between authentic and dubious modes of Being, a tension one can observe, or perhaps imagine, in Darrieussecq's own efforts to present the life in a mode that is at once fragmented, poetic, realist, non-sentimental, and delicate.

The horror of Paula's life is just that – the sovereign, normative forces whose business it is to impose sanctions on Being and becoming. "Children, kitchen, church" comprise the lived horror of the artist who loves, seeks basic necessities like any other, but above all else yearns to paint, and to excel in her vocation. The "fine art," however, exceeds the space of a canvas, the page of the poet, the material of the sculptress. It discloses itself to one working against the cultural odds as an imperative to revise those odds, to shift perspective, priorities, even the very meaning and power balance of authoritarian terms. Religion, patriarchy, marriage. Paula's example bears this prerogative out, however conscious or unintentional it may be. Surrounding each of the prevailing cultural pillars is a sense of religious *inevitability*. Paula and her friends, on the other hand, will revise this orientation in the form of what appears on several occasions as "piety," which they "break … free from its religious cage and return it to childhood and the sacred," Darrieussecq explains. "Piety allows them to see the invisible" (44). They reinvest the sacred with their own gospel. This has remarkable implications for the self at the center, as always, of its course amid competing impulses and agencies. The sacred, stripped of institutionalism, hierarchy, becomes more aligned with a "truth-process" that in turn endows aesthetic, relational, professional actions with inviolability. The sacred, stripped of God but informed by Nietzsche (image, music, text, as Roland Barthes might put it), finds its own way into the lived life that contains the "invisible," the selfhood beneath layers of personality, identity, subject-position. The "cage," of course, has as much to do with an individual's willing adherence to the confines of its bars as it does with the formal, cultural structures of domination.

The horror is overcome in part by cultivating awareness of its machinery, though what emerges in Paula's example – as woman, as artist – is a revision not only of holiness but of sacrifice. In marriage, she confronts Otto's attempts to woo her back after a period of separation with tremendous honesty and assertiveness. "How I loved you," she writes" "… but I *cannot* come to you *now*. I *cannot* do it. And I do not want to meet you in any other place. And I do not want any child from you at all; not *now*" (108). This "now" punches through her letter, as through the advice of her father and the bonds of matrimony, through the prospect – the duty – of childbearing. Men she loves and a child to whose nascent conception she is not entirely averse, these forces must bend to a more personal sacrifice, one that has everything to do with Being and time. A fragment from an undisclosed source, journal or letter, asserts "I think I am living very intensely in the present" (101), which is the only time in which Being is either cultivated or arrested. What is ultimately sacrificed in this time is the self that acquiesces to "publicness," dons a costume (Paula will paint herself nude on occasion), adjusts to conservative expectations, and holds to "natural" standards of Being. Upon leaving Otto, adrift in a liminal between space of old and new self, she writes "I'm not Modersohn and I'm not Paula Becker anymore either./ I am/ Me,/ And I hope to become me more and more" (105-06). From the perspective of history, or feminist ambition, she will fail in this endeavor to become increasingly authentic. She will be killed by childbirth and stasis, by relatively banal sacrifice. Darrieussecq's own revision, however, echoes the unique power of Paula's paintings ("She paints what she sees in front of her: that being-there, that presence in the world" [138]) by re-presenting the life and art with immediacy and innovation. "I want to show her paintings, speak about her life. I want to do her more than justice. I want to bring her *being-there*, splendor" (141-42), aims that also reiterate the problematic but eloquent Rainer Maria: "And at last you saw yourself as a fruit,/ you stepped out of your clothes and brought your/ naked body before the mirror, and you let/ yourself inside/ down to your gaze, which remained strong, and/ didn't say: This is me, instead: This is" (127). Though a prominent presence in Darrieussecq's own requiem, Rilke will pale in its pages next to the comparatively obscure potency and splendor of Paula.

"This is" provokes more questions: how to quantify such a phenomenon? What is it? Is there an epistemology or metaphysics up to the task of the necessary discernment? Is empirical evidence the only form of knowledge adequate to this undertaking? Heidegger certainly made an admirable effort. Barthes is perhaps more realistic, not to mention more enjoyable to read. He claims in the epigraph to his characteristically fragmented, episodic autobiography, *Roland Barthes By Roland Barthes*, that "It must all be considered as if spoken by a character in a novel." All of it, every person, every persona, is susceptible to the re-presentation of fiction in both key senses of the term, as literary narrative and the opposite of truth. All the world's a stage and most of what "is," what we bring to said stage, is the *mere* performance of possibly experienced but not especially conscientious acting (unless one is especially conscientious).

Darrieussecq's Belgian contemporary, Jean-Philippe Toussaint, like other of their (French) peers, explores the boundaries and elasticity of self according to Barthes' "consideration" and in keeping with those qualities that define Motte's "critical novel" in his *Self-Portrait Abroad*, a narrative of seemingly "real" events and attitudes. He compromises both truthfulness and the lack thereof, for example, when, on the first page, he opts to call his wife by her actual name "to help me get my bearings" (Toussaint 7). At one point, as epilogue to a particular anecdote, he concludes "but enough of personal matters" (10), and later, "enough of verisimilitude" (14). Such moments unfold out of what he calls his "daily exercise of irony" (28) that invariably "adumbrates fresh possibilities," as Motte explains. Despite his character's ludic, often irreverent tendencies, there eventually emerges a sense of gravity regarding moments divested of irony, or informed by a relatively melancholic, ironic turn. On a rickshaw in Hanoi, he describes the present, chaotic environment as "fluid … everything flowed listlessly in the surrounding warmth, time and the traffic, life and the hours of the day, my loves and youth itself, I made no effort to hold time back, I consented to get older, accepted the idea of death with serenity" (60). Suddenly, an instance of authentic contemplation and awareness ascends out of jocularity and is all the more impactful as a result of this juxtaposition. The final entry marking his "return to Kyoto," concludes with another such moment in which the protagonist reflects on a former railway station, now abandoned, leaving him "sad and powerless at this brusque testimony to the passage of time. It was hardly the result of conscious reasoning, but rather the concrete and painful, fleeting and physical feeling that I myself was part and parcel of time and its passing" (84). At this point, the "now" of time is as physical as it is psychological, and as affirmative of the self "living very intensely in the present" as it is of inevitable extinction. Here is where the painter, the writer, and the philosopher meet despite divergent milieus, gender, and thus positions in power structures, different capacities for humor and insouciance.

That said, four brief pages prior to this solemn denouement, Toussaint will write the experience of observing a scholar nervously present on "the subject of, let's face it, my really rather wonderful books" (80). It is an attitude diametrically opposed to Paula's tendency to question herself, to demean herself with sincerity rather than irony ("poor little creature that I am" [Darrieussecq 131]). On canvas, we might notice a related sensibility in Finnish painter Axel Gallen Kallela's rich *Démasquée*, which depicts a nude woman sitting erotically and confidently on a sofa surrounded by overtly symbolic objects (a lily, a guitar, a death skull) in a menagerie of dark red, black, and beige colors. The woman maintains an easy smile, a bohemian air that has no problem being the subject of art or a man's gaze. She appears to be exactly where and when she wants to be. For her part, Paula will find her authenticity, and maybe her own cheekiness, behind and on the canvas, as in her most well-known self-portrait in which she is pregnant, an image that does not necessarily square with the timing of her pregnancy. Darrieussecq describes her as possibly "making a game of sticking out her belly, arching her back, her navel protruding. *Just to see.* The self-portrait as auto-fiction. She paints herself as she would like to be, as she imagines herself: she paints an image of herself. Beautiful, happy, a little bit playful" (126). This is what the artist, the woman, may have thought, how she may have aligned her lived experience with art, as when she paints another "young married woman" and between them, painter and subject, "time is reverberating" (78). "It is not," she continues, "about what the girls are dreaming but what they are thinking" (ibid.), and what Paula thought was I am, "there is," "now" in "really rather wonderful" ways.

Would she have wanted to paint the troubled, unmarried, neurotic Eleanor, whose face and corporeal discomfort are embodied so remarkably by actor Julie Harris in the 1963 film version of Jackson's novel, and that reflect a mode of Being not unfamiliar to anyone who knows the quandary of disenfranchisement in the face of one's desire? By the end of her life, Paula adjusts (surrenders?) to maternal – or patriarchal – pressures and premises that are responsible for ending her life. Eleanor also experiences a (relatively brief) burst of selfhood, a Heideggerian "letting of resoluteness," before succumbing to premature death, though she does so without the full range of her conscience, or her consciousness. It is endearing to imagine Paula painting her fellow inquirer into agency and meaning with the hope of being truthful, realist without some demented Nazi imperative of realism, and thus locating the potentiality of becoming the empowered, grounded-in-Being *Dasein* of the "witch" that ultimately surrenders only to a progression of truths, buoyant passions of the moment.

Jean Toomer's Face

Just as it may seem odd to proceed from horror or "weird fiction" texts to a French novelist writing from a feminist perspective on a German painter of the 19th and 20th centuries, it may at first appear a questionable move to follow the latter with a male author/narrator examining, gazing upon the sensual appeal and singularity of a woman. If in the initial transition, clarity emerges around a central, contiguous concern that is the theoretical and thematic focus of this study, the same holds true for the contextual significance of Jean Toomer's "Fern" (first published in 1922, and later in his modernist, bricolage novel *Cane*), relative to the life of Paula. In light of his amorphous racial identity, Toomer, like Ndiaye, resisted racial categorization but wrote on Black (American) experience, the historical horror of which is perhaps best encapsulated in another, often anthologized Toomer story, "Blood Burning Moon." It is in "Fern," however, that *Dasein* takes center stage, as embodied by the titular character, by foregrounding her own equivocal resistance to the culture of her southern American environment and its people. Fern is neither the antipode of Paula and Eleanor nor Zoline's Sarah or Grant's Caroline. Her suffering and her "death" are of another order.

The story's first line is "Face flowed into her eyes" (Toomer, *Cane* 16). How might Paula have painted that face with its eyeward trajectory? How would Darrieussecq write the life of Fern from the perspective of flow? Deleuze poses the broader question of what constitutes a painting: "What does a painter paint? He [sic] paints lines and colors. That suggests that lines and colors are not givens, but are the product of a creation. What is given, quite possibly, one could always call a flow. It's flows that are given, and creation consists in dividing, organizing, connecting flows in such a way that creation is drawn or made around certain singularities extracted from flows" ("Vincennes" 78). From the standpoint of Toomer's narrator, the flow of Fern's face is predisposed as such. Darrieussecq would likely call attention to this, to the protagonist's objectification, at the same time that she could speak to the character's singularity as illustrated by a writer attuned to early 20th century prejudice as a reaction to skin color, to human surfaces and the ideological constructs of racism. It is quite possible that Paula would have created, much as Darrieussecq "creates" Paula's own life, via division, organization, and connection to locate Fern's singularity with ample generosity and consideration.

Toomer's narrator reveals his own sensitivity despite falling in line with other men whose immediate desire appears mechanically activated. He establishes a kinship with the (presumably male) reader immediately following the opening sentence by referring to "your glance" and the fact that "you sought her eyes" positioned above a nose that is "aquiline, Semitic," but follows this bating with the observation, "If you have ever heard a Jewish cantor sing, if he has touched you and made your own sorrow seem trivial when compared with his, you will know my feeling when I follow the curves of her profile, like mobile rivers, to their common delta" (Toomer, *Cane* 16). Here, it is not her beauty that arrests the gaze as much as her suffering. The latter manifests a sense of song, a lament, or a more general quality of artfulness in its dimensions that are soon revealed to be as manifold as they are insular. Consequently, Toomer does not ultimately allow readers to employ the typical mechanism of the desiring gaze. Rather, he imbues Fern with archetypal qualities that keep one at a provocative distance. "Fern's eyes desired nothing that you could give her," we're told, and further, those who seek to possess her develop "a sort of superstition that crept into their consciousness of her being somehow above them. Being above them meant that she was not to be approached by anyone. She became a virgin" (ibid.). Fern is sought after but marginalized, distinctly other in her exceptional alterity that generates a mode of becoming exceeding even the "becoming-woman" of Deleuze and Guattari's category. To become-virgin in the wake of numerous sensual relationships implies something more than entering the radicalism of minoritarian (anti-)structures. It suggests an entirely unerotic denuding of the self that desires according to normative, culturally-sanctioned coordinates.

It is out of such a psychic space that she is able to exercise her critical faculty in her single line of the story, as a question: "Doesn't it make you mad?" The narrator observes "She meant the row of petty gossiping people. She meant the world" (19). In indicting pettiness and the world that enacts it, she critiques a collectively quotidian, ontological structure that maintains itself by enlisting projection, exteriorized self, with ill, egoic intent. *Being* trafficking in the superficiality of inconsequent drama is authentic only to the personality, of individuals and the world, an amalgam of learned traits and perceptions, which leaves Fern profoundly separate from the frivolity that merely passes for what we might loosely call essence.[33] She is essentially herself, as in stripped of excess. There is thus a metaphysical connotation to her critique that lends it all the more weight when she begins to behave strangely, swaying and voicing "plaintive, convulsive sounds, mingled with calls to Christ Jesus," singing "brokenly" in a manner that, the narrator comments, recalls the Jewish cantor's suffering (ibid.). Despite the prefabricated nature of popular Christianity with its pervasive, patriarchal tendencies that impose suffering on women and men, her behavior is hardly in line with the men's (initially) objectifying desires and thus confirms her status as one to whom "nothing ever came, not even I" (ibid.), as the narrator claims matter-of-factly. Nothing ultimately comes to (or perhaps, reaches) Fern because she is in need of nothing but her sense of the sacred as a "mad" counter to "the world." This sense assumes the form of immanence insofar as her eyes are said to "hold God" (ibid.).

The singular quality of the sacred here galvanizes the narrator in his aim not so much to understand Fern as to offer a clear image of her for those willing to approach the abstraction of her contemplative vitality. In her presence, he senses "things unseen to men that were tangibly immediate," his perception of which allows him a modicum of access to the occurrence of her mystical state that is as defined by "anguish" as it is by sanctity (ibid.). It is this acknowledgement that compels him to invite the reader to visit her by the story's conclusion should one be in the area (of Georgia). Again, Toomer shifts the orientation of the narrator and reader alike away from the prospect of Fern's sexual availability to an experience of the "immediate." The inherent tension operating between the imperceptible and the material here is obscurely but arguably linked to Fern's holiness, her ability to hear and embody a version of Heidegger's "call." More specifically, however, the "immediate" is indicative of the insistence on her genuine alterity and inviolability, not to mention her subversiveness as a woman (with mesmeric eyes) and a person who needs, resolutely, only the God by which she is occupied and for the "world" to be better-behaved.

With no apparent painterly or other unique skills, Fern embodies Rilke's testimony regarding Paula's own manifestation of "This is," as opposed to "This is me." The character is less a person and more a phenomenon. Such a quality speaks precisely to the nature of authenticity as this study has been advancing it. There is an immediacy to "is," in contrast to any designation that might follow the verb. The latter's power lies in its minimalism, and even more in its relation to death. When Toussaint gives himself over to the flow of his surroundings in Hanoi, he is able to sanction "the idea of death with serenity." Fern may not be as serene as a clever Belgian author exploring 21st century Vietnam, but the flow of her face yields a vision that is surely the ground for the tranquility of life in death.

The Strangeness of Emmanuel Bove's *Armand*

As Paula's critical example indicates, the weight of our creative and critical endeavors, our painting, our music, literature, film, scholarship, is forever vulnerable to the relative insubstantiality and "leveling down" of "fallenness," particularly in the age of social media. Yet the *time* of aesthetic or scholarly production is arguably more aligned with *Being* in the sense of Heidegger's "resoluteness" of *Dasein* than that which feeds digital self-promotion. Granted, neo-Nazis and earnest, uniquely out of touch Composition and Rhetoric pundits who deny the value of literature and other identity fanatics are generally resolute in their own enterprises, though their determination is guided by ideology; they aspire to forms of domination and operate out of "the they" as both abstraction and as collective, fascistic, political orientation. On the other hand, like rabid supporters of a deluded president, they are also human beings questing for agency and cultural relevance, not to mention financial security. But the perseverance required of art and informed critique has a way of shaping time to fit the present moment in a manner that correlates with a truth of said moment beyond personal ambition. The "call" of *Dasein*, we may remember, comes from within as from without, not as ideology but as *memory*. "Forgetting the truth of Being in favor of the pressing throng of beings unthought in their essence" is thus the great heresy in the face of Being and time.

Social media induces an automatic occupancy of time without an occupant, time grounded in the re-presentation of predictable details that emerge from (or are mechanically cultivated in) the lived life – our relentless sound bites, memes, images that plunge us into a present time that is strangely not our own. This common scenario generates a certain risk in terms of our missing out on the unorthodox, the detritus, the overlooked, the inadvertently negated of life. Heidegger's insistence on listening (rather than obeying [*Basic* 330]) as a condition of freedom applies to seeing, or insight, as well. Elsewhere, Martin Jay refers to the "hegemonic role [of vision] in the modern era" (*Downcast* 14) to account for a particular theoretical perspective that arose in the last century, one that is surely all the more accurate in its assessment in the current milieu and that consequently precipitates a responsibility on the part of those so inclined to *remember*, to consistently gauge the quality of vision's attentiveness, its conscientiousness, and the scope of its range between interiority and exteriority. As with Jack Torrance in Stanley Kubrick's *The Shining* (1980), failure to see holistically (in the Overlook Hotel, no less) carries severe repercussions: alienation, violence, self-absorption, oblivion, death. Time may be reduced to a carrier of dis-ease, the mad impulse to replace the "truth of Being," the truth of a given juncture, with prescribed visions, tunnel perceptions. So the text intervenes. It diagnoses and advocates for veritable awareness and discernment.

While key aspects of the "serious" or "critical novel" are manifest in a variety of fictions, Motte's category tends to apply to 20th and 21st century French fiction (from particular publishing houses) for a reason. He focuses on those writers who "share a crucial will to make French fiction *new*" (*Fiction* 13-14) through stylistic as well as conceptual innovation. Why "crucial?" The impending death of the novel, not to mention the author? Because the world needs inventive fiction to help us transcend banal, bourgeois, or perilous ways of thinking and being? While book formats may be in process of shifting, for better and probably for worse, we are still far from calling in the hospice worker, which is why the second option has long been and will remain a vital orientation of literary "will." Essentially, the critical edge refers to an exceptional level of sophistication, which is not to imply smoking jackets, cravats, fur coats, or social hierarchy. Rather, the term speaks to a specific, historical relationship to intellectualism that informs contemporary writers in a culture known for its 18th/19th century revolution, its *nouveau roman*, and its May 68,' among other things. Here, sophistication has meaning, as it does for the current notion of the "elevated horror" film (*The Witch* being a prime example) that creates controversy by distinguishing itself and thus (seemingly) distancing the entire horror genre from aesthetic quality, when it fact it does the opposite. In this context, elevated refers to pushing the genre even closer to its potential by eschewing the formulas that satisfy the general moviegoer (as opposed to the connoisseur) and line the pockets of suits who have nothing to do with art, not to mention "critical" art. It is an argument that hinges on the question of authentic alterity. A novel or film may exceed boundaries or expectations by exploring uncharted content, but if its form remains tethered to convention, it is unlikely to break the kind of ground that signifies "newness," that challenges the reader or viewer to reevaluate life as well as art. Certain French writers are especially advanced in this regard.

Born approximately seventy years before Darrieussecq, Emmanuel Bove died in 1945, prior to both the *nouveau roman* (though Nathalie Sarraute's *Tropisms* was published in 1939) and the more contemporary new, new novel as practiced by such writers as Darrieussecq, Toussaint, Jean Echenoz, Marie Redonnet, and Christian Oster. His *Armand* nevertheless displays characteristics of "critical," sophisticated fiction in every way. Its plot is sparse – a man encounters an old friend, Lucien, still impoverished as he once was, makes a move on the friend's vulnerable sister, Marguerite, despite being "kept" by a loving, older woman, Jeanne, and reaps the consequences – as is its tight, streamlined language. The titular protagonist develops, but only in so far as he becomes relatively selfless. None of the novel's characters are one-dimensional; Bove offers the challenge of ambiguity, with no easy designations as to a singular authenticity or inauthenticity. In fact, the text itself, in its Proustian attention to detail, its eccentric and at times profound observations, wears its alterity above and below its surface. *Armand* is finally concerned with the existential and societal condition of being a stranger among strangers and presents this predicament via a literary style that accommodates rather than mitigating the dilemma of immeasurable otherness; what Sarte calls hell and critical horror identifies as the ultimate source of its provocation.

As first-person narrator, Armand's attention to quotidian phenomena, though indicative of a specific personality, defines the ethos of the novel and its universe that is hardly divorced from a preponderant "truth" of the human condition. When he first visits Lucien's bleak apartment, he notices that his friend's face is "covered with a thousand meaningless marks" (Bove 34). In addition to the scourge of common acne, it is difficult *not* to find meaning in these marks as scars that reflect psychological and physical adversity more or less on the surface of every human being. During his second visit, he observes Lucien move toward his bed while "his drying foot-prints remained in front of his dressing-table. He picked up his socks, turned them the right way round because they got inside out when he took them off, like mine" (50). Such correspondences accumulate in the novel to align not only the two friends – between whom class is ostensibly a recent but significant barrier – but Armand's steady trajectory toward insecurity with the reader. His impropriety with the younger and equally destitute Marguerite (he kisses her in her apartment) is shocking, not simply because of its unethical crudity but because it invariably strikes the reader as catastrophically stupid and unlike the behavior of an individual who has achieved stability and something at least resembling love. After Lucien explains the situation to Jeanne, Armand is compelled to confront her as his partner sits quietly, unnervingly awaiting an explanation that never quite arrives. He merely circumnavigates her chair, claiming "when I passed behind her, I could see the reverse side of the chair-back, covered with some fabric I had never noticed before. That I should notice an unfamiliar detail at such a serious moment terrified me. Perhaps others would follow until they were so numerous that they would change my life" (100). And this is exactly the point. Much ado about noting. To the extent that Armand recognizes and contemplates the immediacy of his environment, which includes himself and his symbiotic role in various "events," he is "forced," in Badiou's sense of the word, to come to terms with his life as one among others with whom he shares trials, tribulations, and meaningful, if not poignant revelations.

While navigating this final, melancholy discussion with Jeanne in which she is asking him to leave *her* apartment, Armand notices this small feature of his comportment: "My fingers were trembling, especially the little one, because it is weaker" (101). What becomes apparent in Bove's novel is that every part of the body/mind is susceptible to such weakness in that each character oscillates, physically and psychologically, in a push-pull toward and away from authenticity. Armand, of course, is distinguished by the fact that his awareness of this process manifests as narrative, another literary correlate thus being Jean-Jacques Rousseau's *Confessions*, though with Armand/Bove there is no manifesto concerning self-expression. There is only the moment that consists either of an effort to *seem* or the reality of Being, the latter more often than not emerging out of hardship, as amusingly idiosyncratic as certain observations may be.[34] Armand's disingenuousness is commonly rationalized as an intention to assuage the brunt of his friend's economic condition. "So that he should not reproach me for having changed," he observes, "I tried to recover my former bashful and uncouth manners. I was ashamed of my warm overcoat and especially my silk tie. I pretended that I took no care of my clothes and when a drip fell on to my coat I let it make a stain" (10). Eventually, he will go so far as to assert an overt alliance with Lucien: "In obedience to some interior command which I have never been able to explain, unless it was that I simply wanted to humble myself, to show myself in another light, to put myself on Lucien's level, I murmured: 'I am not happy'" (39). He is unable to explain this event, though he certainly tries, and what he produces by way of explanation suggests intentionality whose source is nevertheless the dominion of unconsciousness. What does this razor's edge between agency and mechanical direction say about the veracity of his unhappiness? Is he telling a white lie with confidence or succumbing to the psycho-choreography of conscience, or some other mental impulse? What we do know is that Armand's well-being is ruptured by the time Jeanne confronts him. And yet, even here, there is a margin of error in terms of the case he makes for himself when he concedes the fact that

"Everything was over. My happiness no longer depended on myself. Great anguish flooded over me. I could not be gentler or more tender than I had just shown myself to be" (94). While his "anguish" appears genuine, in "showing" himself, he has merely performed contrition, which calls into question the quality of his initial happiness. However, he has also realized the hazard and, perhaps, the value of endearment.

For his part, Lucien is frequently portrayed as attempting to gauge how to behave in the presence of his relatively privileged friend. "He was always trying to guess what was considered proper behavior" (8), Armand observes – without judgment, it should be noted. On the other hand, there is a pitiable quality to Lucien that nevertheless shifts once he is informed by his "child" (67) sister that Armand has behaved inappropriately toward her. He becomes not only socially perceptive but ethical.[35] Likewise, Jeanne, Armand discloses, has her own deceptive inclinations stemming from the fact, for example, that "she is tall" and consequently, "tries to appear absent-minded, artless and easily surprised" to "emphasize her femininity" (20). Strange indicators of femininity given her strength in the inevitable separation and Armand's ultimate recognition of the buoyancy she maintains in her womanhood. Collectively, these characters demonstrate the impossibility of applying the "ethical ideology" of humanism to their – and our – mutual condition. They exhibit the nuances of everyperson's tightrope walk through a life of performing in the real that is itself in pantheistic relation to lived experience, always already a force of knowledge for those with the capacity to learn. With or without cognitive awareness, they learn from and, in the case of the two friends, evolve *into* each other in terms of both class status and ethical insight. Though he vacillates, Armand knows the experience of feeling "completely as [he] should be," then "[speaks] with animation, [his] movements are easy" leaving him compelled to claim "I am another man" (15). It is this "other man," these "other people" who suddenly, in moments of clarity, find themselves empowered by authenticity and over the course of the novel set the stage for an exceptional incursion of ethics – even happiness – into the doldrums of mere pleasure-seeking, self-regard, and isolationism.

Moreover, the "other person" within the individual is alone capable of knowing the reality of shared humanity and vulnerability. Not long after they first reunite on the street, Armand notices something at once shocking and banal in his companion: "glancing at Lucien again, I became aware that he was made of flesh, as I realize I am when I look under my tongue in a mirror" (10). Such otherness is not only a productive aspect of the human being in its wisdom and understanding, it is physical – salivary ducts, frenula, glands – flesh that requires attention, a varied costume the delicacy of which one has in common with every other person. Armand is constantly reminded of an earlier, struggling chapter of his life in the presence of Lucien, who "spoke with detachment, dropping his eyes before he finished his sentences, but managing always to remind me of my former life" (31). The irony that will become increasingly substantial by the novel's conclusion is the fact that these uncomfortable moments (certainly for Armand, and perhaps for the reader) signify authentic ways of being. They reserve no room for acting, the politics of identity, however transient they may be. They reduce the person to this interior other who, comfortable or not, has no choice but to be radically cognizant of Being.[36] Like Lucien, Jeanne betrays this quality when confronting Armand about his behavior, with her "whole being before" (85) him, much to his alarm and discomfort. Later, just before they say goodbye, he notes "neither of us had spoken without using the other's Christian name. At the moment of parting, the names took on a new significance. They were the only part of the being we were leaving that remained to us" (105). The termination of their relationship imminent, their forenames become signifiers for the "truths" of two "other people" between whom an inevitable but melancholic fissure is necessary. *Dasein* may be ensconced in the real, though it is not always congenial.

That said, the assertion of *Dasein* in the face of the world's inauthenticity is the portal to empowerment – not necessarily the kind that amasses wealth or cultural relevance but one whose weight in the lived life generates strength and personal resolve. In the uncomfortable minutes prior to lunch with Jeanne and Armand, the latter observes how "a feeling of self-esteem led [Lucien] to make me understand that he had just as much right to be there as I, that it was only luck that made the difference between us" (19). Luck or no luck, what is at stake in the understanding of this microscopic "event" is a sense of dignity. By virtue of their impoverishment, both Lucien and Marguerite are haunted by this latter word. The brother fluctuates between embodying the indignity of his abjection (and taking it out rather aggressively on his sister) and declarations of "truth" that hit the protagonist where he is most vulnerable, while Marguerite, in the awkward exchange with Armand, begins manipulating the skin of her face because "by obliterating herself she wanted to destroy the last part of her which retained any dignity" (57). Her body, to which Armand is attracted, is the only aspect of her life that she can control, so she attacks it, choosing an injurious self-effacement as a proxy for her remaining morale. This is the real in which she floats, doubly abject as a consequence of being a woman and barely capable of fending off equally deprived (of money, propriety, contentment) assailants. The two siblings will not be redeemed in Bove's narrative universe beyond the fact of their having *been* and the harrowing prospect of their becoming.

Eagleton claims that "at the root of our most lofty conceptions lie violence, lack, desire, appetite, scarcity and aggression" (*Why* 146). He goes on to quote Adorno who notes "'the horror teeming under the stone of culture'" and Walter Benjamin on "'class struggle [as] a fight for the crude and material things without which no refined spiritual things could exist'" (ibid.). We see manifestations of such horror in the relatively tranquil but abbreviated life of Darrieussecq's Paula as much as in the plight of James Baldwin's Sonny (about whom we'll have more to say in the next chapter), not to mention any text that operates under the banner of horror-proper. Despite his focus on mortality (and due in part, no doubt, to a subject-position of non-Jewish, male, Nazi-sympathizer), Heidegger is more optimistic in his appraisal of the human condition. "Man is the shepherd of Being," he contends, and as such "he gains the essential poverty of the shepherd, whose dignity consists in being called by Being itself into the preservation of Being's truth" ("Basic" 245). This account fails to take into consideration cultural dynamics that boil "under the stone" of civil society, though its argument for dignity (as representative of Being) in the face of unwieldy life circumstances is not without validity or power. "Refined spiritual things" sometimes emerge from the tumult.

By the time Armand is on the streets, nowhere to go, no room to call home and presumably lacking money, he gravitates toward his previous, dilapidated neighborhood, uncertain of his next move. Standing at the peak of a hill, he allows the familiar scene to imbue this otherwise obliterating new situation with a sense of calm reflection, whereupon his "sufferings become less great. Little by little they melt into the sufferings of everyone around me … Then the world seems less distant, its joys and sorrows deeper and more of a piece" (Bove 110-111). Further on, as the novel concludes, Armand notices children playing on a "sloping street … the little ones higher up, the bigger ones lower down, so that their chances were equal" (111). He becomes the "shepherd" here, the adjoining resident in Being, which puts no food on the non-existent table but elevates his perspective in relation to others as well as to his own *Dasein*. Significantly, he is also "thrown," to use Heidegger's oft-repeated term, into authentic alterity to the degree that he is literally homeless while having, in this pivotal "event," transcended homelessness as "oblivion of Being," that condition of which Heidegger warns that plays no favorites according to class, race, gender, sexual orientation, etc. Armand's quiet revelation makes the many-banded "stones of culture" "of a piece," levels the field of conceptions lofty and prosaic, and recognizes, through witnessing a particularly equable expression of childhood, the fact that horror is as adulterated and culturally conditioned as it is burrowed into the recesses of the all too human flight from Being.

Chapter 6

– James Baldwin's Blues as Sound, Listening, and Agency

Some revelations are less quiet. In his popular 1957 story "Sonny's Blues," James Baldwin portrays the freedom offered by engagement with art, and the active gift that is listening. While Baldwin's characters face the horrors of racist violence, poverty (itself a form of institutionalized racism), disease, addiction, and above all, loss, they triumph over life's various forms of darkness by learning to actively engage with their lives' narratives. This grasp of agency is realized only through active presence with the Other, a process mediated by music. Baldwin does not situate the potential to embrace freedom or to love solely in musicians or artists such as the titular Sonny; rather, he demonstrates that the ability to love is a skill that anyone can develop if they offer themselves to listening, to something beyond the urge to recognize or confirm the self and its attendant perspectives willingly, authentically. Baldwin thus illustrates the value of Silverman's conception of "ceaseless textual intervention" and "the active gift of love," the capacity to "acknowledge the other as other," by demonstrating that the power to love, to reconcile, to acknowledge, and to affirm, is a process, and thus a skill firmly within the grasp of everyone. By reconciling with his free-spirited brother in the wake of successive family tragedies, Baldwin's narrator translates Silverman's conception of "the active gift of love" from theory into practice through which love is understood as necessary for survival within the violence, ephemerality and divisiveness of the world – which Baldwin metaphorically transmutes into darkness – given that these darknesses, these separations and losses, are often more visible than love and light. As in horror proper, darkness pervades "Sonny's Blues" as an ever-present obstacle to love's fulfillment, as it does to varying degrees for everyone. Such darkness acts here as a facilitator of the listening that must precede authentic, selfless love, the trajectory of which can only be subversive where listening is otherwise a tenuous anomaly.

Baldwin makes use of darkness as a fluid, capacious metaphor representing racist violence, poverty, escapism and ignorance, the "othering" capacities of the mainstream media that markets restrictive ideals, anonymity and temporal separation, and literal death. Throughout the story, darkness accompanies loss and fosters the belief in separateness and difference, a belief that breeds violence and alienation from others and the self, as it gives rise to victimization, a means of self-identifying that can suspend one's belief in one's own agency. Darkness, as nightfall, as mortality, is a force of nature, perpetual, unavoidable, Other in the largest sense, but Baldwin also casts human actions as "dark," forces of separation and loss. Baldwin demonstrates that the presence of darkness, perhaps of necessity, catalyzes the process of becoming *Dasein* and makes possible ethical relations to the other. In this sense, he is carrying out the work of Heidegger, for whom *Dasein* must "[hold] itself out into the nothing" (*Basic* 103). Darkness, as oppression, as literal, obscuring nightfall, as death, as fear, reveals the nothingness or the state of anxiety that functions as a ground of Being against which the *Dasein* forms an authentic self.

Darkness is first tied to entertainment and addiction, implicitly communicating the lure of pleasure and the role media plays in demonizing those it does not represent; by aligning them with darkness, Baldwin insinuates that these hedonic and victimized self-conceptions are misrecognitions that perpetuate the loss of the authenticity. The earliest mention of darkness appears when the narrator, a high school teacher, observes the boys in Harlem and recognizes in them his own youth: "all they really knew were two darknesses, the darkness of their lives, which was now closing in on them, and the darkness of the movies, which had blinded them to that other darkness, and in which they now, vindictively, dreamed, at once more together than they were at any other time, and more alone" (18). Immediately, darkness is couched in language connoting crampedness, confinement, living in marginalized, impoverished communities, and isolation. The description of the youths' deluded love for the movies that both unites them and leaves them "more alone" implies pop-culture's role in disseminating exclusionary ideals, ones that tend to shy away from poverty, shabbiness, or "other" bodies in a capitalist thrust that favors wealth, masculinity, whiteness, and identity-forming advertisements. Baldwin persists in casting darkness as giving rise to deluded self-conceptions rooted in representation and non-representation when he describes the housing projects in Harlem by writing that they "[look] like a parody of the good, clean, faceless life – God knows the people who live in it do their best to make it a parody. ... They don't bother with the windows, they watch the TV screen instead" (25). In comparing the domestic lives of Harlem's Black residents to a parody and emphasizing the role of television in the residents' lives, Baldwin communicates that the African American communities have internalized the status of "other" when compared to the ubiquitous white Americana ideal. Television, movies, and other readily accessible images of a "better" life, or one established as "normal" through sheer circulation in the media, figure here as a kind of voyeuristic addiction, not self-denial as much as self-neglect. In a letter to his older brother, Sonny, who has just gotten out of jail, writes "I feel like a man who's been trying to climb up out of some deep, real deep and funky hole and just saw the sun up there, outside. I got to get outside" (22). This passage, with its allusion to Plato's "Allegory of the Cave," illustrates the falsity of the self-as-Other, of the self as heroin addict, of the self addicted to pleasure.

Darkness also metaphorically stands in for temporal separation and death, a loss of not only self, but also other. When driving through Harlem and reminiscing with Sonny, the narrator notes that "the cab moved uptown through streets which seemed, with a rush, to darken with dark people, and as I covertly studied Sonny's face, it came to me that what we both were seeking through our separate cab windows was that part of ourselves which had been left behind (24-25). Baldwin's characterization of the residents of Harlem as "dark people" is more than skin deep; it speaks to the oppression of and the misrecognitions shouldered by its denizens. While they come seeking "light," they find only "disaster," speaking to poverty, violence, escapism, drug abuse, and the other attendants of oppression. But here, in the darkness of the night and the cab, the narrator recognizes his own loss, the losses of his brother, and the losses of the people walking the streets. In the darkness (and in the black, figurative night, as Jackson's Mrs. Dudley might say), in the memory-choked place that is Harlem, the narrator and Sonny recognize the past, too, as a kind of darkness, an interminable loss. Recalling a moment from childhood after hearing a story from his mother, the narrator recalls his own dawning awareness of mortality: "For a moment nobody's talking, but every face looks darkening, like the sky outside. ... The silence, the darkness coming, and the darkness in the faces frightens the child obscurely. He hopes that the hand which strokes his forehead will never stop – will never die" (26-27). Here, darkness is identified with time, with death, and the impossible desire for immortal companionship. Darkness and death are both facts of nature, insurmountable and isolating, and a symbol for dispossession.

Listening is central to the functioning of "Sonny's Blues" as a love story, but before Baldwin can show the process of "ceaseless textual intervention" and its role in the cultivation of love, he represents shallow, self-seeking listening, a style of listening which is actually grasping and insisting on the self in lieu of making space for the other; an auditory correlate to dark, malicious forebodings. While listening to the mocking laughter of his high school students, the narrator notes that "Perhaps I was listening to them because I was thinking about my brother and in them I heard my brother. And myself" (18). Here, listening is not about understanding whatever is unfolding at the present moment, but about grasping one's own past, reinforcing one's own personality. Poor listening, or self-seeking listening, also figures as a closedness to spirituality. Baldwin illustrates this when the narrator makes light of Sonny's spiritual proclivity to reify his own "sensible" existence when the younger brother gets "hipped on the idea of going to India.... I used to say that it sounded to me as though they were getting away from wisdom as fast as they could. I think he sort of looked down on me for that" (24). Baldwin makes overt the narrator's desire for the confirmation of his own wants and hopes for others during his first dinner with Sonny after his release from jail, writing that "I was trying to remember everything I'd heard about dope addiction and I couldn't help watching Sonny for signs.

… I was trying to find out something about my brother. I was dying to hear him tell me he was safe" (26). While well-meaning, this self-seeking listening bars the narrator from actually engaging with what Sonny says, as he is only listening for what he wants to hear, or building a "profile" of Sonny as a doctor might. The narrator's insular style of listening gives rise to a pejorative attitude towards Sonny and "artistic types," which he compares against his white-collared, more traditional lifestyle: "I didn't like the way he carried himself, loose and dreamlike all the time, and I didn't like his friends, and his music seemed to be merely an excuse for the life he led. It sounded just that weird and disordered" (36). This rigorously self-confirming attitude serves only to alienate Sonny and the narrator from each other.[37]

In contrast with the narrator, Sonny is a gifted listener, as he consistently recognizes and rejects self-seeking listening in others. In a conversation about jazz and Sonny's musical aspirations, Sonny rejects his older brother's ingratiating, slightly patronizing offer to consider Sonny's chosen vocation, incisively grasping that it does not come from a place of sincere curiosity. When his brother says "'I'm ignorant. I'm sorry. I'll go out and buy all the cat's records right away, all right?'" Sonny dismisses the "offer," answering "'It don't,' said Sonny, with dignity, 'make any difference to me. I don't care what you listen to. Don't do me no favors'" (32). In the same vein, Sonny confronts his older brother, stating "I hear you. But you never hear anything I say" (34). Baldwin aligns listening with love and with authentic familial feelings when he describes the narrator's frustration at Sonny's intimacy with the artistic residents of Greenwich Village, complaining that "he treated these other people as though they were his family and I weren't" (36). When discussing the ubiquitous nature of suffering, Sonny chastises his brother for his dispensing of advice: "'But nobody just takes it,' Sonny cried, 'that's what I'm telling you! Everybody tries not to. You're just hung up on the way some people try–it's not your way!'" (41). Through Sonny, Baldwin more or less overtly highlights the narrator's judgmental listening style and foreshadows the need for the discovery of alternate means of communication that is less spectral, in the sense of phantasmatic, more somatically, emotionally invested, and thus indicative of the active gift of love.

In addition to representing perceptive listening in conversation through Sonny, Baldwin also demonstrates how listening constitutes loving in Sonny's receptiveness to art and ear-training. Sonny's intuition and authentic presence are first revealed when he begins his music training, teaching himself. The narrator comments "he had graduated, in the time I had been away, from dancing to the juke box to finding out who was playing what, and what they were doing with it, and he had bought himself a set of drums" (30). Sonny's listening progresses from enjoyment to very concerted efforts to understand the sounds being made; his efforts evince his love for music and the feelings of those who make it. Sonny also symbolically repudiates restrictive middle-class consciousness and elitism when he eschews the narrator's classist fear that Sonny will become a jazz musician, or a "good time" person. Sonny laughingly tries to assuage his brother's fear of his artistic vocation, and his laughing tone implicitly questions his brother's stance: "He sobered, but with difficulty. 'I'm sorry. But you sound so–scared!' and he was off again" (31). He becomes-ghost again, eluding the grasp of his older brother as perhaps another mechanism of instruction. Sonny vanishes, though unlike the narrator, whose relatively bourgeois confusion and oblivion keeps him from recognizing the value of alterity, Sonny does so in a state of perceptive sobriety. Baldwin aligns sensitivity to music, as "textual intervention," with empathy when Sonny comments on the voice of a gospel singer in the street: "listening to that woman sing, it struck me all of a sudden how much suffering she must have had to go through–to sing like that" (41). This quote also highlights the healing capacities of music and the arts in general by making clear the relationship between suffering and the development of alternative, artistic means of self-expression and constitution. This connection is made again when Sonny talks about making and learning to listen to music, explaining that "You can't talk it and you can't make love with it, and when you finally try to get with it and play it, you realize nobody's listening. So you've got to listen. You got to find a way to listen" (42). The "horror" of alterity, productive and otherwise, challenges one to "make love" in a manner that is exceptional indeed.

Baldwin demonstrates the necessity of "darkness" (or nothingness, in Heideggerian terms) for the cultivation of love, as it is family tragedy that catalyzes the narrator's journey towards authentic presence and selfless listening. Towards the beginning of the story, the narrator encounters one of Sonny's acquaintances who uses heroin and the two talk about Sonny's release from jail. Though initially dismissive of him, the narrator is shocked into listening, and into holding out hope for his brother, whom he also dismissed: "'Tell me,' I said at last, 'why does he want to die? He must want to die, he's killing himself, why does he want to die?' He looked at me in surprise. He licked his lips. 'He don't want to die. He wants to live. Don't nobody want to die, ever'" (21). But Sonny's personal darkness, along with the narrator's, is essential to progressing the life and Baldwin's narrative; the same can be said of the larger terrain of cultural darkness with which they and their readers must contend. This claim does not negate the sorrow of tragedy, but ultimately points, in Vonnegut-like fashion, to the nothingness at the center of both life and death, a core emptiness the discursive correlate of which can be reduced to a "so it goes" detachment, such as that of an author relative to characters, or a holy person whose vision is wider than the insulating boundaries of the *moi*.

Still, Baldwin wants the reader to feel. When the narrator's mother recounts the story of her husband's brother's violent death at the hands of white motorists, she concludes with the charged observation "the world ain't changed" (29). She also makes explicit the value of listening by telling the narrator, whom she charges with caring for Sonny, "You may not be able to stop nothing from happening. But you got to let him know you's there" (30). In addition to his mother, the narrator's wife, Isabel, also models listening as the active gift of love throughout the sickness and death of their daughter: "Isabel says that when she heard that thump and then that silence, something happened in her to make her afraid. And she ran to the living room and there was little Grace on the floor, all twisted up, and the reason she hadn't screamed was that she couldn't get her breath. And when she did scream, it was the worst sound, Isabel says, that she'd ever heard in all her life, and she still hears it sometimes in her dreams" (37). It is tempting to reflect on other texts here, other events that dramatically shift the conditions of Being. Two in particular star actor Donald Sutherland: Robert Redford's *Ordinary People* (1980) and Nicolas Roeg's *Don't Look Now* (1973), to which we might add, in keeping with the first part of this study, John Carpenter's *Assault on Precinct 13* (1976) in which a young girl is shot point blank in scene that remains shocking in the 21st century. The death of children in fictional narratives is hardly taboo, though it certainly challenges any impulse to advocate for darkness. It forces (and aesthetically institutionalizes) feeling. The rich irony is that in both the lived experience of loss and in facing up to the figurative death of a Blackwoodian depersonalization, presence and acute, selfless listening are essential. To support and care for his wife, or "to let her know he's there," Baldwin's narrator learns to listen, to offer his presence. Moreover, his understanding of listening as presence, of the active gift of love, is made apparent when he recognizes the limitations of speech. When he wants to reassure Sonny of his love and to promise to remain in his life, he recognizes that speech is often largely for the speaker, reflecting that "I wanted to promise that I would never fail him again. But it would all have sounded–empty words and lies. So I made the promise to myself and prayed that I would keep it" (42). In making such a promise, the narrator resolves to demonstrate his love for Sonny through action, the offering of a self that has, in a sense, died to itself and to the stories that have allowed him to retain his nearly unbreachable bulwark of convictions and formulas of being.

And yet, "textual intervention," as a kind of guiding, often lacerating, wounding tool with which to chip away at the ramparts of self, is, we maintain, fundamental. Baldwin is obviously as interested in music, which figures as an alternative means of self-expression and constitution, as he is literary discourse. In order to show how music functions as "text," Baldwin must demonstrate the need for alternative texts. As a high school teacher, the narrator figures as an agent of mainstream, middle class enculturation, thoroughly familiar with normative standards and texts, both the texts in the curriculum intended to shape his students into ideal citizens and the movies and ideals the young people imitate. So insular is the narrator that the reality of his brother's life and suffering is only accepted when it is reported in the newspaper, a thoroughly mainstream and "reputable" source: "Then perhaps I just stared at the newsprint spelling out his name, spelling out the story. ... I couldn't believe it: but what I mean by that is that I couldn't find any room for it anywhere inside me. I had kept it outside for a long time. I hadn't wanted to know" (17). Despite his disdain for Sonny treating his artist friends as family, the narrator holds Sonny's counterculture at an arm's length. Once the narrator confronts his remoteness from his own brother, he begins the work of reconciling, yielding to his brother's art as his authentic self-presentation.

Baldwin casts certain forms of music as thoroughly "other" and musicians as occupying a primal state of alterity and authenticity through his pattern of comparing music and musicians to the inhuman or relating music to anxieties surrounding social and economic status. For the narrator, music is associated with low social status, reflecting that "I simply couldn't see why on earth [Sonny'd] want to spend his time hanging around nightclubs ... It seemed – beneath him, somehow. ... I had always put jazz musicians in a class with that Daddy called 'good-time people'" (31). Baldwin establishes that there is something innate and authentic about making music when the narrator and Sonny's high school acquaintance walk through Harlem, past a boy who's whistling "seemed to be pouring out of him as though he were a bird ... just holding its own through all those other sounds" (18). When the narrator is reunited with Sonny, he sees Sonny as unfamiliar, vulnerable, almost inhuman: "He looked very unlike my baby brother. Yet, when he smiled, when we shook hands, the baby brother I'd never known looked out from the depths of his private life, like an animal waiting to be coaxed into the light" (23). Similarly, Sonny addresses his favorite jazz musician, Charlie Parker, by using his nickname, "Bird," which aligns him with animals rather than humans (31-32). This association with animals belies music's role in countercultural movements, which discard many barriers erected by enculturation, familiar ideologies, and politeness norms. Sonny briefly lives with Isabel and her family, a time that Isabel confesses "wasn't like living with a person at all, it was like living with sound. And the sound didn't make any sense to her, didn't make any sense to any of them– naturally. ... It was as though Sonny were some sort of god, or monster"

(35). By so thoroughly uniting with sound, his artistic vocation, Sonny is shown to be fully authentic and in some ways, post- or meta-human in his insights and communicative capacities; he not only becomes-animal but acquires the psychic dimensions of monstrosity, godliness, and thus, fecund subversiveness informed by authentic, aesthetic alterity.

There is a powerful sense here of music's authentic reflection of lived experience in so far as it identifies music with body and life. When the narrator's mother recounts the murder of the narrator's and Sonny's uncle, the moment of his death is also a kind of grotesque music due to the guitar that he carried on his back: "Your father says he heard his brother scream when the car rolled over him, and he heard the wood of that guitar when it give, and he heard them strings go flying, and he heard them white men shouting, and the car kept on a-going and it ain't stopped till this day" (29). Similarly, the guitar is described as part of the brother's dead body, as the mother states "And, time your father got down the hill, his brother weren't nothing but blood and pulp" (29). The narrator identifies Sonny's instrument as an augmentation of his body when he watches him play, reflecting that "I had never before thought of how awful the relationship must be between the musician and his instrument. He has to fill it, this instrument, with the breath of life, his own. He had to make it do what he wants it to do. And a piano is just a piano" (46). Here, awfulness is conflated with breath and life rather than negative aberrancy. Music is also identified with life in a less physical way when Sonny claims it as his life's purpose. When defending his decision to become a jazz musician to his brother, he claims that "I think people ought to do what they want to do, what else are they alive for?" (32). Through the repeated identification of life and body with music, Baldwin communicates how musicians occupy a state of alterity, a separate kind of body with different limitations, or ethics, for that matter.

In other words, Baldwin situates music as a deliberate means of expressing and constituting an authentic self by demonstrating how the creation of music gives characters a more complete narrative control over their singular narratives and suffering and consequently enables them to harness this deepened sense of agency to relate to others; in a sense, music and art emerge as a kind of experience bared outside of the body. Sonny notes the sense of control he has when seriously listening to music and compares it to doping, what becomes an essential sensation. Additionally, Baldwin makes explicit the kind of formal control offered to the musician when the narrator listens to Sonny perform for presumably the first time in their adult lives: "the man who creates the music is hearing something else [than his audience], is dealing with the roar rising from the void and imposing order on it as it hits the air. (45) This statement is an epiphany, for the narrator finally understands Sonny's attraction to music and opens himself to the possibility of listening to the order Sonny imposes, his alternate means of self-constitution and the drug-like need of this "void." Music functions as a true textual intervention when it creates the possibility of authentic relations – the recognition of self and other – between people, as opposed to a monolithic, univocal self. One rarely hears music – it is an astonishing claim.

The role of music as catalyst for authentic relations is on display beyond just Sonny's interactions with his brother. When Sonny and his brother pass a street performer, the narrator recognizes a connection between the singer and her listener, noting that a singer "whose voice dominated the air, whose face was bright with joy, was divided by very little from the woman who stood watching her ... Perhaps they both knew this, which was why, when, as rarely, they addressed each other, they addressed each other as Sister" (38). Despite their implied estrangement, Baldwin casts music as a means of communion between the singer and the woman entranced by her song. As a jazz musician, a tradition often governed by improvisation, Sonny is uniquely able to recognize music as an alternative form of dialogue. Crucially, the narrator finally understands Sonny's music as authentic self-expression, a true autobiography unburdened by the misrecognitions brought on by oppression, victimization, mainstream media, even personal tragedy. In the climactic scene, "Sonny's fingers filled the air with life, his life. But that life contained so many others. ... Freedom lurked around us and I understood, at last, that he could help us to be free if we would listen, that he would never be free until we did. ... I heard what he had gone through, and would continue to go through until he came to rest in part. He had made it his: that long line, of which we knew only Mama and Daddy. And he was giving it back, as everything must be given back, so that, passing through death, it can live forever" (47-48). "It" constitutes something both personal and universal, figures as an art that accomplishes more than egoic, self-conscious posturing. It is a fully self-authored expression of self, one that beautifully illustrates the agency of the artist and enables the listener to recognize the reality of their experience and narrative, to behold and love the other as other.

Baldwin does not represent music, or even the process of textual intervention, as a panacea to the problem of suffering, depicted throughout "Sonny's Blues" as darkness, the pervasive "trouble" whose animality is feral rather than naturally, organically propitious. Rather, it is an act that reminds people of their agency, gives them a choice in how they respond to the inevitable darkness. Attempts at connection, through the deliberate "textual intervention" offered by music or no, figure as the only productive answer to darkness. When coping with the loss of his baby, the narrator suddenly feels a pang of desire to interact with Sonny, reflecting that "I was sitting in the living room in the dark, by myself, and I suddenly thought of Sonny. My trouble made his real" (37). In his suffering, he realizes that Sonny has suffered, too, and that Sonny likely knows how to cope. Baldwin explicitly identifies music – textual intervention – as the "light" to repel the very real existence of suffering, writing of Sonny and his band that they "were keeping it new, at the risk of ruin, destruction, madness, and death, in order to find new ways to make us listen. For, while the tale of how we suffer, and how we are delighted, and how we may triumph is never new, it always must be heard. There isn't any other tale to tell, it's the only light we've got in all this darkness" (47). Baldwin never eliminates suffering, instead positioning it, threateningly, on the margins of even the most agency-affirming, loving acts. The narrator recalls the world "hungry as a tiger" even during his epiphany while listening to his brother, and when he gifts Sonny with a drink, he sees it again: "For me, then, as they began to play again, [the gifted drink] glowed and shook above my brother's head like the very cup of trembling" (48). Music, musicians, listeners, are all rendered still vulnerable, but as possessing a choice in the matter of how to relate to suffering and each other.

In many ways, "Sonny's Blues" functions as a love story that acknowledges the integral place of art in the process of creating loving consciousness, and by extension, subversive *Dasein*, as evidenced when Sonny, living with Isabel's family, "afflicts" them with the tenacity of his musical practice, "as though [he] were some sort of god, or monster," the two ascriptions, like agency and darkness, as complementary as they are opposed. This reading is made even more apparent by Baldwin's non-fiction. In a letter to his nephew, he writes of love's necessity to survival: "We have not stopped trembling yet, but if we had not loved each other none of us would have survived. And now you must survive because we love you, and for the sake of your children and your children's children" (*Fire* 7). In another work of non-fiction, Baldwin explains his solution to racial violence and discrimination in terms that closely mirror Silverman's conception of "ceaseless textual intervention," explaining that "if we – and now I mean the relatively conscious whites and the relatively conscious Blacks, who must, like lovers, insist on, or create, the consciousness of the others – do not falter in our duty now, we may be able, handful that we are, to end the racial nightmare, and achieve our country, and change the history of the world" (*Fire* 105). "Sonny's Blues," then, is a story in which people "insist on, or create, the consciousness of the others" in the face of oppression, of illness, of poverty, of violence, of mortality. Sonny's very name, as a homophone of "sunny," establishes him as capable off fending of the darkness that is separation, by virtue of his becoming at once abject and exemplary of **how to carry out a "truth-process" of ceaseless textual intervention** in the name and, far more importantly, in the act of love.

Chapter 7

–The Motherhood, (Re)birth, and Aborted Doubling of Sylvia Plath and Amélie Nothomb

Sylvia Plath's *The Bell Jar* and Amélie Nothomb's *Strike Your Heart* dramatize the problem of identity with the two most pervasive models of (educated, privileged) womanhood, constructing this bind as a deathgrip: does a woman devote herself to family, nurturing, and self-sacrifice, or to personal ambition and artistic and professional attainments? Plath's novel, *The Bell Jar*, usually renowned for its visceral representations of misogyny and mental illness and commentary on mothering vs. working, also functions as a horrific account aligning the female subject position itself with captivity, the threat of violence, and dehumanization. As such, this feminist tour-de-force articles the main binary plaguing modern womanhood. *Strike Your Heart*, set in the 1970s and published in 2018, shows this binary reinforced by second-wave-feminist maintenance that it doesn't exist, a dismayingly relevant problem even after the feminist watersheds of the 1960s and 1970s. In both works, motherhood looms as a rite of passage that slays the woman's previous self. After surviving a suicide attempt and a car accident, respectively, and a series of abusive relationships with mother-figures, Plath's Esther Greenwood and Nothomb's Diane achieve rebirth by rejecting the examples and adaptations of their potential role models; instead, they recognize the woundedness of the women around them and chart alternative paths for themselves towards greater authenticity in which their personhood is subsumed by neither the selflessness of motherhood nor the dependence of childhood.

Birth signifies both a new life and a death for the mother in *Strike Your Heart*. Nothomb portrays the haughty and image-conscious Marie's pregnancy as a loss of self. After her graduation from secondary school, Marie thinks "'From now on, I'm the one who matters, at last it's my story, it's not my parents,' or my sister's'" (Nothomb 9). Her new and treasured life, bolstered by her sense of independence, is slain when she conceives. Nothomb writes "On the rare occasions when Marie was not asleep and indulged in thought, she would conclude, 'I'm pregnant, I'm nineteen years old, and my youth is already over'" (16). Nothomb asserts that Marie is no longer the main character of her own life's story after the birth of Diane: "Olivier placed the baby in her arms. She looked at her child and thought, 'It's not my story anymore. It's yours.' It was January 15, 1972. Marie was twenty years old" (18). The date, which Nothomb emphasizes by virtue of including it at all, becomes both a birthdate and a deathdate: Marie marks the day as the end of her youth, agency, and importance. Interestingly, Marie's loss of self-authorship, is emphasized when her suggested name for her baby, "Olivia," after her father, is rejected in favor of "Diane," due to her supposed divine good looks (18). Here, Nothomb illustrates the child's elevation to divinity at the expense of the mother, implicitly demoted to caretaker, servant to the Goddess.

Diane, the precocious and willful protagonist of the novel, recognizes that her mother's resentment for her is born from more than simple spite, but from the sacrifices surrounding mothering. Following the birth of her little brother, Diane reflects on the meaning of motherhood and justifying her deification of her mother: "The little girl's love for her mother was so great that it could even encompass what her own birth must have meant to Marie: resignation, the end of her faith in some kind of ideal. Nicolas's birth had not sealed her fate in any way, and that too was why Maman showed him her affection. When she saw the goddess kissing the little boy, leaving her out, Diane managed to move beyond her pain and remember that someday she would become Queen, not out of personal ambition, but in order to hand the crown to her mother and console her for everything in her life that seemed so constricting" (40-41). Diane's worshipful desire to ameliorate "everything in [Marie's] life that seemed so constricting" proves impossible; as for Marie, motherhood grows from labor (both the birth and the act of nurturing) into a whole identity. In naming the ambivalent mother figure Marie as she did, Nothomb likely pokes fun at

Catholicism's obsession with and deification of the Mother, Mary. Not only does her story now belong to her children, Marie resigns herself wholeheartedly to the script of motherhood after resenting it through two terms and childhoods when she gives birth to her third child. Nothomb writes of Marie's third child, Célia, that "Célia was a sort of redemption for her. With a child in her arms, she at last stopped seeing herself from the outside. However extravagant her maternal tenderness might seem, it allowed her to view things from another angle than that of the envy they might arouse" (52). While her sense of self is no longer dependent on the approval (or, more realistically, the imagined and projected approval) of others, Marie loses herself (and her good sense) to the role of doting mother, this time at the expense of her children. Her maternal devotion is so strong that it practically eclipses the possibility of other minds: even the object of her love becomes an outgrowth of Marie's mother-ego. Diane is openly rejected and ignored, while Célia is smothered. At the tender age of six, the younger child seeks help from her older sister, crying "No, it's true. Maman loves me too much, she never leaves me alone" (58). Thus, Marie's sense of self is totally subsumed by the maternal archetype; she lacks even the self-awareness to gauge her differential treatment of her children as she grows accustomed to her new ego.

Marie's maternal ego overcomes her to the extent that her children see her as a terrifying, predatory God, and holiness itself emerges as a horrific solipsism. Diane's younger brother Nicolas tells her that "he would stay at home, 'to stop Maman from eating Célia as if she were some coconut cake'" (50). Nothomb intervenes to underscore the reality of this metaphor: "This was no mere image: Marie's excessive love for Célia evoked the swooning of certain thirteenth-century saints when swallowing the communion host. It was holy gluttony" (50). In *Strike Your Heart*, neurotic motherhood and selfhood work to dehumanize both the mother, who loses authorship and centrality in her own life's "story," and the children, who figure as props tethering the egoic and unaware mother to the world and have little say in their family lifestyle, growing up to see themselves as largely passive accessories of the mother who grow to reenact her lifestyle, worshippers of an ineffectual and absent God.

Plath shows the female body and mantle of motherhood as similarly dehumanizing in *The Bell Jar*. She represents the patriarchal lens's dehumanization of women by frequently aligning women with animals, especially birds. Like women, who are expected to become housewives, birds are caged; like educated women, birds can speak, but their speech is regarded as merely an amusing trick, not meaningful communication; like women, birds are valued for their reproduction and capacity to provide nourishment, as people buy and eat both eggs and birds. Esther's habit of identifying women with animals and birds is an outgrowth of her awareness of and anxiety about the status of the female body–and, by extension, female lives–as commodities, trophies. Through this habit, Plath renders much of *The Bell Jar* a captivity narrative. As objects of male desire, women are transmogrified into subhuman animals; this benefits men, freeing them to "hunt" without concern for the subjectivities of women. During her time at *Ladie's Day*, Esther joins another writing contest-winner, Doreen, in a jaunt through New York. When the two accompany a local radio show host, Lenny, to his apartment, Esther sees the mounted heads of animals on his walls. Lenny claims more than just animals as trophies. Plath showcases Lenny's trophy-mentality when Esther observes that Lenny looks at Doreen "the way people stare at the great white macaw in the zoo, waiting for it to say something human" (Plath 11). This symbolically casts Doreen and Esther as prey, too. Female sexuality is constructed as devaluing, animalistic, whereas sexuality bears no consequences for men. This is shown through Eric, the college student who believes that sex with a woman he loved "would be spoiled by thinking this woman too was just an animal like the rest" and tells Esther that if he loved anybody he would never go to bed with her (79). Even sex within marriage cannot protect women from being "animal," so there is no possibility for full human dignity even for the chaste housewives who do all that is expected of them, i.e. "putting out" and bearing and raising children.

Plath represents the pregnancy and birth through even starker personhood-annihilating images. Plath's descriptions of encounters with the medical establishment, which reduces women (even those women who only engage in sexual acts within the socially permissible bounds of marriage) to bodies, horrorifies Esther, who fearfully infers that the only conventional occupation for women is to breed. During her courtship with Buddy Willard, a medical student, Buddy suggests the couple go watch young doctors deliver a baby. Before they go to look at the pregnant woman, Buddy shows Esther jarred embryos: "the baby in the first bottle had a large white head bent over a tiny curled-up body the size of a frog" while "the baby in the last bottle was the size of a normal baby and he seemed to be looking at me and smiling a little piggy smile (63). In this scene, Plath compares the undeveloped human children to animals and writes the embryos in a group and in jars, pluralizing and depersonalizing the would-be-children, while also making the process of human birth resemble the laying of a clutch of eggs, debasing or animalizing it. When they move on and she finally sees the pregnant woman, Esther comments that the "woman's stomach stuck up so high I couldn't see her face or the upper part of her body at all" (Plath 65). Her protruding stomach covers her face, thus obscuring her most identifying features, depersonalizing her. In this grotesque image, Plath conveys the fear that Woman does not have an identity, is nothing more than a vessel for a child. A coworker of Buddy's, Will, attempts to steer Esther away from the birth, saying that "You oughtn't see this ... You'll never want to have a baby if you do. They oughtn't to let women watch. It'll be the end of the human race," underscoring male control over female bodies and birth (65). Medicine and pregnancy wards emerge as male-dominated centers for the reproduction of patriarchy.

Reproduction, then, is more important than personality, or at least female personalities; in this sense, the mechanisms of culture at large take priority over individual desires, leaving no room for the subjectivities of women who do not want to be reduced to motherhood. Plath reinforces this message when she writes that "Later Buddy told me the woman was on a drug that would make her forget she'd had any pain and that when she swore and groaned she really didn't know what she was doing because she was in a kind of twilight sleep. I thought it sounded just like the sort of drug a man would invent" (66). Plath even identifies the vagina as a wound that needs to be treated when, after the birth, Esther observes that "Will started sewing up the woman's cut with a needle and a long thread"

(67). In this image, Plath constructs the female body as damaged, a painful space to occupy.

Many of the social pressures the institutions and individuals apply to (and by) women are more subtly dehumanizing. Women and women-run publications write Woman as a nurturer, a less harsh presentation of the consumable body than the masculine, medical practice of treating women as bodies, vessels for sex and birth. The viability of *Ladies' Day's* publication depends on a home-making audience; as such, the nurturing, motherly image-ideal is actively constructed by writers *and* their audience, creating a positive feedback loop that makes ubiquitous and naturalizes this image-ideal. Thus, women who don't conform to or feel comfortable with this ideal, such as Esther (and, by extension, Plath) must choose to either toil to embody it or refashion and resell it. Esther's job with the women's magazine is meant to be a reward for her academic prowess and skill as a writer, but the kinds of writing positions available for women mainly consist of advising women on homemaking, meaning that Esther has not strayed far from the domestic sphere and that there are not very many opportunities for women; femininity becomes an insular industry. Plath conveys the link between Esther and the magazine's work in her description of "the glass eggbeater of *Ladies' Day* revolving doors" (41). Esther feels trapped while working for *Ladies' Day* because of the elite women-only hotel, the Amazon, in which she has been lodged. She notes that the wealthy women that stayed in the Amazon had gone to posh secretarial schools but spent their time "simply hanging around in New York waiting to get married to some career man or other" (4). Though she is not planning on becoming a housewife like the other clients of the Amazon, Esther is still captive to expectations of women through her writing assignments.

Moreover, Plath's protagonist internalizes both the mainly-female enforced conception of women as mothers, housewives, beautifiers, and nurturers, and the male, medical conception of women as subhuman breeders, and finds that there is no happy way to live with both. She despises the inane interests of most appearance-obsessed women and compares them to parrots, who merely imitate human speech, while she volunteers in a maternity ward, which she identifies as their cage. Plath's comparison of women to parrots does more than make fun of the young ladies' conventional hobbies: it also constructs their situation as tragic captivity and demonstrates Esther's own internalized misogyny.

In *Strike Your Heart*, rather than depicting women's professional ventures and mothering as two sides of a patriarchal coin, Nothomb positions employment and motherhood in opposition. Nothomb sharply reveals and criticizes the culture of "choice feminism," which constructs a woman's deciding to quit working and mother full-time as a personal choice, not an adaptation to workplace misogyny and inadequate institutional concessions to working mother. Nothomb first implicitly conveys the devaluation of mothering and the subtle binds of choice feminism when Marie's husband, Olivier, seeks help from his mother-in-law to support his languishing bride: "Olivier went to see his mother-in-law, but her told her something completely different: her daughter was in the throes of postpartum depression, and only the prospect of work gave her the will to live. Her begged her to be so kind as to look after her granddaughter" (22). Olivier casts motherhood as a fatal, hopeless pursuit, and professional endeavors as the only source of hope and meaning for a woman. Interestingly, Olivier asks Diane's grandmother to care for her, thus deflecting the responsibility of parenting onto a woman, even though this means sending her out of her nuclear family's household. The message is clear: child-rearing is the province of women. Nothomb again presents motherhood as a personal and professional hazard when Olivia Aubusson, Diane's brilliant research mentor complains

"I don't know which are more macho: the male students or the male faculty."

"Do you think that has anything to do with the fact that you're not a full professor?"

"It's bound to. Particularly as I had a child, ten years ago. They never forgave me for it. But if I hadn't had a child, I'd have been judged even more harshly. Even when you teach at university you still can't get away from their provincial mentality" (78).

Olivia is implied to have had a child in part to escape condemnation for the "inadequate womanhood" of childlessness, but faces a double-bind, stigmatized as not wholly dedicated to her work because of her child. Later, Nothomb reveals that Olivia wholly neglects her daughter, Mariel, who lives in their empty apartment and earns terrible marks in school as a casualty of her parents' careers as academics. Given this, a reader would be forgiven for regarding Olivia's comments about motherhood as spurious, but her suggestion that parenthood is unfairly constructed as exclusively women's labor rings true even almost forty years after the novel is set: "'Diane, don't you think it's dreadful, the way they make mothers feel guilty nowadays? Have you noticed that every pretext is valid to make them feel ashamed they don't look after their children properly? But never a word about fathers'" (107). Published in 2018, Nothomb's *Strike Your Heart* operates as an examination of both what it means to be mother and child and scathing criticisms of the societies that make mothers choose between nurturing and working, and the resultant emotional neglect and abuse at the expense of both mothers and their children.

Plath never represents a woman living and succeeding without somehow conceding to patriarchal ideas about women, somehow resigning to domesticity. As a result, her own self-conception is based on the idealized mother-nurturer, i.e. consumable, woman. Plath communicates this via the image of the fig tree: figs, as both food items and symbols for female sex organs, are representations of the normative conception of woman, and by sitting at the "crotch" of the tree, Esther's visions remain grounded in–confined to–sexuality and birth. Even two of her considered futures, a life as a housewife and a career as the literary editor Ee Gee (a derivation of "Jay Cee" and allusion to Esther's fixation with eggs) are mired in either birth and domesticity or making a career catering to them. Later, Esther proposes that "my vision of the fig tree and all the fat figs that withered and fell to earth might well have arisen from the profound void of an empty stomach" (Plath 78). In context, her stomach is literally empty because she is hungry, but the phrase "profound void of an empty stomach" also suggests an empty womb. Here, Plath implies that Esther believes the problem of her empty stomach would be solved if she were a more traditional woman, more willing and able to produce food and children. The horror of the fig tree is that it only offers a life of mothering.

Birth figures as a site of woundedness for Diane and Esther, too, not just their mothers. Nothomb broadcasts Diane's acute awareness of and trauma due to the separation of birth: "Diane was a good little baby. She only cried at birth" (20). Out of the womb, Diane loses any chance at intimate or loving contact with her mother and finds herself forced to navigate a neglectful childhood; Esther, smothered by her practical, secretarial mother is constrained by archetypal femininity and trapped between mutually exclusive life trajectories. In her essay on Plath's conflicting views of motherhood, which she designates the Demeter/Persephone complex, psychoanalytic scholar Bracha Ettinger writes that Plath's work "expresses a delirium-like desire of a mother to return her children to pre-life and non-life in her womb … the same womb whose infertility and menstruation were not so long ago deeply lamented. Death wishes appear as a desire to dismother and a desire to disbirth, to de-mother and unmother Mother. The subject does not ask why she should go on living. She asks Why have I been born" (Ettinger 139)? Death, then, is not only a looming spectre, but a chance to re-experience the comfortable oblivion of life in the womb, complete union, the antithesis of the separation that is birth. The impulse towards dismothering and disbirth is just as present in Nothomb's *Strike Your Heart*. Both Diane and Esther are haunted by a desire to return to pre-birth and pre-separation, pre-psychic fragmentation. This desire is illustrated through their relationships to eggs.

For Diane, eating eggs literally constitutes a relationship with herself pre-birth. During her pregnancy, Diane's mother Marie develops a powerful craving for eggs. She demands that Olivier leave work and prepare them: "he peeled them delicately and took them on a tray to Marie in her bed. The young woman devoured them with terrifying delight (Nothomb 16). That her husband makes the eggs for her represents Marie's passive relationship with her own pregnancy. She eats the eggs, symbolic of the potential for birth but also of abortion, as they are unfertilized. Nothomb mobilizes eggs as an ambiguous image that suggests both Marie's craving for abortion or *not* birthing and for acclimation to and acceptance of her pregnancy. Later, Marie grows to hate eggs, emblematic of her carrying Diane: "'Now, just the sight of them makes me nauseous,'" she asserts (44). Diane, not wanting the food to go to waste, accepts them, musing that "When Maman had me in her tummy, she ate them all the time … Did that explain why this particular meal had such an effect on her? She trembled with pleasure and emotion" (ibid.). Diane, elated at the possibility of sharing an experience with and thus identifying with her pregnant mother, whom she has deified, grows to love eggs.

Eggs are poignant symbols for the time before birth. Just as Esther loves eating eggs, all of her suicide attempts suggest birth or a return to the womb in some way. That Plath implicitly compares suicide, the ultimate abdication of choice, with birth, reveals how deeply Esther dreads motherhood and how fervently she wishes her birth/death could be avoided. She says of slitting her wrists in the tub "I thought it would be easy, lying in the tub and seeing the redness flower from my wrists, flush and flush through the clear water, till I sank to sleep under a surface gaudy as poppies" (147). The image of this suicide, with its warmth, red color, wetness, and clearly defined boundaries resembles a womb. In her most abstract suicide attempt, Esther tries to exhaust herself swimming to a far-off, egg-shaped rock, making this effort a death by the pursuit of the mere idea of reproduction, as represented by the egg. Again, this suicide attempt constitutes a symbolic returning to the womb, watery and dark. Esther eventually turns away frustrated, explaining that "The egg-shaped rock didn't seem to be any nearer than it had been when Cal and I had looked at it from the shore … The gray rock mocked me, bobbing on the water easy as a lifebuoy. I knew when I was beaten. I turned back" (161). Esther's fondness for eggs (and thus the output and skills of housewives) and desire to die or return to the womb, to non-existence, both figure as failures.

Plath identifies sexuality and giving birth with death even more starkly when Esther, undergoing treatment at a psychiatric ward and granted time away from the ward, practices a "new, normal personality" on a man to rid herself of her virginity. Virginity, she reasons, is a hypocritical mark of "purity" idealized by and used to attract men. She loses it to "get even" with her suitor, Buddy Willard, who has lost his virginity but only continues to pursue Esther while under the impression that she remains a virgin. She sets her sights on Irwin, a young professor with "the pale, hairless skin of a boy genius" (228). Curiously, in her pursuit of sex, Esther chooses a man who himself resembles a baby, perhaps an ominous portent of the consequences of the deed. After her loss of virginity, Esther hemorrhages, bleeding so profusely that Joan, her inmate at the psychiatric ward, calls an ambulance to assist her. While Esther nearly bleeds out, literally injured by penetrative sex, she recalls "a worrisome course in the Victorian novel where woman after woman died, palely and nobly, in torrents of blood, after a difficult childbirth. Perhaps Irwin had injured me in some obscure, awful way, and all the while I lay there on Joan's sofa I was really dying" (232). As we learn from Darrieussecq's rendition of Paula, the Victorian novel is hardly off the mark.

Esther cannot become a mere housewife, nor can she elude the problems of living and the ultimate need to make decisions about her future by returning to the womb. Diane also cannot return to pre-birth or win any kind of healing or unitive love with her mother. To achieve authentic selfhood, to overcome the struggle of bearing manifold, mutually exclusive expectations of women, the pains of rejection, and a deeply felt sense of separateness, Esther and Diane must attain rebirth through different means: rejecting potential doubles or archetypes off of which to pattern themselves, ending toxic relationships, and living in accordance with their own authentic, purposefully abject principles. Esther and Diane, reborn, live for their own sakes.

Diane accomplishes her rebirth by recognizing and rejecting the examples of the manifold doubles, mother-mentors, she encounters throughout her life. Nothomb makes a playful show of doubling: Diane's best friend's Élisabeth's parents, who take Diane in and raise her as their daughter after her grandparents die, are literally named Madame and Monsieur Second (Nothomb 116). But doubles also cut more insidious figures, offering Diane neurotic and selfish examples and modes of being. When Marie discusses her youngest daughter Célia's running away with Diane, she questions Diane for her alleged closeness with "a woman my age," Olivia (84). Diane is sensitive to this and more or less explicitly raises the possibility of doubling: "Was she crazy to think that she had detected sarcasm in her mother's allusion to that fact that Olivia and she were the same age? How could they even be compared?" (87). Initially spurring the idea that her petty mother and an accomplished academic could be similar, Nothomb prods Diane to confront their shared jealousy and profound lack of love for their children when she recreates a hurtful scene from Diane's childhood. During a family brunch, Marie's sister offers her niece a piece of chocolate: "Marie stopped her: 'Out of the question. It's fattening.' 'Oh, honestly, Marie, your daughter is thin as a rail!' said Brigitte. 'And she has to stay that way,' said Marie" (36). Diane recognizes the subtext: "I don't want my daughter to enjoy herself" (ibid.). Years later, when Diane offers Olivia's daughter Mariel chocolate, Olivia answers "'It's out of the question. ... They're fattening.'" When Diane objects, saying "'Mariel is as thin as a rail!'" Olivia responds "'And she has to stay that way'" (104).

As Diane's academic mentor, Olivia also figures as a possible double of Diane. Nothomb first raises this possibility in dialogue between Marie and Diane: "'Olivia? How funny. That's the name I had chosen for you'" (84). This exchange suggests that, were Diane to continue her career following Olivia's example, she would also continue enacting her mother's hopes for her firstborn. In recreating Olivia's example, she is also recreating that of her mother. The Olivia/Diane doubling persists when Olivia takes credit for Diane's thought. Explaining her motive for studying cardiology, Diane tells Olivia that "'I was impressed by a quote from the work of Alfred de Musset: *'Strike your heart, that is where genius lies'*'" (76). Later, after Diane labors to help Olivia publish the dozen articles she needs to produce to become a full professor, Olivia lifts Diane's inspiration by using the same quote when she delivers a speech to her colleagues to accept full professorship: "'... and I knew at once that I would devote my future to the study of the human heart'" (97). Similarly, when Olivia seeks to publish another article to maintain her standing at the University, she plagiarizes Diane's dissertation (123). Diane finally acknowledges the similarities between Olivia and her mother when Olivia asks to use the intimate, informal pronoun *tu* (as opposed to the formal *vous*) with Diane, who works not only as her research assistant, but also as a tutor for Mariel, her daughter. Olivia admits that "'I thought of it now because I heard Mariel saying *tu* to you.'" Enraged, Diane thinks "how could I have thought this was sign of friendship, when it was only jealousy toward her daughter?" (122)

Diane's rebirth and progression towards authenticity and genuine love for self and other begins when she elects to identify with Mariel, Olivia's stunted daughter, rather than her cold and successful mother. After establishing parallels between Marie and Olivia, Nothomb offers Mariel up as a double for Diane when Diane reflects "How could there be any similarities between herself as a child and that poor traumatized kid? Above all, how could the oh-so-brilliant Olivia Aubusson resemble her mother in any way? She refrained from digging any deeper" (105). Diane struggles to think critically of Olivia, her mentor, until she has sustained contact with Mariel. Making time to tutor Mariel, the tactful Diane "carefully avoided asking awkward questions such as 'Didn't your mother or father ever explain to you that...' so that the little girl would not realize that she was suffering from a grave parental deficiency" (108). After supporting the attention and affirmation-starved young girl, Diane grows to hate Olivia for her neglect of her child, who obviously loves her. While the former has become "cold," in the words of her mother, to cope with her own neglect, she processes her own trauma via Mariel.

Like Diane, Esther is surrounded by potential mother figures, mentors, and doubles. The first, Jay Cee, the famed editor at *Ladies' Day*, shares a name, Jay, with birds. Though she is a witty and accomplished working woman who has prioritized her job over having children, Esther cannot completely dissociate her from ideals of female beauty and domesticity: "Jay Cee had brains, so her plug-ugly looks didn't seem to matter. ... I tried to imagine Jay Cee out of her strict office suit and luncheon-duty hat and in bed with her fat husband, but I just couldn't do it" (Plath 6). Though Jay Cee has an intellectual career as a literary editor, she is not out from under the influence of the patriarchy. Hers is a publication that instructs women on fashion, recipes, and how to style homes, and she favors male writers over female writers. Through the reality of Jay Cee's dismayingly patriarchal work and Esther's inability to stop imposing the normative conception of women onto Jay Cee, Esther comes to realize that even the most exceptional and accomplished women do not live lives independent of patriarchal ideality. Plath summarizes this disheartening but provocative realization when Esther observes that "Jay Cee wanted to teach me something," and "all the old ladies I ever knew wanted to teach me something ... I suddenly didn't think they had anything to teach me" (6).

Philomena Guinea, whose name recalls guinea fowl, is a famous novelist and the sponsor of Esther's scholarship (40). She tells Esther that "she had been very stupid at college," seemingly dismissing her college education as valueless (41). Eventually, Philomena Guinea pays for Esther's psychiatric care, for "at the peak of her career, she had been in an asylum as well" (185). Plath's specification that Philomena Guinea's hospitalization was at the peak of her career insinuates that she was hospitalized at least in part *because* of her career. Through this decision, Plath aligns the writerly woman with insanity, and thus radical alterity. Unlike Jay Cee, Philomena Guinea cuts a countercultural figure as a single woman writer who supports herself; she identifies her life as contrary to the traditional roles for women and implies that she wants the same for Esther, for she threatens to withdraw her financial support for Esther's psychiatric care if "there was a boy in the case" (ibid.). After being medicated in the asylum and gaining weight, Esther notes that "it was a good thing Mrs. Guinea hadn't seen me like this, because I looked just as if I were going to have a baby" (192). That Esther compares her psychiatrists' "cure," which causes weight gain, with pregnancy, suggests that pregnancy is the mark of normalcy and sanity for women; similarly, another patient in the psychiatric ward with Esther, Mrs. Tomolillo, is released after she helps to "[dish] out everybody's food like a little mother," modeling maternal behavior and thus demonstrating that she is "cured" (180). Though Philomena Guinea has made enough money off of her writing to live in a mansion, a life that most would consider successful, she is enfeebled and explicitly compared to a bird when juxtaposed with a man: "next to him, like a frail, exotic bird, the silver hair and emerald-feathered hat of Philomena Guinea, the famous novelist" (184). This avian comparison marks her as unfree, and somehow still subhuman. Similarly, her mental health struggles and desire to steer Esther away from romantic involvement further underscore the need for reconceiving of gender roles and Esther's sense of captivity.

Another potential mentor figure is Dodo Conway. Esther regards Dodo Conway, whose name brings to mind the fat, docile, and stupid bird with contempt. In Plath's introduction of the character, her piety and fecundity are emphasized: "A serene, almost religious smile lit up the woman's face. Her head tilted happily back, like a sparrow egg perched on a duck egg, she smiled into the sun. ... It was Dodo Conway" (116). Dodo's head, which was obviously serviceable, given her Barnard education, is transfigured by Esther into eggs, suggesting that all of her intellectual powers have gone into making her seven children. Though Esther regards her with horror, she admits that "Dodo interested me in spite of myself" (116). Dodo's lifestyle may be interesting because hers is the lifestyle that faces the least social opposition, the life that seems most viable.

Plath encapsulates the danger of faithful doubling through Joan the lesbian, a peer of Esther's throughout college and within the psychiatric ward. Interestingly, Joan, too has dated Buddy Willard, the emblem of hypocritical patriarchal expectations for women and benign oppressor. Esther reflects "Joan was the beaming double of my old best self, specially designed to follow and torment me," underscoring their similar experiences and "model behavior" as Ivy League-adjacent young students, and romantic prospects of "successful" men like Buddy (205). When they are reunited, Joan explains that she followed Esther's example: "I read about you [in the newspaper articles about surviving a suicide attempt], and I ran away" (195). Chillingly, Esther is the only model that seems to have reflected Joan's lived experience. When Esther begins her recovery in the psychiatric ward in earnest, she reflects that "In spite of my profound reservations, I thought I would always treasure Joan. It was as if we had been forced together by some overwhelming circumstance, like war of plague, and shared a world of our own" (225). Joan's attraction to women in general, and Esther in particular, as Joan regularly calls on Esther during their treatment and makes advances on her, may mark Joan as a foil for Esther and potential "double," as her experiences literally mirror Esther's. Her lesbian attraction may be mobilized as a symbolic surrender to doubling and imitativeness, rather than authenticity and an independent, self-forged life trajectory.[38] Crucially, Joan is close with her psychiatrist.

When she cannot "merge" with or double Esther through a romantic union, she later concludes that "I'm going to be a psychiatrist. ... I've had a long talk with Doctor Quinn, and she thinks it's perfectly possible" (224). When Joan goes missing, the psychiatric staff question Esther, demonstrating their closeness and implying their representation to each other as foils (234). Finally, Joan is found dead by suicide, representing the full surrender of autonomy. She has completed suicide where Esther has failed: as such, she is a chilling reminder of Esther's plan. Perhaps Esther realizes the doctors' insinuations during the questioning, as she thinks "Suddenly I wanted to dissociate myself from Joan completely" (234).

Like Diane, Esther's recovery begins with her rejection of her mother and refusal to reproduce the example of another woman. Esther's mother, dutiful but unimaginative and smothering, visits Esther throughout her institutionalization and issues unhelpful statements such as "I knew you would choose to be alright!," revealing her complete failure to grasp her daughter's suffering (145). When Esther is sent to a psychiatric ward for full-time treatment, she finds that her doctor is a woman, whereupon Esther is shocked, reflecting "I didn't think they had woman psychiatrists" (186). As a professional and accomplished woman, Dr. Nolan may seem like another future, another fig for Esther's fig tree. Esther even explicitly imagines her as a glamorous mother figure: "This woman was a cross between Myrna Loy and my mother" (186). This makes her another potential role model, yet Esther refuses to idolize her as such. Esther's first breakthrough in therapy occurs under the care of Dr. Nolan, apparent from her statement, "I hate my mother," to which the psychiatrist replies "I suppose you do" and issues a knowing smile, sealing the statement as a sign of progress (203). After spending most of the novel functioning as a near kaleidoscope stuffed with imagined futures reproducing the lives and examples as the women around her, Esther never fantasizes of being or imitating Dr. Nolan. Instead, she moves forward as Esther, embracing her body and autonomy, and leading a new, authentic, non-archetypal life.

In rejecting lives of reproducing the images of the women around them, Diane and Esther abort their previous mentors, or, to use Ettinger's term, dis-mother them and themselves; their rebirths figure as a psychic killing of the mother. Plath makes this clear during Esther's interviews to leave the psychiatric hospital. Fixing her gaze inward, Esther listens to "the old brag of her heart: 'I am, I am, I am'" (244), signalling a newfound sense of groundedness in her body as well as of autonomy. Plath explicitly characterizes Esther's self-liberation from the images of mother-mentors as a rebirth when Esther reflects that "there ought to be a ritual for being born twice" (ibid.). For Esther, this "ritual" symbolically follows the contours of rebirth. Her last suicide attempt via sleeping pills, the one that catalyzes her commitment to the psychiatric ward, is mired in birth imagery, complete with crowning, moaning, and a "slit" or "wound" standing in for the vaginal opening: "I felt the darkness, but nothing else, and my head rose, feeling it, like the head of a worm. ... Someone was moaning. ... a slit of light opened, like a mouth or a wound ... through the thick, warm, furry dark, a voice cried" (170-171). Her first conscious word, of course, is "Mother!" (171). The second part of her "ritual," her real and final rebirth as an independent woman, is her passage through the psychiatric interview room's swinging doors, another symbolic vagina. Whereas both Esther and Diane's killing the mother and rebirth into authentic living are figurative, Mariel's rebirth is a more literal dis-mothering. Mariel murders Olivia on Diane's birthday. Diane recognizes this as a message to her, due to her own closeness with and rejection of Olivia as a mother-mentor: "To commit the act on the evening of her birthday, the murderer must have loved Diane" (Nothomb 135). The murder itself is another of Nothomb's nods towards doubling: after Diane discovers that Olivia plagiarized excerpts of Diane's dissertation for her own article, she reflects that "She's a member of my thesis defense jury. I'll grit my teeth until tomorrow. Then I'll break off with no explanation. Otherwise I'll end up killing her" (123). Recognizing the deep woundedness in Mariel that was inflicted by her mother, Diane recalls Mariel's birthday, February 6th, and stays at home all day. When Mariel approaches her, Diane welcomes her:

At 23:54 there came a very quiet knock on her door.

"Happy birthday," she said immediately to the girl she let in.

"I have nowhere to go," said Mariel.

"This is your home." (135)

Mariel's murder of Olivia on Diane's birthday constitutes a purging of the haunting example of the selfish, abusive mother, so constrained by modern femininity as to reject their daughters, from both her own life and that of Diane's. In returning to Diane on her own birthday, Mariel herself is reborn into a life in which love is possible.

Chapter 8

– The Being, Nothing, and Revelation of Virginia Woolf

In "What is Metaphysics?," Heidegger criticizes the totalizing belief in science that haunts Western thought. Scientism, he establishes, means privileging matter over experience, and thus overlooks "the original question" of what it means to be. He argues that positivistic allegiance to science, and the resultant treatment of science as a capacious quasi-religion for resolving all queries, contribute towards a fundamental misrecognition of self, things, Being, and what it means to be amongst beings. Heidegger summarizes that science "gives matter itself explicitly and solely the first and last word" (*Basic* 94). Guided by positivism and scientism, mainstream thought and academic disciplines both tend toward the exhaustive exercises of defining, measuring, and splitting the world into categories, granting us a sense of control over the physical world. Yet every name and description remains inadequate. A "thing," Heidegger notes, is a designation for a unity of experience (156). We can create a sign, but the sign merely points to, never encompasses, the signified. The most fundamental "signified," that which Heidegger calls the nothing, offers us a more authentic understanding of things and beings in relation to the latter. The experience of the nothing grants the ability to penetrate the veil of "thingness," both physical phenomena and the superfluities of ideologies. Woolf's spectral, profoundly interior-oriented short stories serve as dramatizations of Heidegger's theory of metaphysics by acquainting readers with absence and misrecognition, and as such, with the capacity to recognize the miasma of "thingness" and the nothing.

According to Heidegger, nothingness necessarily precedes the cognitive act of negation, which follows its example (*Basic* 97). As such, the nothing is the most original state, the ground of Being, and beings must relate to it. Despite the nothing's primacy, science, humanity's dominant means of understanding the known universe, is unable to comment on the nothing. Heidegger observes that "When "the Nothing" is seriously pursued, "The idea of 'logic' itself disintegrates in the turbulence of a more original questioning" (105). The "more original questioning" includes inquiry into the origin of matter, of moral questions, of concerns such as "Why are there things instead of nothing?" In a culture of materialism, and the scientism that follows, physical concerns and natural disciplines take precedence over moral and artistic disciplines, obscuring essential facets of humanity and what it means to be a being. As we have established, science, the knowledge of Things, cannot comment on meaning, being, or reckon with the nothing. Yet even thought experiments and logical reasoning fail us: "We can of course think the whole of beings in an 'idea,' then negate what we have imagined in our thought, and thus 'think' it negated. In this way we do attain the formal concept of the imagined nothing but never the nothing itself" (99). Thus, the nothing emerges as a spectre that assails scientific and philosophical thought. The nothing is unobservable, invisible, elusive, yet it is fundamental to existence; as such, it must be reached through some other means. Yet without *some* relation to the nothingness, one's Being, or self, "could never be related to beings nor even to itself. *Without the original revelation of the nothing, no selfhood and no freedom*" (emphasis our own, 103). For Heidegger, and, we will argue, Woolf, it is the experience of the Nothing that awakens us to being and to authenticity.

Almost paradoxically, in this age of science, medicine, entertainment, and the Human Development Index, self-fulfillment remains elusive, obscured by manifold distractions, and loneliness runs rampant. Heidegger exposes the fundamental misrecognition that is scientism (no doubt exacerbated by capitalist culture's materialism), or a life submerged in "thingness," cognizant merely of matter, and not of nothing and being. He synopsizes modern scientism and materialism's myopia as "[relating] to beings themselves in a distinctive way and only to them" (109). This insular state is equally applicable to gossips across time (as shown through Julia's recollections of hearsay in Woolf's "Moments of Being"), or to someone seeking out a passionate love through a personal advertisement or dating app while presenting themselves as a few photographs, a list of likes and dislikes, an archive of television quotes. This everyday submersion in cataloguing likes and dislikes, like science's knowledge claims and exhaustive cataloguing of matter, occlude the immediacy necessary for wonder and revelation. In both the exclusively materialistic lifestyles, exhaustive explanation emerges as an obstacle, and the revelation of the nothing is lost. In turning to "being in our preoccupations … we let beings as a whole slip away as such and and the more we turn away from the nothing. Just as surely do we hasten into the public superficies of existence," as thus give up the means to self-knowledge and authenticity (104). The secret of being, Heidegger implies, is private and revelatory.

In spite of the importance of the experience of nothingness, Heidegger observes that we cannot bring about the "original mood," "the most proper sense of unveiling" by ourselves, noting that "We are so finite that we cannot even bring ourselves originally before the nothing through our own decision and will" (100; 106). The nothing is not reducible to and precedes the conceptual categories of emptiness and absence, which, congealed into thoughts, become things, words, signs referring to physical states. Because of this, desire of the nothing annihilates it, renders it invisible.[39] Though we cannot will the revelation of the Nothing, art can guide us to a realization of nothingness, the ground of Being.

In "Literature and Life," Gilles Deleuze claims that "Writing is a question of becoming," and that "Becoming is also 'between' or among'" (*Essays*, 1, 2). He proclaims that "literature begins only when a third person is born in us that strips us of the power to say 'I'" (3). In reading, we can recognize bits of ourselves in others, exercise empathy, and glimpse into becoming, seeing how each person–being is the product of physical and social forces, being acted on and acting among things and other beings. Art is, if nothing else, emotionally affecting; Heidegger foregrounds the affective nature of experiencing the nothing when he writes "anxiety reveals the nothing. More precisely, anxiety leaves us hanging because it induces the slipping away of beings as a whole. This implies that we ourselves–we humans who are in being–in the midst of beings slip away from ourselves. … In the altogether unsettling experience of this hovering where there is nothing to hold onto, pure Da-sein is all that is still there" (*Basic* 101). One becomes attuned to Being and a sense of continuity independent of things and current circumstances during the experience of anxiety: even when alienated from all else, consciousness, awareness, the thing that looks, remains. Heidegger also offers the emotional experiences of boredom and love as means of realizing the nothing. Of boredom, he writes that "drifting here and there in the abysses of our existence like a muffling fog, [it] removes all things and human beings and oneself along with them into a remarkable indifference. This boredom reveals beings as a whole" (99). Of love, Heidegger is more abstract, stating that "Another possibility of such revelation is concealed in our joy in the presence of the Dasein–and not simply of the person–of a human being whom we love (ibid.). Love, then, is something more than fixation, something more than the desire for revelation. Woolf, in her profoundly introspective phenomenological novels and especially her short stories, captures the "question of becoming." We will examine her stories "A Haunted House" and "Moments of Being" as catalysts for the experiences of boredom, anxiety, and love, respectively; each reveal the nothing and revelations towards Being, authentic selfhood, and freedom in a manner that is as subversive as it is elegant.

Woolf centers "A Haunted House" around a pair of phantoms searching through a house, providing exhaustive, list-like descriptions of the house's furnishings; this narration dramatizes a life submerged in "thing-ness" at the expense of nothingness, as well as the deep boredom and sense of lack that provoke the search. Woolf's introduction to the story implies the narrator's limited perspective, as well as that of the searching ghosts. She begins the story with "Whatever hour you woke there was a door shutting" couching the narrator in a sleep-stupor, a liminal state of consciousness and an experience not unlike Heidegger's "indistinguishability" that expediates the nothing (Woolf, *A Haunted* 3). Woolf's main characters survey the house, naming objects, searching for visible phenomena: "From room to room they went, hand in hand, lifting here, opening there, making sure–a ghostly couple" (ibid.). In "lifting," "opening," – and perhaps most significantly, "making sure," – interacting with their material surroundings despite their own implied immateriality, Woolf shows the ghostly couple to be acutely aware of an emotional, perhaps spiritual lack: i.e. deeply bored. Instead of finding the object of the search, the ghostly couple find reflections, seeing that "the window panes reflected apples, reflected roses; all the leaves were green in the glass" (ibid.). These reflections are symbolic of misrecognition, perhaps emerging as a 20th century equivalent to Plato's shadows on the cave wall. In directing the ghostly couple's attention towards the glass windows rather than the apples or roses themselves, Woolf shows their attunement to mere things over the living i.e. beings. Similarly, the listing of reflections points to absence, to misrecognition.

Woolf depicts the ghostly couple in dialogue, recounting their shared past with the house, but their reminiscing has an abortive quality. Rather than describing their experiences, the ghostly couple keep their recollections brief, as if they cannot recall how they felt, or they are overwhelmed by the multitude of "things." Together, they drone: "'Here we slept,' she says. And he adds, 'Kisses without number.' 'Waking in the morning–' 'Silver between the trees–' 'Upstairs–' 'In the garden–' 'When summer came–' 'In winter snowtime–'"(4). Woolf ends their discussion of their (past?) experiences by foregrounding the present situation of the house, implying either severance from the past or the past's simultaneous presence within the present, writing "The doors go shutting far in the distance, gently knocking like the pulse of a heart. Nearer they come; cease at the doorway" (ibid.). Additionally, the couple "cease at the doorway," stopping just short of some form of passage, of completing their search. The ghostly couple's incomplete inventory of the home and aborted summaries of their past lives suggest a quality of lostness amongst things, as does their very presence in the house. The ghosts have left something, we are led to infer, unfinished; their lives' promises were not quite fulfilled, selves not realized.

Just as the ghostly couple fail to find the object of their search, lost in their fixation on things, not beings as a whole, the sleeping narrator and their spouse fail to observe the ghosts: "Our eyes darken; we hear no steps beside us; we see no lady spread her ghostly cloak. His hands shield the lantern" (ibid.). In their shared obliviousness to each other, and in their occupation of the same house, the ghostly couple and the narrator and their spouse emerge as doubles to each other, a confusing series of identifications and mis-identifications that perfectly illustrates Heidegger's conception of beings relating to themselves and *only* themselves. This anticlimax represents the cognitive and affective insularity that precedes the revelation of the nothing.

Woolf resolves the story through confrontation: a confrontation between the ghostly couple and the "real" sleeping couple, a confrontation of her reader, and ultimately, a confrontation of our relationships to things and to the lifestyle that favors misrecognitions over Being. Woolf begins her confrontation of the reader via metafictional direct addresses early in the story. By using the second-person pronoun, "You," she positions the reader, murkily, in the events of the story, drifting but unable to interact with the two couples: lost, and thusly in the same position as her story's actors. The narrator, initially, is undisturbed by the ghosts' search, and anticipates the reader's reactions to the ghosts' plight: "But it wasn't that you woke us. Oh, no. 'They're looking for it; they're drawing the curtain,' one might say, and so read on a page or two. 'Now they've found it,' one would be certain, stopping the pencil on the margin" (3). In believing in the ghosts, in assuring themselves of the success of the search, Woolf implies, the reader, too, is searching, and perhaps looking for the wrong object, drawing the wrong conclusions. Here, Woolf suggests the murkiness of the reader's own "thing-ly" submersion. Woolf's direct address of the reader positions her or him as a mere spectator, making the reader's removal from the story very real, and creating another means of dramatizing absence, revealing the nothing. In making central characters ghosts, Woolf makes real the dead, memories, and absence. The invisibility of the searchers, as well as of the spectating reader, and the seemingly simultaneity of past and present convey the paradoxical presence of absence, the seminal nothing. Woolf's development of absence sustains a feeling of being lost, the same experience Heidegger names as anxiety, one of the emotions that brings on revelation.

Woolf also transmits the problem with "thingness" when she constructs the house as a character in its own right, one made significant and livable due to its vacuity, the emptiness demarcated by the structure.

Woolf makes apparent the fallacy of giving matter "the first and last word," as Heidegger may term it, by representing matter as something that separates and obstructs mutual understanding, writing "So fine, so rare, coolly sunk beneath the surface the beam I sought always burnt behind the glass. Death was the glass; death was between us; coming to the woman first, hundreds of years ago, leaving the house, sealing all the windows" (4). Here, death, as in *The Haunting of Hill House*, equates to separateness. Structures, the trappings of materialist society, become monstrous in their own right, masquerade as shelter, as belonging amongst other beings and things. Woolf's personification of the house offers another relation to materials and to domesticity, revealing one in which that the house is not made a character by virtue of its physical presence, but the lacunae it offers. The house is useful for its emptiness, not for its structure, as Eleanor misrecognizes: this emptiness renders it a livable shelter and directs the reader towards interiority. The house responds to the ghosts' search, pulsing as if alive: "'Safe, safe, safe,' the pulse of the house beat softly. 'The treasure buried; the room…' the pulse stopped short. Oh, was that the buried treasure?" (ibid.). Throughout her personification of the house, Woolf underscores emotions and memories, the "experience" of the house rather than its structure, or "thingness." So the house becomes a symbolic body, a heart, one that the "treasure" inhabits. She even shows the house speaking, albeit silently, writing 'Safe, safe, safe,' the pulse of the house beat gladly. 'The Treasure yours'" (ibid.). The treasure is love, the primal basis of which is nothing.

The climax of the story emerges as a revelation of the nothing, a celebration of the absence that underpins presence, and a glimpse into Heideggerian "beings as a whole." When Woolf reveals the treasure, she effectively offers it to the reader, the ghostly couple, the (now wakened) narrator, and even the House, who are all implied to claim it: the ghosts "seek their hidden joy…… 'Long years–' he sighs. 'Again you found me.' 'Here,' she murmurs, 'sleeping; in the garden reading; laughing, rolling applies in the loft. Here we left our treasure–' Stooping, their light lifts the lids upon my eyes.... Waking, I cry 'Oh, is this *your* buried treasure? The light in the heart'" (5). The invisibility of the object of the search points to interiority, not a "thing" but the experience(s) of it, not something, but its underpinning of nothing. The past-ness of the ghostly couple that necessitates the simultaneity of past and present, the seemingly animate "heart" of the house which shelters *because* of its hollows; the metafiction that establishes the reader as anticipating, somehow part of the story yet passive in it; the immateriality of the "light in the heart," and the narrator's confrontational last words all reveal the nothing. In being able to interact with the ghostly couple, to feel the pulse of the house, *and* recognize the true treasure as ultimately interior, as lived experience, the narrator transcends beyond "comprehending the whole of beings in themselves," and instead "[finds] oneself in the midst of beings as a whole" (Heidegger, *Basic* 99). Now aware of absence, of the existence of nothing that makes possible the existence of something, of Being, the narrator can live with a deeper understanding of their place in the world, freed by virtue of their cognizance of their Being. Awakened to nothing, a being has the liberating, self-affirming opportunity to decide for oneself what it means to be and to love, with or without a body.

Whereas in a "A Haunted House," Woolf dramatizes the revelation of the nothing as catalyzed by boredom and anxiety, in "Moments of Being" Woolf reveals the nothing through a relatively overt experience of love. In the latter story she illustrates the Deleuzian challenge to move beyond Being and towards becoming, as well as towards the Heideggerian mode of health, wherein one is able to perceive "beings as a whole," rather than sinking into dehumanization of science and material culture and publicly affirmed image-ideals. Image-ideals status, gossip, the best pins, all feature in "Moments of Being" as those things Heidegger might name as "the public superficies of existence" (104). The instances dramatizing the revision of subjectivity, the recognition of one's own misrecognition and inauthenticity, represent a particular moment of Being, one that has nothing to do with a sense of self as static, but rather a self-in-progress, a narrative center of gravity. Deleuze describes this movement towards a state of "becoming" in feminine, i.e. subordinate or "minor," terms: "Becoming does not move in the other direction, and one does not become Man, insofar as man presents himself as a dominant form of expression that claims to impose itself on all matter, whereas woman, animal, or molecule always has a component of flight that escapes its own formalization. ... Even when it is a woman who is becoming, she has to become-woman, and this becoming has nothing to do with a state she could claim as her own" (*Essays* 1). Interestingly, in describing his conception of life as a process, Deleuze designates femininity as revolutionary, thus constructing "becoming-woman" as both an acceptance of one's social marginality and refusal to pattern one's self-conception off of dominant ideality. "Moments of Being" depicts a female pupil, Fanny Wilmot, falling in love with a cultured older woman, Julia Craye. Radically, Woolf represents a young woman recognizing her internalization and projection of the circumscribed normative role for women onto her companion, projections that are viscerally disrupted by a kiss, a show of love. This homoromantic disruption renders the story as one of Fanny's "becoming-woman" by voiding her culturally transmitted, patriarchal schema for evaluating the lives of women, including her own, and opening her to new, more authentic ways of living.

Through Fanny's thoughts about Julius Craye, Julia's dead archeologist brother, Woolf depicts the cultural (and by extension, political, economic, *material*) eclipse of the feminine by the masculine. Fanny's habit of attributing Julia's aloofness and eccentricity to her dead brother constructs Julia as a byproduct of her brother's lifestyle. The names Julia and Julius invite comparison, of course, as they are the feminine and masculine versions of each other. Yet Julius seems to be constructed as the more important, influential partner in the relationship between the gifted siblings, as in Fanny's conversations with local socialite Miss Kingston: "'The famous archaeologist'–as she said that, ... there was in Miss Kingston's voice an indescribable tone which hinted at something odd; something queer in Julius Craye; it was the very same thing that was odd perhaps in Julia too" (Woolf, *A Haunted* 105). In "Moments of Being," Julia is quite clearly defined against her brother, as is woman against man in Simone de Beauvoir's *The Second Sex*, which famously states that Woman is "determined and differentiated in relation to man and not he with reference to her; she is the inessential in front of the essential. He is the Subject; he is the Absolute. She is the Other" (26). This constructs masculinity as "default" or normative, effectively othering

Julia and, by extension, femininity, even Fanny. Thus, in recognizing and loving Julia, Fanny is, symbolically, loving the nothing.

While Fanny's recollections represent a policing of femininity, for they still position Julia as defined by relation (or in her case, non-relation) with a man, Fanny's imagined – projected – accounts explaining Julia's refusal to marry also reflect an awareness of and discomfort with the normative feminine position and even homoromantic desire. They also represent a succumbing to Heidegger's "public superficies of existence," and a regard for the relations between things and other things, not Things and the question of what it means to be. Woolf writes Fanny as recognizing Julia as peculiar due to both Miss Kingston's gossip and her unwed status, with Fanny noting that "None of the Crayes had ever married" ("Moments" 104). Indeed, she initially rejects Julia's attempts to relate to her, or to the lives of "regular" people in her description of mundane home goods, like Slater's pins, but Fanny takes it upon herself to find some means of understanding Julia, of escorting her back into normalcy. Fanny establishes the difference, then recognizes her desire to span the gulf when she thinks "She knew nothing about pins–nothing whatever. But she wanted to break the spell that had fallen on the house; to break the pane of glass which separated them from the other people" (ibid.). Here, as in "A Haunted House," material objects (discrete, easy to produce and touch and understand), though transparent, emerge as separating beings from other beings, leaving beings lost amongst things, yet Fanny is fascinated by Julia's supposed isolation and presumed loneliness. Both Fanny's initial judgment of Julia and her subsequent attraction to her eccentricity hint at an alienation from the town gossips labeling Julia and her brother "queer" and from the mainstream cultural norms they represent.

The need to account for Julia's marital status at all insinuates the "[Freudian] radically deidealizing screen or cultural image-repertoire, which makes her body the very image of 'lack'" described by psychoanalytic theorist and art historian Kaja Silverman, and thus Fanny's internalization of the patriarchal devaluing of women (33). It also hints at the feminine desire to love a privileged subject "in a way that compensates for the [perceived] impossibility of self-love" (34). When imagining Julia's courtship phases, Fanny tacitly acknowledges Julia's attractiveness, noting that she would have been pursued "with her good blue eyes, her straight firm nose, her air of cool distinction, her piano playing, her rose flowering with chaste passion in the bosom of her muslin dress" (Woolf, *A Haunted* 107). The language making up Fanny's thoughts also suggests an awareness of the projection, a private sanction of homoerotic desire. When considering Julia's claim that Kensington was the nicest part of London due to its gardens, which Fanny uses as a basis for a hypothetical garden stroll date, she notes that "One could make that yield what one liked" (107). Fanny's imagining of Julia's romantic past and rejection of a marriage proposal (or proposals) reeks of discontent with the subordinate station of women, as she characterizes the proposal as "a moment of *horror,* of disillusionment, of *revelation,* for both of them" (emphasis our own, 108). Afraid, Fanny imagines Julia lamenting the loss represented by marriage: "I can't have it, I can't possess it, she thought. … The scene could be changed … but one thing was constant–her refusal, and her frown, and her anger with herself afterwards, and her argument, and her relief–yes, certainly, her immense relief" (ibid.). A complicated issue, Fanny construes the rejection of marriage proposals as a decision followed by cognitive dissonance and the loss of a certain domestic respectability, but mostly relief, imagining Julia relishing her freedoms: "She was so thankful that she had not sacrificed her right to go and look at things when they are at their best … she had not sacrificed her independence (ibid.). Though at the end of the daydream, Woolf at least implicitly reveals that "it" refers to Julia's independence, she suggests that Julia uses her independence to experience beauty; as a designation for experience, "it" may represent the totality of Julia's being.

Julia represents, at least for Fanny, an authentic woman, an alternate schema for Being. In Fanny's imagined proposal, a life schema patterned on the masculine science, Being, personhood, and feminine illogic, nothing, non-personhood, explicitly emerges as horror and abjection. This scene represents a moment during "which the female subject [protests] her forced identification with lack" (Silverman 33). Through these imagined explanations for Julia's independence, Woolf both illustrates the social pressures and noncompliance that make Julia a pariah and suggests

Fanny's values, her projected desire to keep her right "to go and look at things when they are at their best," a right she admires Julia for keeping.

Through Fanny's relationship to Julia, Woolf represents a feminine desire for self-same love, which implies the ability to love oneself and others who belong to the same group(s) in background information she provides about Fanny and Julia. Fanny is aware of their closeness, which she contemplates when recalling how "she had played Bach beautifully as a reward to a favourite pupil (Fanny Wilmot knew that she was Miss Craye's favourite pupil)" (Woolf, "Moments" 105). There is also a moment of founded identification with each other when the two women discuss men and their ambivalence towards them: "'It's the use of men, surely, to protect us' ... 'Oh, but I don't want protection,' Fanny had laughed, and when Julia Craye, fixing on her that extraordinary look, had said she was not so sure of that, Fanny positively blushed under the admiration in her eyes" (106). Here, the two coyly acknowledge that they do not desire those whom they were socialized and presumed to want.

Woolf completely dispels Fanny's daydreams concocted to explain the behavior of Julia with a kiss, a somatic union prefaced by the recognition that Fanny and Julia occupy the same space–an image that represents occupying the same subject-position. Crucially, Fanny recognizes and loves the culturally denigrated subject position, Woman, the negative, the nothing, relative to Man's positive and Being. When considering why Julia moved from Edinburgh, where she lived with Julius, to a house in England by herself, Fanny thinks "Was Miss Craye so lonely? No, Miss Craye was steadily, blissfully, if only for that moment, a happy woman. Fanny had surprised her in a moment of ecstasy" (110). This moment of recognition, of Fanny seeing that Julia is happy, not lonely, not painfully aware of the lack located in women's bodies and the lies of patriarchal power structures, places Fanny on the very same side of the window as Julia, in the same space rather than walled off: "She sat there ... while behind her was the sharp square of the window, uncurtained, purple in the evening, intensely purple after the brilliant electric lights which burnt unshaded in the bare music room" (ibid.). This imagery alludes to and repudiates Fanny's initial understanding of Julia as somehow "walled off" from others. By positioning Fanny as looking both outside the window–judging Julia for her inherited(?) "peculiarity" and pitying her for her loneliness–and looking out from within it, Woolf highlights the absurdity of Fanny's negative, male-centric judgment of Julia when she in fact occupies the same space: the female body. The descriptions of the lights as "unshaded" and of the "bare" music room suggest the clarity needed to see what truly animates and motivates Julia and the inherent revelatory character of love.

Upon recognizing that Julia is happy absorbed in her music, fulfilled, not frustrated, Fanny abandons her assumptions about Julia. This process is completed with the kiss, which offers a new means of Being and interacting in the world for Fanny and ends her misrecognitions of Julia and the disbelief in the capacity of women to love women (extending, it is implied, to themselves). While Fanny observes Julia, Woolf writes that "All seemed transparent, for a moment, to the gaze of Fanny Wilmot, as if looking through Miss Craye, she saw the very fountain of her being spurting its pure silver drops" (ibid.). Woolf goes on to write that "She saw Julia–Julia blazed. Julia kindled. Out of the night she burnt like a dead white star. Julia opened her arms. Julia kissed her on the lips. Julia possessed it" (111). Woolf previously refers to "it" in Fanny's daydream of Julia rejecting a proposal. Here it returns again, more clear in its implication that "it" is more than bodily autonomy, more than the refusal to be closeted, but rather the very *experience* of that body: the true self, the marriage of body and mind. "It" is one's right to Being. In Fanny's previous imagining of Julia's inner life, she repeatedly assumes a frustration on Julia's part, an inability to "possess" beauty, with Fanny imagining Julia saying "I can't get at it; I can't have it" and her grip being characterized by "a perpetual frustration" (105). Julia is recognized as possessing it, is reconfigured as whole instead of lacking, freed instead of victimized. Fanny also discards her water imagery and imagined association of Julia with rivers and fountains for fire imagery, signaling a sea change in Fanny's thought and a willingness to consider new paradigms, new means of understanding people. She sees the Julia in front of her, sees and embraces Julia's self-presentation rather than her own characterization of her teacher. The acceptance of and usage of different imagery associated with Julia suggests the beginning of a truly loving relationship, one founded on "recognition of that other as an other" (Silverman 43). True to Heidegger's revelatory characterization of love, in "Moments of Being," love emerges as the cessation of projection and the willingness to accept another's Being rather than potentially limiting visions of one's own.

Chapter 9

– The Stranger Solitudes of Philippe Sollers

The projects of writing books, composing a complicated musical score, painting, be they hyper-realistic or modernist minimalism, or contemplating the depths of one's mysterious, revivifying ground in emptiness outside the ideally redemptive boundaries of love and companionship, all require solitude. People, other egos, chat and frolic, regale us of their dramas or seek advice, along with providing necessary stimulation, intimacy, or other essential, inspiring aspects of the human experience, while authenticity – of aesthetic, intellectual, or spiritual practice – demands the reclusive sensibility. There is no escaping this reality that is as much of a conundrum as one makes it, though it may be especially challenging in the arena of love, no matter the nature of affiliation. Barthes speaks of the "difficult paradox: [that the lover] can be understood by everyone (love comes from books, its dialect is a common one), but I can be heard (received 'prophetically') only by subjects who have *exactly and right now* the same language I have" (*Lover's* 212). Goethe's Werther asks when the lovers' "inmost souls are tormented by terrifying passion or torn with grief, can you [who are not in this frame of mind] afford them the slightest consolation?" (*Sorrows* 49). We share in the proclivities of desire, perhaps even in the need for creative awakenings, and yet circumstance dictates empathy. How resolutely authentic – anchored in a fundamental solitude and thus aware of Being – we are in a given situation determines one's ability to see oneself in the other and vice versa regardless of the dynamic. Augé addresses this issue more sociologically in characterizing the "ritual paradox" as "always lived individually and subjectively; only individual itineraries give it a reality, and yet it is eminently social, the same for everyone, conferring on each person this minimum of collective identity through which a community is defined" (*In the Metro* 30). He is speaking specifically about the "non-place" of the Parisian metro, although most social situations have an element of ritual for which sociology provides no shortage of terms. Maybe the central paradox for the individual lies in the intricacy of having to negotiate authentic Being born of interiority in the multitudinous spaces of life's generally inevitable exteriority.

Augé twice refers to this incongruity as "strange" in terms of the given public space in which the negotiation is enacted and as a quirk potentially subject to the demystification of ethnology. We are all "solitudes" interacting with other solitudes in "*boundaried*" environments, subject to various rules and expectations, a notion that is deceptively simplistic (30-31). Of course, the individual alone samples the swarm of the mind's thoughts at any moment, alone in thinking and feeling, reacting or responding. In public, we conceal, more or less successfully, our "deliriums," "desires," and "illusions" (34), and yet, pathological or not, they emerge from a shared human experience. Both sides of the wall that separates the asylum from the mass public represent degrees of one another, the narrator of Zoline's story, or that of Charlotte Perkins-Gilman's "The Yellow Wallpaper" exemplifying this truth. In this regard, Augé's version of homelessness perceives its sufferers as "black holes in our daily galaxy" that provoke his interest in the "sacred disquiet they arouse" (48). Why "sacred?" Might such fissures in the daily landscape provoke at least a sense, perhaps even the inevitability, of what Eagleton calls sacrifice? In any event, Being is certainly at stake in this "disquiet," as is alterity to the extent that "something of the other exists in the self, and what belongs to the self that is in the other is indispensable for the definition of the social self, the only one that can be formulated and fathomed" (39). In the depth of our fathoming, of our love, resides the possibility of our prophecy toward the other, to use Barthes's example, the ability to divine the other as ourselves and thus a mutual course toward a "home" walled by windows rather than rigid, concrete boundaries.

Between Bove and Darrieussecq is Philippe Sollers in terms of the timeline of his writing life and the nature of his "critical novel." At once highly observant, realist, romantic, and honest, his first book, *A Strange*

Solitude, expresses the wandering, questioning intentionality of Bove's narrator and the general optimism of Darrieussecq's Paula despite obstacles to the fruition of her art and fulfillment. Another first-person narrative, the novel's protagonist presents a love story, though one in which the beloved, in her exceptional authenticity, places the world in a new light and the lover under the heightened scrutiny of his own conscience and consciousness. "My book," he exclaims, "would be a battle narrative, a history of labor with myself in order to reach that one quality which had been refused me: simplicity" (Sollers 96), a quality that surely evades us all on occasion, if not in most circumstances, and has a great deal to do with solitude for which one must often wage such a "battle" requiring the "labor" of "resoluteness." Like Bove's vulnerable, urban wanderer, Sollers's young, precocious narrator (he is sixteen when they first meet) moves through Paris and other environs with a skeptical eye, though his skepticism is relatively quick to broaden into a larger sense of selflessness: "I was walking. Nothing seemed real: to see something, I had to begin with someone" (73). Prior to this realization, he is able to reflect on his initial, domestic experiences with Concha, the older Spanish nurse/maid who inhabits the family home in his formative years, and specifically their "affair (which brought me into the world)" (50). It is through an ongoing process of refining his "simplicity," in solitude, that he is able to contact the world and its human face with a comparable fidelity to immediate truths.

That the relatively privileged narrator and the nurse are having an affair certainly provokes issues of class and power. However, their age difference (she is in her thirties), and most importantly, Concha's stolid disposition combined with her aptitude for unambiguous pleasure and playfulness inhibit the dynamic's traditional power imbalance. She is the "someone" who will, over time, allow him to see with greater clarity "something" that eventually assumes the form of himself and the events of his life relative to the "world," which naturally includes others, other "solitudes" who share, consciously or not, one's struggle for substantiality. On the other hand, clear, developed perception of external phenomena also implies a critical faculty. Concha, equally invested in her own pleasure, "instructs" by way of example, as a model of embodied, astute observation and detachment. "No 'effect' impressed her; she was really an impossible person" (37), the narrator claims. We could just as easily substitute "affect" here, which opens up the word "impossible" in terms of its implications of social alterity; one who is unimpressed by affectation may have a difficult time navigating conventions of social decorum, the drama of dinner parties, all the prattle and performativity. Her impossibility is what drives her authentic, organic investment in being. "She paid no attention," he observes, "to those farces by which we carefully magnify our tastes and even our incapacities in order to acquire a special 'sympathetic' quality to account for ourselves as a *personality*" (36). The relation to Gurdjieff's notion of personality as the amalgam of everything that is merely learned by the individual, as opposed to his sense of "essence" that we may align with Heideggerian Being, cannot go unnoticed here. Nor can we (that is, anyone inhabiting a current Western milieu) entirely distance ourselves, or at least our cultures, from the "farce" of endless, now normative "magnification of tastes" for the sake of constructing said personality. In Concha, "there was not the slightest trace of duplicity" (42).

"There was nothing in her character of hysteria, none of the disturbing obsessiveness of vice," the narrator explains. "She moved through her life with an absolute availability and an absolute detachment. Yes, in a sense she *was* solitude, the transition between two incommunicable worlds" (110-111). "Availability" and "detachment" would appear to contradict one another unless the latter is recognized as the condition of an "absolute" variety of the former. To be detached need not equate to indifference stripped of ethical concern. If detachment coincides with Concha's distinct "impossibility" – as fundamental non-compliance with affectation – then it fosters rather than eschews a quality of being amenable not to the superficiality but to the immediate *time* of the world, to what it presents in the moment. It is "absolute detachment" that allows her to *be* or embody a productive, radically impossible solitude just as Baldwin's Sonny becomes-sound or Nothomb's Diane assumes the position of total acceptance in the face of murder. Despite her general composure, the narrator implies that she fully and elegantly occupies a liminal space between the environments of self and other – "incommunicable" in that

language is invariably insufficient to forge a completely stable link –
though environments capable of meeting, however obscurely, in the space
of absolute solitude where reactionary judgment holds no sway.[40] Concha
embodies alterity, which, contrary to a prefabricated "otherness," allows
"her character [to harmonize] so well with her surroundings" (45). She
occupies a becoming-solitude.

Nonetheless, in witnessing Concha exchange with a younger friend
from Spain, the narrator is forced to acknowledge the fact that "social
categories persist even within a caste regarded as inferior" (48). Like
Bove's Jeanne, or any number of characters outlined in this study, Concha
is entirely human, susceptible to hierarchies despite her distance from the
world's folly. For his part, the narrator is aware of his own and other's
contributions to this folly quite early on. He notes the "airs," common to a
sixteen-year-old poet, for example, "that make people forget how stupid
you are" (8).[41] His lover, of course, is hardly deceived in this regard.
Relative to Concha, he observes this phenomenon in his friend and mutual
flirt, Beatrice. He "[smiles] to think that by an undeniable sense of theater
which she made a rule of life and pleasure alike, Beatrice had succeeded
only in provoking an unfavorable comparison" to Concha (65). There are
levels of theatricality in the lived life, from childlike teasing, innocent of
hardened deception, to having some vague self-awareness of the
loquacious personality with which one interfaces, with a world that steps
aside when one enters the room. Beatrice is not without her own
sophistication and savvy, which is why she and the narrator find common
ground, in as much as this is possible under the conditions of everyday
incommunicability. That said, she does not meet him where he grasps, in
his own solitude, "that murmur of the mind which is simply a field of battle
where a thousand stupidities clash without ever diminishing each other"
(87). His book as well as his mind becomes a "battle," as opposed to an
innocuous palliative bent on distraction from the world's incessant noise.
He confronts the quagmire of competing voices and allegiances to a point
of locating not only his personal "strangeness" but his own
"impossibility."

For most of us, subjectivity, be it genuinely "strange" or merely
bourgeois and identity-driven, manifests as a revolving door of situations

that may or may not become "events." With an inversion of Badiou's vocabulary that nevertheless corresponds to the philosopher's ideas concerning ethics, Sollers's protagonist asserts "You cannot explain people by events but only by what, in them, resists events" (130). A Badiouian update of this claim would, of course, substitute situations for events, thus foregrounding the value of resisting "the they" (be they traditional humanists or something more abstract, something that works its way into the recesses of one's psychology) who govern and enforce hegemonic social structures. The narrator is not unaware of his own tendency in certain instances to be little more than "an exhausting oscillation, an irremediable transition" (70). At one point, he even sounds like Jackson's Eleanor to the degree that he becomes temporarily absorbed by "I": "Here I am – I thought – here I am, 'me,' mind and body, sauntering, tracing my purposeless stroller's route like these ghosts who oblige my attention" (85). For better or worse, his own "ghosts" are anything but phantasmagoric, at least on the surface, their flesh, their personalities readily apparent. He also diverges from Eleanor in ultimately bringing purpose (rather than deadly "surrender") to his "stroll" amid the challenges of achieving agency. He does so in part by inverting the aimlessly "sauntering" "me" by contrasting it with the "person" who performs or prevaricates. The "me" transforms in such a manner as to be "capable not only of seeing all this kind of luminous absence, but of weighing it, of judging, of laughing at it … And in this passionate detachment from myself, the absurd at last became marvelous: a reality marvelously absurd" (89). "Strangeness" will again emerge from the dichotomy between inauthenticicity's quality of absence and what he later experiences as the "final ecstasy" of "absolute emptiness" (92), approaching a kind of inexplicable mysticism as it does.[42] Only the "marvelously absurd" real can accommodate the essential balance of Being and non-being.

Sollers's novel is finally a love story, though like those examples of his later collaboration with Kristeva and Badiou's "praise," it portrays, as J.D. Salinger puts it, "a compound, or multiple … pure and complicated" love (*Franny* 49). The narrator eventually leaves home, and thus Concha, to pursue his studies in Paris. She occupies his thoughts, to the point of obsession at times, and yet his is still a process of coming of age that precipitates questions and concerns not only about desire but around the nature and possibilities of being a self. Like Salinger's siblings in *Franny and Zooey*, for whom love operates as a gateway to self-development as well as to familial intimacy, Sollers's narrator excavates his solitude for a more genuine form of Being, one that is up to the complex task of selflessness in union with another. For this reason, he determines, after an earlier meditation on the value of music, that "you must use yourself like an instrument ... you must know how to *play yourself*" (Sollers 88). What this might look like is not entirely clear here except for the fact that it is inextricably linked to consciousness, and specifically the "voluntary" development of consciousness (126) that presumably implies a cultivation of awareness regarding the balance or imbalance of personality and essence, the fulcrum of which determines nothing short of authenticity. To "play oneself," then, would mean tipping this scale to centralize Heidegger's "call of conscience" in the psycho-somatic experience of everyday life, toward the nothing. It would also confer understanding, with the narrator, that "love does not mean longing to achieve the other – which would be impossible – it means permitting the other to discover himself as profoundly, as vastly as he deserves" (137). While the lover and his beloved eventually relocate one another and move deeper into their relationality, they ultimately separate, with Concha fully embodying her sorrow now, and leave one another nonetheless to the fruits of their individual self-discoveries. What this means for the narrator is being "as far as possible from the world's stir and strategy," living out of the joyful "certainty of being inaccessible" and "no longer shamefully glued to some illusion" (148). Contrarily, those who exhibit overt *accessibility*, for which there are ample opportunities in the 21st century, digital and otherwise, are prone to the games people play in our efforts to "achieve" another, or the fulfillment of some obsequious strategy. The narrator simply discovers, in keeping with the novel's epigraph, "the courage to be happy."

Locating this courage entails his having "worked at [himself]" (50). For the narrator, such work evolves over the course of his life and the novel, beginning with mining his past for new "presents" and loving, first out of adolescent self-absorption and later with greater selflessness, and eventually working toward the development of consciousness as an enriching safeguard against the world's debilitating artificiality. There is much to critique in the world, though dysfunction and what Gurdjieff calls waking "sleep" begin with the individual who learns from a cultural environment and regurgitates the spoils of this education back into the larger community amid the minutiae of a social existence. The mind's stupid, incessant "murmurs" become us, and not in the sense of enhancement. In this regard, Ouspensky alerts us to "a fact of tremendous importance, namely, that *we do not remember ourselves*; that we live and act and reason in deep sleep, not metaphorically but in absolute reality. And also that, at the same time, we *can* remember ourselves if we make sufficient efforts, that we *can awaken*" (*In Search* 121). It is possible that of all the characters who occupy this study, Jackson's Eleanor is the most deeply embedded in an "absolute reality" wherein the competing "murmurs" sounding in the protagonist's mind collide with those that are present but relatively concealed in others. The author makes certain that the fundamental power of this reality is felt from the novel's first sentence, while the slowly unfolding horror of the novel ultimately lies in the absolute real being stretched out in such a way as to spill over into the lived experience of the reader, to remind us that we are all to some degree Eleanor. Sollers's protagonist, like others, is acutely aware of this condition, one that can operate as a source of horror or, in his case, as inducement for transformation.

On the other hand, this notion of pervasive sleep is a hard sell. We publish books, lead seminars, train for marathons, prepare exquisite dinners, care for children and the dying, make decisions crucial and mundane. How can one be "asleep" and flesh out such a rich existence as *I* have? I am a community leader, an experienced yoga instructor, a successful ad executive, an expert plumber – how would I have accomplished any of this in a state of slumber? I have a favorite color and frequently ponder my knowledge of entomology. I am also widely respected on social media. I am so engrossed in life that I barely have time to sleep. The question, of course, is whether or not we have immediate access to time – the present moment of self-other awareness – through the medium or condition of Being. "Absolute reality" suffuses this moment with the mechanical clashing of thoughts, emotions, and their concomitant behaviors that descend upon, absorb, ignore, or rip through others, and, according to Gurdjieff/Ouspensky, pervades most every hour of a given day in a given life. "Self-remembering" is simply a practice of temporarily stopping the murmurs, of locking into the moment of oneself stripped of all identity or personality-laden accoutrements. This is not to say that one can completely escape the impact of ideology, but the instance of remembering oneself generates, or preserves, a "truth [that] forces knowledges," as Badiou claims, that "returns to the immediacy of the situation, or reworks that sort of portable encyclopaedia from which opinions, communications and sociality draw their meaning" (*Ethics* 70). In "self-remembering," the "encyclopaedia" of the self is bracketed to allow for greater objectivity in the unique time of the situation. It is only in such a moment, a point in time unique by virtue of its alterity relative to a sleeping, impersonating world, we would argue, that authenticity is possible.

Conclusion

– "It's Me I Have to Kill:" Contamination, Monochrome, and Mist

One of the central aims of this study is to highlight the primary delusion, common to individuals and collectives of all stripes, that identity is innately authentic and enduring, while simultaneously affirming the foundational nature of race and sexual/gender orientations. We propose a general outline of human experience: from the moment one fears or desires and attaches a sense of self to the compulsive interiority, up through Descartes' famous dictum on thinking and Being and, later, to the contemporary "selfie." Every thought, expression, or emotive reverie signaling "I am" this or that person carries the charge of self-deception and equivocation to the degree that the edifice of the subject/individual, like Hill House, "might stand for eighty more [years]," with "walls [continuing] upright, bricks [meeting] neatly, floors … firm, doors … sensibly shut" (Jackson 3), but inevitably succumbs to the garden variety vicissitudes of illness, loss, death, aloneness. Shakespeare's seven ages on the world's stage dramatically underestimates the developmental process; one's ages number in the trillions, a near infinitude contained only by the start and finish of the beating heart. What is equivocated is this reality that functions, mechanically, under the dictatorship of "dominant fictions." And yet some fictions impose upon rather than support the scaffolding of domination.

Ligotti's "psychic imposition," mentioned at the beginning of this study, was published in 1985. In an effort to pursue the value (and it goes without saying, the literary legitimacy and import) of subversive literature in the 21st century, we might further inquire into the merit of "contamination," the bringing to the fore of uncomfortable, inconvenient truths (or "truth-processes"), that to some extent inspires each of the texts operating in the second half of this study but finds its knife edge and aesthetic apotheosis in critical horror proper. What exactly is the nature of subversive literature's imperative "imposition" in a milieu ripe for its particular instruction? And what makes the latter so inclined, whether it knows this condition is the case or not?

Subversive Horror Today and Yesterday

At the time of this writing, three seemingly unparalleled phenomena have occurred and are still occurring simultaneously in the US, though there are and will likely always be precedents: a global pandemic that reached a fever-pitch of death and denial in the rapidly aging New World, ongoing murders of Black Americans whose guilt or innocence is given no consideration or due process at the hands of police, and a compromised, weirdly ongoing transition of power from a thoroughly incompetent, egomaniacal, pseudo-fascistic president to a slightly dull, visibly enfeebled but well-meaning incumbent whose otherwise ordinary sense of dignity appears nearly archaic in context of the previous administration. The death toll of the first of these has steadily climbed to well above the number of people who lost their lives in New York City during the September 11th attack in 2001 and will doubtless continue to rise. Mere mention of 9/11 amongst certain demographics tends to provoke a moment of disquieting, solemn patriotism that congeals, as so much right-wing ideology does, around vague notions of loss and freedom. The deaths of approximately 3000 lives certainly constitute significant loss, the culprit behind which, a visible, conspicuous enemy, exacerbates the necessity, for those vengefully inclined, of retribution for the sake of returning as much as possible to a collective consciousness tainted by images of iconic buildings falling and bodies leaping. But remove that palpable antagonist, add the prospect of survival in the event of contraction (not to mention an infected president who showcased his recovery in a Dadaistic display of bravado for all the world to see), and staggering numbers of loss no longer carry weight for some. Only an absurdist, capitalistic notion of freedom remains, much to the detriment of some, and perhaps their loved ones.[43]

The second American catastrophe, informed as it is by a history of enslavement, polite bigotry, and every self-serving whip's lash in between, is curiously aligned with the first in that its point of origin is indeed a haunting series of past events while its current manifestation has taken multiple cues from the third instance in the form of unmitigated cultic leadership and tribalism. Donald Trump needs no exhaustive analysis here beyond the obvious claim that he has at once consistently sought to further disenfranchise people of color and cater to those for whom racism and cultural insularity are ways of life and being. It is as though the much-lauded Karl Edward Wagner's story, "Sticks," that concludes with an illustrator whose final creative contribution is unknowingly to a book of genuine, humanity-destroying evocation, who upon this grim revelation amid a steadily approaching, demonic ghoul intent on leading him away, can "only follow" (224), has come to doomful life. In the reality of the 21st century American political landscape, a ghoul tweeted incongruous words and people hungry to contribute, illustrate their identities, locate meaning in populist congregations, absorbed the conjuration, allowed it to inform them given the leader's dramatic sense of urgency and adolescent charisma. Now this demographic does the same with unfathomably silly conspiracy theories. They follow, and a virus flies its planes into a million-plus buildings and counting, while authoritarian cannibals gun down lives that matter.

Is provocative, subversive literature redundant in this epoch of senselessness and fatality? To answer this question with scholarly rigor requires one to discern the critical in critical horror. In other words, when horror qualifies as both imperative and culturally or psychologically diagnostic, hardly redundant, it is, rather, revelatory. We would argue that the texts from the first section of this study, as overtly imbued with genre tropes as they exceed them, bear this out. And yet, even a cursory, cross-cultural look at the massive popularity of horror is equally illuminating. We will return to this observation later. In elaborating on the application of such texts, it is useful to remain with the implications of "critical," particularly in its diagnostic function.

In so far as concluding an average day with the perusal of Netflix or comparable film/television streaming services has become *de rigueur* in the average (certainly American) household, our collective reliance on the particular selections and formatting of said offerings is evident. That this phenomenon generates a level of cultural homogeneity is equally clear. Despite the sheer quantity of options at one's disposal, the algorithmic determinations inherent in these platforms, like some Brian Enoesque generative music bereft of primary, creative intentionality, limit the range of possibilities, and in so doing, restrict creative input into how one occupies Being and time when the day's labor is not demanding attention. Most relevant to horror, however, is the ever-increasing number of content/trigger warnings that precede a given film or show, an astonishing recent example of which, situated alongside the certainly valid "extreme violence" and "rape" tags, is "fear." People of today must be warned that they are about to witness or experience fear. Fear can be both rational, as in the somatic response to unexpected confrontation with someone masked and armed, or irrational, paranoiac, as in pervasive panic concerning one's life being generally tread upon. Nevertheless, it is universally foundational in its correlation with death, the great leveler and reminder of prioritization in terms of how one inhabits life and values death. Fear can be more or less transcended by the individual whose foundation is supplanted by the development of productive detachment or stoicism, though for most it is a factor of life with which one must become reconciled, especially in its habit of striking, from without or within, unpredictably.

In an effort to make the populace feel as safe as possible in front of their screens, in the spaces of their schools, places of employment, etc., taking measures to reduce if not eradicate the unsavory tendrils of fanatical hate speech and behavior is both sensible and essential. In the face of the latter's delusion, the reasonable person identifies a clear danger to self, democracy, and critical thought in the way one might identify an obvious terrorism threat. Fear, on the other hand, operates more like an imperceptible virus, one that will not necessarily kill us, that differs from physical illness and malevolence-induced trauma in that it may actually instruct in the expansion of personal depth and substance. To place "fear" in the category of "safe space" content warnings is to chip further away at the breadth of human experience, which is not to say that discomfort is preferable or to be wished upon another; only that it is intrinsic to education in any given context. Today, education, in keeping with populist cultural mandates, is inclined to indulge and pamper, and consequently runs the risk of infantilizing, arresting development as though distressing representations onscreen, in fiction, in art, are tantamount to the villainy of marching, unhooded white supremacists, overt homophobes, or misogynists enacting their overt violence. The vulnerable, collective status-quo self, that paradoxical individual-cum-super-egoic, social media aggregate, becomes the fulcrum of conflict and "resolution," of interpretive meaning, as opposed to the original point of provocation, however vile or innocuous. In the space of critical aesthetic work, fear is neither contemptible nor harmless. It haunts, rather, or is the product of strategic haunting that warrants the purity of its shocking disclosure without intermediary censorship.

We might conceive of this nebulous confusion on the part of heresy hunters as Deleuze and Guattari's minoritarian and majoritarian forces having folded into one another. The former can refer to an aesthetic or political orientation that produces a community whose *raison d'etre* is to operate within but ultimately against the grain of prevailing cultural norms. In other words, in contrast, majoritarian "implies a state of domination" (Deleuze and Guattari, *Thousand* 291), while minoritarian solidarity may at once utilize and subvert the language, as in discourse, intelligence, or prophecy, of oppression. Neither is determined by quantity but by compulsion or dynamism, respectively. The powerful, ethical conscience of the left, invariably functioning in a field of right-wing political forces, has slowly morphed, in some quadrants, into an agent of authoritarian tendencies (such as prescribing censorious interpretation, erecting small fortresses around words, any siege of which may carry dire consequences in the social arena), thereby undermining the very mechanism of the psychic/social apparatus's capacity for what Deleuze and Guattari famously call becoming. This conundrum brings us back to Badiou's consideration of ethics as highly specious when practiced according to the authority of standardized presuppositions, as opposed to the immediate nature of events and their processes. "Fear" as a content warning is one such event, a profound incursion into the public psyche the seeming insignificance of which speaks to the actual power and insidiousness of ironically "conscientious," majoritarian territoriality.

In situating fear as an ominous, parental admonition, then, the incursion becomes yet another potential fortification of self (*it is right that I be warned of fear or discomfort*), as opposed to self-inquiry that might willingly and skillfully examine the value of discomfort in its arresting immediacy, especially in the context of aesthetic practice (*fear can provoke insight*). Han distinguishes between the positivity of data- or information-driven culture and the negativity of philosophical thought, the former being "*additive* or *detective*" and the latter "*narrative* or *hermeneutic*" (49-50). The simplicity and moralistic reductiveness of "fear" is an additional layer of data, for which someone else, "the they," has done the detective work, which makes it "positive." Self-inquiry, which often demands some level of philosophical thought prior to intuitive insight, on the other hand, is negative in the sense of being "exclusive, exquisite, and executive" (51). While the hermeneutic process is necessarily animated by "tension," data-based culture "*falls apart* into mere information" (50). It is fascinating how a claim about information in the postmodern age can so easily be grafted onto the self that yields *Dasein* to the safety and relentlessness of "mere information" or embraces the negativity of "tension" and thus critical self-inquiry. And yet, there is also an argument to be made regarding literature. Han quotes Michel Butor's contention that we (in France, and really, in the West, at least) are "living in a literary crisis" (ibid.). Literature Studies in the age of Digital Humanities is one example of this crisis, though, more generally, as literary and other modes of language/expression are sanitized by the culture at large, their productive negativity is stripped of the "wholly Other" (51), the unknown that is at once immanent and exterior, that which resists formulas and commodification of both language and Being. Subversive literature opens the lines of inquiry into precisely this otherness.

For his part, Lovecraft asserts the "dignity of the weirdly horrible [tale] as a literary form" (*Supernatural* 12). To conceive as dignified any cultural manifestation commonly viewed as "horrible," not to mention the *horribile dictu*, seems anathema in today's climate. On this note, he continues: "Against it [the horror text] [is] discharged ... a naively inspired idealism which deprecates the aesthetic motive and calls for a didactic literature to 'uplift' the reader toward a suitable degree of smirking optimism" (ibid.). When the imperative of safety (from a virus, a deadly law-enforcement officer, a ranting, deceitful, tweeting maniac) regresses into a cult of safety, critical horror provides a productive, ameliorative riposte. Lovecraft was a great admirer of Guy de Maupassant's *The Horla*, a narrative in diary form that evolved into three versions, the first of which is especially adroit at wielding the flag of "contamination." The narrator is clear in his assessment of the populace, even as he is ravaged by a shapeless, invisible presence. "The people," he claims, "are an imbecilic herd, sometimes stupidly patient and sometimes ferociously rebellious" (Maupassant 16). And yet, "those who run it [the Republic] are also fools; but instead of obeying people, they obey principles, which can only be inane, impotent, and false because of the very fact that they *are* principles, that is, ideas imagined to be definite and immutable, in this world where we are sure of nothing, since light is an illusion, since sound is an illusion" (17). Each level of the text, from his critiques of the "herd" and the foolish leaders, to the narrator's own struggle with sanity, hinges upon ascribing power to "ideas imagined to be definite and immutable," power that, of course, becomes very real indeed when one is accosted by a specter, or the taboo of fear, or a would-be-dictator who believes his own illusion. Thus "we are appallingly subject to the influence of our surroundings" (24), to the power of delirious, rampaging imagination, and, entrenched in the hell of other people or of our unequivocal aloneness, "we people the void with phantoms" (16). The one in particular comes to possess the narrator, dictating his every movement, with those few exceptions when he is able to step outside the sinister occupancy and reflect via his innate intelligence. The "we" of his incriminating claim would seem to reach into the 21st century to speak to our own "homelessness" and distance from ontological depth. We are like him to the extent that we can say, from the vantage point of our provocative, if ephemeral, detachment, "I can no longer want anything; but someone wants for me; and I obey" (28).

If there is an off-putting sense of melodrama here, it is certainly borne out when, in another moment of clarity, he elects to burn his house down as a means of finally evading the Horla (literally, the "out there"), with little consideration, incidentally, of the servants inside. However, as is expected in critical horror, it is never as simple as extinguishing the evil with one's weapon of choice because the evil has likely gotten inside, it is "in here," where we generate our enemies and succumb to flimsy ideas that nevertheless calcify as identity. The Horla remains: "No... no... of course not... of course he is not dead," the narrator exclaims by the story's end. "So then – it's me, it's me I have to kill!" (43). And herein lies the tremendous value of "contamination," horror that enters the home and the body, the beleaguered psychology, and concomitantly, issues an affront to the boorish, shortsighted reliance upon a reactionary notion of safety. The figurative suicide is the only enduring access point to authenticity. It may assume any number of guises, be undertaken by anyone regardless of subject-position or ideological certitude, though clearly some positions are more amenable to self-effacement than others. Maupassant's narrator is unnamed. He is us when the phantoms howl in the deceptive quietude of a mind always struggling to adhere to an untenable coherence, or what Lacan calls "misrecognition" ("*meconnaissance*") (*Écrits* 6). Critical horror tells us that we must die to perceive and inhabit the home of Being.

This condition has always been the case. From the terrorizing episodes of ancient to biblical mythology to the horrors of Dracula and Dr. Frankenstein, to Jack the Ripper narratives to Stephen King to Blair Witches and fatal, online Zoom films, horror ensures death, at least for those whose ethical compasses don't quite measure up or whose stupidity and arrogance lands them into the unforgiving clutches of a violent force. Eugene Thacker puts it this way: "It's all in your head. It really happened. These mutually exclusive statements mark out the terrain of the horror genre. And yet, everything interesting happens in the middle, in the wavering between these two poles – a familiar reality that is untenable, and an acknowledged reality that is impossible" (*Tentacles* 5-6). The between space is the promise of death, if not the literal death of a character then the demise of a protagonist's former sense of self. Blackwood's Mr. and Mrs. Bittacy exemplify this space that is safe only for the one capable of listening to what the "evil" has to teach, as in the case of Baldwin's two brothers; though as is indicative of fiction whose horror is estranged from the tropes of critical horror proper, redemption is finally available to both characters, even as "the world waited outside, as hungry as a tiger, and … trouble stretched above us, longer than the sky." Safety from the world's racist and omni-phobic menace is absolutely essential, as long as "everything interesting" is given its due.

In light of this orientation, the genre's vast popularity may seem counter-intuitive. It presents a paradox: fictional narrative that imposes the "impossible" reality of death captivates not only the "herd's" attention but currently generates a hauntological desire for past visions of horror that came into being during more permissive eras. An obvious example is Netflix's own relatively gentle *Stranger Things* series (content warnings: "fear, language, gore, smoking") that is popular enough to produce an array of marketing products.[44] Occasionally bloody, more often endearing but always building to the reveal of a gargantuan, Lovecraftian threat, the predominant draw of *Stranger Things* is arguably its 1980's setting, complete with the fashion, synthesizer soundtrack, and social mores of the time. People wore their hair and their general self-performances differently then. It was a time defined in part by the cultural line it rode between tolerance and indulgence, antipodes that are readily apparent in the series. Naturally, the inclusion of a Reagan/Bush campaign sign signifies the weight of privilege, racism, potential nuclear devastation, and thus the real and present danger of overindulgence. On the other hand, the simplicity of dualistic good versus evil dynamics allows room for both antagonism and a cultural landscape defined less by the representational excesses of language or body fears and more by a kind of broad-minded resilience in the face of adversity. Even such a phenomenon as the laughable satanic panic of the age was met by the heroic efforts of popular musicians offering counter arguments; in retrospect, at least, the ascription of good and evil was *reasonably* difficult. *Stranger Things* gives the contemporary viewer an adolescent but no less effective window into a past whose endurance speaks to, among other things, the value of this razor's edge, the poles of which, in their neon aesthetics and extravagances, fostered a climate wherein Parental Advisories on albums were gleefully subverted by the very fact of their enticement.

The "interesting," to return to Thacker's term, assumes a relatively adult, gritty substance in the example of Grady Hendrix's influential 2017 *Paperbacks from Hell*. Less a study and more an introductory catalogue of 1970s and 80s horror novels, many long out-of-print, *Paperbacks from Hell* maintains, in its own jocular discourse, that the writers with which it is concerned "delivered books that move, hit hard, take risks, go for broke. It's not just the covers that hook your eyeballs. It's the writing, which respects no rules but one: always be interesting" (Hendrix 9). This imperative assumes many forms in the larger field of said novels, though of particular note here are those texts that conflate the "interesting" and the critical. They do so by pushing beyond the sensationalism of "going for broke" (outrageously violent acts, pornographic sexuality destined to dovetail with outrageously violent acts, stereotypical satanic excesses, etc.) into weightier realms of classic or modernist literature. Joan Samson's *The Auctioneer* is removed from the nuanced work of Shirley Jackson only in its conventional foregrounding of dialogue; Michael McDowell's *The Elementals* rivals and surpasses the tension and atmospheric Southern Gothic of Flannery O'Connor's penetrating stories. Ken Greenhall's *Elizabeth*, which we will consider in some detail, presents a literary aesthetic akin to contemporary versions of the *nouveau roman* (actually, the new, new novel) in the balance it strikes between Motte's "critical novel" and critical horror.

Elizabeth begins with a fourteen-year-old girl's parricide and concludes with her request to a long-since perished witch, with whom she has been communicating via a mirror image, to abort her child, the father of whom is her lascivious uncle. In this sense, the novel embodies the sensationalistic tendencies of its milieu (1976), pushing against the grain of what many of the time (and doubtless today) might have conceptualized as common decency, all the while fulfilling expectations of those hungry for alterity. "I first came to live with Grandmother about a year ago, after I killed my parents. I don't mean to sound callous. Let me explain" (Greenhall 4), the titular Elizabeth asserts. And while the reader learns to take her explanations seriously (she really does not mean to sound callous), it becomes equally clear that she wants to provoke us with the chilling reality of her keenly felt inclinations and, ultimately, her ever-

evolving *Dasein*. Aside from various animal "familiars" that come to
signify aid in her process of development, her *being there* has its ground,
ironically, in the mirror. "I am a young woman," she maintains. "My
mirror tells me so, and the eyes of men tell me so. When I was younger, I
saw James, my father's brother, look from our dog to me without changing
his expression. I soon taught him to look at me in a way he looked at
nothing else" (3). The precariousness of locating one's value in the mirror
image, Lacanian or otherwise, is not lost on the reader; nor is the
problematic nature of her reliance on sexual control of men. Nevertheless,
she remains aware that "there is really no way to know whether your
mirror shows you what others see or what is really there" (ibid.) and is
consistently inquisitive about what is in fact *there*, the nature of which
evolves throughout the novel. Her self-awareness extends to the
discernment of self, its limitations as well as its capacity for becoming:
she comes "to realize that consciousness was not unalterable, but could
grow into many forms. Later I learned that some of those forms bestowed
strength" (119).

The novel's sexuality, be it overtly or mildly aberrant, is crucial. From
her relationship with James to his wife's more or less clandestine affair
with Elizabeth's female tutor, the sexually abject is carefully proportional
to the young woman's empowerment as natural. The lesbian relationship
is presented as a rather poignant effort on each woman's part to fulfill
herself and stave off a meaningless existence. In much the same way that
Elizabeth senses the value, perhaps the inevitability, of allowing her
dysfunctional, oppressive parents to die at the hands of an occult force, her
use of sex as power over men ("Last night I met James in the attic, and we
did things we seldom did – things that caused him pain" [31]) clarifies her
budding strength amidst patriarchal social structures. [45] Well beyond
Nabokov's own infamous title character, the example of Elizabeth,
however, is likely far from amenable to the contemporary, culturally
sensitive reader. She kills, fucks, and compounds her power through the
portal of what is "really there" in the mirror image, herself as becoming-
witch in all of the journey's grisly, unsavory details, not to mention its
exceptionally dark humor. Greenhall, by extension, is hardly the writer of
a 21st century, politically correct demographic that is ever-cognizant of

pressure points and an increasingly amorphous catalogue of taboos and sensitivities, with only the vaguest artistic gestures or concessions toward decadence or edginess. By the novel's end, Elizabeth's intention to abort her child (whom some readers may initially be inclined to celebrate as a potential incursion of familiar, stabilizing domesticity in the protagonist's highly checkered life) by means of witchcraft signifies her insistence on nothing and no one coming before her potential and may very well stand as the moment current, competing political ideologies find themselves mutually aligned against a very "nasty woman" indeed.[46]

Of course, by its very nature, horror "goes for broke" to the extent that it invariably seeks to push boundaries not only of "nastiness" but of living and dying. Its more extreme manifestations are not always merely reactionary in their violence. Perhaps the most notorious novel to be inducted (and thus reissued) into the *Paperbacks from Hell's* selective roster is Mendal W. Johnson's *Let's Go Play at the Adams,'* originally published in 1974. Current, public reviews frequently find the book being accused of blatant misogyny and repulsively sensationalistic violence; and in fact, its highly articulate, psychologically astute discourse represents astonishing levels of brutality, directed predominately at a woman, twenty-year-old babysitter Barbara. Subject to rape, torture, and finally a truly repulsive form of murder, Barbara's life is erased for no other (apparent) reason than boredom – on the parts of five kids, ages 10-17. The two youngest' parents are in Europe for two weeks, prior to which the children have concocted a carefully-crafted "game" of abduction that begins with uncomfortable bondage and slowly proceeds to death. And yet, to identify this narrative as reactionary is itself a reactionary stance given the nuance of Johnson's key, Badiouian events that reflect truths, however inconvenient, about life, death, and what it means to be human.

Johnson's own interpretive stance on the novel that developed over the course of time, according to which Barbara is symbolic of an unrealistic, bleeding heart left, the absent parents indicative of a disconnected right, and the children aligned with middle America, is, by the author's own admission, and in the view of Hendrix, finally more complex than this reduction (quoted, Johnson, 9). While the eldest child, Dianne, explicates the game as essentially an enactment of social

Darwinism, she does not speak for them all, thus leaving the reader with the unsettling conclusion that they are yearning for experience well beyond the routines of their quaint lives. "They were so close to doing something marvelous now," Dianne thinks regarding the inevitability of murder, "something out of sight, something *real*, that they couldn't let it be stopped" (236). They long for the real. Once they arrive at this experience, however, it is destined to be yet another plateau subject to the very boredom of their otherwise mundane lives. Barbara, on the other hand, comes to observe "the hopeless, alien strangeness of another complete, isolated human being" (242) in each of her captors, compelling her to reach the conclusion that "no one can bear to know humans and bear being human" (267). This is her epiphany in death that does not annul her goodness relative to the others. The property on which the horror occurs may now be "sick" ("a fundamental sorrow infected the very ground") (274), though, as Hendrix argues, this illness does not represent "a plunge into cheap nihilism but a soaring, near-psychedelic consciousness as Barbara meets her fate with sublime grace, transcending into a higher state of awareness" (7).[47] Hermeneutics does not lessen the repulsive, deeply problematic nature of her death, but it does centralize a form of death as essential to transcendence.

Nevertheless, Barbara may still be seen as emblematic of a gullible but no less primal goodness, and the children, in their current-day Trump hats and rabble-rousing, are the masses itching for a spoon-fed liminality based on tawdry, adolescent notions of freedom. It is surely not a coincidence that Johnson gives the latter the name of the "Freedom Five." *Let's Go Play at the Adams'* earns the ire it receives from many readers and is certainly not beyond critique, though it epitomizes the value and radicalism of critical horror as a tool for contacting authentic, as opposed to prefabricated states of Being, especially in an age of censorious impulses emerging from rather unexpected places.

The significance of *Paperbacks from Hell's* popularity, then, suggests not only a resurgent interest in the literary styles of a genre during an earlier era, but a collective impulse to revisit certain of the cultural forms and sensibilities of that era. While far from a movement (insofar as it relies, to a large degree, on the raw consumerism of what can be quite expensive, now vintage titles and has no unified political creed), this aggregate of readers displays elements of an authentically minoritarian intentionality. Using the traditional language of horror to redefine the genre from within, in their provocative intelligence and literary vitality certain novelists produced minor literature and proactively created a "people," "a collective enunciation that is lacking elsewhere in this milieu" (Deleuze and Guattari, *Kafka* 18). What is articulated in *Paperbacks from Hell* and absorbed by a community of readers is, among other things, an appetite for a healthy cultural and personal permissiveness, a penchant for transgression, or in Deleuzian terminology, investment in productive becoming. Any other mode of becoming is negatively self-defeating: becoming-addict, becoming-bigot, -misogynist, -religious fundamentalist, -homophobe, becoming-willfully sensitive, etc. So these books have a contemporary function; in their most banal manifestations, they merely hearken back, however entertainingly, to an era of egregious dominations, microaggressions that no longer seem small, while at their most sophisticated, they invoke the heresy of authentic alterity. *"There are only collective assemblages of enunciation,"* Deleuze and Guattari tell us, "and literature expresses these acts insofar as they're not imposed from without and insofar as they exist only as diabolical powers to come or revolutionary forces to be constructed" (ibid.). Critical horror of any age can only be diabolical. It must deal in death and subversive, unsanitized declarations of "absolute reality." It is therefore revolutionary, a political project, to the extent that revolutions are comprised of individuals who are "necessary, indispensable, magnified, because a whole other story is vibrating within" (17) the reading self for whom advance notice of discomfort can only compromise the power, and empowerment, of that story.

But what of nostalgia, that often unruly, sentimental intoxication capable of removing one entirely from the present that is always already replete with the force of the moment? We do not discount the fact that compulsive return to the familiar trappings of an idealized past is not without peril, even when the epoch is characterized in part by delightfully infernal statements of purpose and entertainment. Hauntings can be as stultifying and reactionary as they are subversively pleasurable and inspirational. In her study of the haunted house in American horror fiction, Rebecca Janicker cites Leslie Fiedler in his contention that "the political thrust of American gothic is essentially conformist and reactionary ... at its deepest level of implication" as a consequence of having "identified evil with the id" rather than the super-ego, as common to the European gothic (*Literary* 15). The id, of course, houses the past as present, unconscious, neurotic impulses that manage to surface one way or another. Though it may be too hefty of a generalization to align a psychic apparatus to an entire nation, Janicker's engagement with 20th century American history yields the persuasive claim that "after 1975, the basic impulse of America's political and military leaders (as well as many other Americans) was not to forge a new relationship to the world but to reconstruct a lost identity of triumph" (135). Here, right wing identity is exposed as the most pernicious of identities in that it removes one not only from the immediacy of Being but seeks to inflict its dominance over others. It depends upon sentimentality; its nostalgia informed by an embryonic becoming-fascist. Critical horror aspires to frighten, unsettle, de-center, illuminate. The "identity of triumph" endeavors to make America great again by way of disenfranchisement, legitimized prejudice, and even, on occasion, pop-intellectualism in the guise of establishing order as an antidote to "postmodern" chaos.

Monochrome and Mist

Jackson's Eleanor dies, as do we all. Though the final tragedy of Eleanor's demise lies in the inevitability of its literalism. She surrenders, as only she can in Jackson's universe, to the most unhealthy, the most death-driven force imaginable: herself, under the weight of debilitating alienation. The alternative might have landed her narrative in the second half of this study, as a representative of the self's figurative death that temporarily diminishes the countless pulses and molecular implosions of self-exhibition/preoccupation/promotion. Paula Modersohn-Becker appears to have contacted this exceptional death before succumbing to relatively mundane tragedy. The figurative termination of being-death-in-life is the elevation of Being, or non-being, over and against personality, and is thus the critical ground of authenticity.

Language, too, is mortal. Just when it seems to be working beautifully in our favor (words of romantic love and conquest; the eloquent interview response or oration), it escapes the speaker or interpreter into a "beyond" where nothing is quite as it seems and all meaning is finally dispersed upon a Fulciesque landscape with no apparent end. With Lovecraft, then, the contemplative user of language must come to terms with the reality that such a central part of life is in fact "from beyond," and that accessing it – not to mention enunciating it, in public – is not without a certain danger. A single slip, a discursive misstep, and the date goes sour, ravishment becomes resentment, the interview, the graceful monologue, are blown. And yet, Ouspensky holds that "there will always be people to whom words are more precious than anything else" (*In Search* 157), including but not limited to literature professors, evangelical rabble rousers, men and women on the verge of a nervous breakdown in Almodóvar's Spain or at any other global location. Communicating oneself via conversation on or offline is for some more important than, to reference the common phrase, being oneself. This is not to say that articulation is inherently inauthentic; only that language is too cloudy, or swampy, or haunted, to encapsulate the breadth of a moment's truth. Literature and poetry may come close, though their ultimate value rests in the veracity of their *extension* of meaning across a particular discursive spectrum and into the lived life of a reader. "Peanut" does not mean "tennis racket" but both terms can occupy a range of meaningful, even poignant, nodes within a literary or social context; they can even share that context. Literature collates and designs the ambience in which seemingly disparate terms flourish and inform. Nevertheless, the "beyond" is always already on the other side of the door, around the corner, another dimension where the only real possibility of health and well-being lies in arresting compulsive thought and shutting up on occasion.

Sollers's protagonist argues that "there [is] no truth save in the difficulty of expression; … at first you must stumble and weigh your words, separate them with difficulty (there are so many ties), not take pleasure in them but accept them with all their possibilities and weaknesses (seeking that rare state of intensity and control); that you must be simple and passionate, and if you permit yourself to use a language at all, it is almost in despair of the result" (*Strange* 108). A strange predicament indeed, wherein pleasure, if it has any relation to language usage, equates to "intensity," "control," and despair lurks in the shadows of expression. He is referring to the "haunted" voice of a singer whose musical enunciation reveals its difficulty in both form and content. Likewise, Darrieussecq observes that when Paula "looks around at human beings again [after having devoted attention to paintings at the Musée du Luxembourg], she realizes they are more surprising than the story told by artistic conventions" (*Being* 84). It is perhaps the failure of language, of art, to complete its representation – its surprise – that produces disconsolation, or a ghostly, uncertain atmosphere. The key in Paula's case, however, is to reach out, brush in hand, to an aesthetic environment and touch the "beyond," beyond convention. Her portraits evince strange spaces between realism and a thick, paint-heavy flatness that nonetheless contains rich contours and shadows, as seen in her *Clara Rilke Westhoff* (1905). That her work was deemed "degenerate" by Nazis is a credit to her ability to make something unique and, if not indicative of total representation, then pleasurable in the sense of evoking a productive quality of "surprise." Darrieussecq's reference to the Lacanian notion of there being "no sexual rapport *that can be written about*" (62), unexpectedly sandwiched between bittersweet details of the painter's marriage, manifests its own surprise by virtue of its spatial incongruity and its potential application to the relationality of a reader. No language can fully capture lived experience, though it can doubtless pave the way for rare states, as Sollers puts it, as long as its composition frustrates Nazis and eschews convention.

And as long as it contributes to the figurative death of the reader, viewer, or listener. What is to be gained from the danger of aesthetic outer limits is the knowledge that it behooves us to be quiet on occasion, to recede from ourselves and the myriad components and diversions that go into (in)forming the daily, hourly task of being oneself, as distinct from Sollers's "intoxication of banality" (*Strange* 126) that magnifies and locks one into the present of that Being. This benefit is especially potent when "death" is reflected in the lack of overt, animated structure. Badiou, for example, speaks of painter Kasimir Malevich's *White on White* (1918) as "a subtractive thinking of negativity" that "can overcome the blind imperative of destruction and purification" (*Century* 55). How might the painting accomplish this? A gray-tinted square, tilted at an angle within the cream-white square of the canvas, it might appear to the casual viewer as the annihilation of art, of representation held dear, with no further value outside of its mere existence, like any mechanically reproduced object. And yet its minimalist beauty is widely celebrated (currently at New York's MOMA). The central question is what, if not merely the "sacredness" of representational art, is it negating? Badiou's response is complex: "instead of treating the real as identity, it is treated right away [by the painting] as a gap. The question of the real/semblance relation will not be resolved by a purification that would isolate the real, but by understanding that the gap is itself real. The white square is the moment when the minimal gap is fabricated" (56). *White on White* negates reified identity that commandeers the real by presuming the latter's natural basis for its designs, unverifiable beyond its own cultural domination, identity that can assume any form, from white supremacists to Appalachian snake handler, from "cosmic pessimist" to prideful collector of high-end art and Audis. *White on White* negates identity by virtue of its neutrality in the face of both hegemony and humanist representation. It kills the self in desperate, unending search of its personality-bound self. It is also a "moment," synchronic as much as diachronic, defined by the expanse of an interval, as opposed to a consistency of "truth." The "gap" of minimalism, for one neurotically ensconced in some version of Lacan's "mirror stage" as life orientation, proves "impossible" in much the same way that Sollers's Concha is said to be "impossible," by not reflecting the identity of one's desire.

Badiou goes on to further specify the nature of *White on White's* provocation in relation to the "passion" for identity, for what is ultimately "a passion for the authentic ... that can only be fulfilled as destruction" (ibid.). Here we must part ways with the philosopher on the crucial issue of authenticity's viability and legitimacy as praxis. That Nazis, from the "ordinary" variety such as Heidegger to those who would gladly entertain another holocaust program, seek their own identity-entrenched sense of authenticity is without question. At stake, however, is not simply hegemony but a "passion" that negates the very ego that would lower itself to intolerance, extremist or otherwise. It is undoubtedly true that "purification is a process doomed to incompletion" (ibid.) when speaking about racist fantasy, though when the "minimalist gap" becomes its own conscious orientation counter to the narcissism of excessive identity-formation, it develops in the lived life as empirical self-knowledge – invariably incomplete and thus unconcerned with essentialist purity, but present to immediate "truth" as embodied process. The painting, then, by way of its spaciousness and angular, subversive stillness, assists, if it is met with complimentary attention, in scaling back the self with all its authoritative expectations around art, time, perspective, etc., and serves Malevich's poetic advocacy for its unique "moment:" "Erase, be quiet, stifle the fire if fire it be,/ so that the corset of your thoughts may be lighter,/ and not rust" (quoted, 57). Without the gaping capaciousness of authenticity instrumental to Being, we are probably enslaved to that excess of self that tightens around thought and body alike to the great detriment of passion and the productive death.

If *White on White* is not quite ground zero for minimalist painting (a solid white canvas? a canvas with no paint? a mime painting in air?), Japanese sound artist Sachiko M's related 2007 album *Salon de Sachiko* is not Cage's well-known "4:33" (consisting of four minutes and thirty-three seconds of silence while the musician(s) follows movements instructing the opening and closing of a piano fallboard, for example), though it comes close. Like the square within the square, brief or occasionally extended "glitch" sounds, created from a no-input sound mixer over the course of exactly sixty minutes, inhabit a dominant background of silence to inform the listener of a human presence, digital though its manifestation might be. Form is clearly the centerpiece here, as opposed to content (be it lyrical or conventionally structural) that would serve to ground the listener in familiar musicality – and thus subjectivity. And yet, the medium is not quite the message in this case; it is too stripped down and the musical gestures so spare and refined that meaning is utterly reduced to the raw fact of Being in time. In other words, the "salon," which operates as both living room and exhibition space, becomes "home" to *Dasein*. This may seem a trite supposition until one sits with the piece in its entirety and encounters the manner in which it potentially provokes the "fire" of discomfort, boredom, rampant, associative thought; in short, reaction rather than response. Were the stark, miniature flares to be substituted with piano or staccato violin notes, it would come within closer range of Morton Feldman's austere but nonetheless lush brand of minimalism, though as it stands, there is arguably a purity to *Salon de Sachiko's* strictly high frequency, digital blips and bleeps, and its silence, but a purity without nationalism, without country, race, or gender. In this hyper-minimalist space, there is constructed a room for the simple pleasure of listening.

Heidegger famously writes of Friedrich Hölderlin's poem "Homecoming" as being equally bereft of any national allegiance and finally invested in the prospect of the poet's fellow human beings "[finding] their essence" (*Basic* 241). Home may be where the heart is but it is more profoundly where Being is developed, where access to something akin to Gurdjieff's "essence" may blossom and thrive, or deteriorate. Blackwood's David Bittacy finds his home amongst the trees who love him; Grant's Caroline struggles against unknown forces to maintain her home in quaint Oxrun Station; Hill House instructs its inhabitants to "Help Eleanor Come home;" Ligotti's Spare operates a home of both abject horror and cosmic revelation; Darrieussecq's Paula pushes against the grain of home as patriarchal structure and finds her most fruitful, dynamic abode on the canvas; Bove's Armand loses the home that was never quite his and locates fellow-feeling; Sonny finds his home on the stage, in jazz; Plath and Nothomb's protagonists are reborn; Woolf's heroines become via a productive nothingness. In each case, the stimulation of "essence" is dependent on the space of one's achievement or repudiation of authenticity. Cosmic or social forces encroach upon one's efforts for better or for worse, though in each example the individual retains an opportunity to think and act according to the dynamics of a "truth-process," to make "home" a psychological environment governed either by personality or essence. In this sense, homecoming signifies the paramount moment or process in the cultivation of authenticity.

"Home" assumes a richly august – and majestically minimal – quality in Paul Willems's story "The Cathedral of Mist" that opens with a critique of contrary stone: "Stubborn, it fulfilled only its destiny, which was to endure. It focused its immense, compact strength inward, on itself. And it pitted all its inertia against those who tried to distract it by moving or carving it" (49). It is more than tempting to relate this characterization to the intoxication (and toxicity) of conservative, Don't Tread on Me values. Bereft of anchorage in immediate, ephemeral, "process" time, its vision is future bound. Its "home" is more a fortress than a sanctuary, weighed down by the "inertia" of domestic protectionism, its interiority the glorification of a "stubborn" ego, as embodied by Hugh Crane's Hill House. But the focus of Willems's text is on a different analogy, one that celebrates rather than derides. A father tells the story of the architect of this unparalleled cathedral to his son, and of his adventure there. He speaks of the "steam" on a "bed of warm air" creating "[drops] of water [that] moved to sustained song" which in turn "traveled to a very deep place inside" visitors (50-51). Willems presents a literal but improbable phenomenon here that nevertheless has ramifications for one who is amenable to its miraculous properties and spiritual allure. In this architectural space, a cathedral constructed of mist, "prayer took on greater fervor ... because it was not expressed in words;" rather, "you became words," moved toward "everything" and "nothing," toward "beneficent emptiness" (52). Like anyone who, in productive, Deleuzean transformation, becomes-other, a traveler in the ethereal mist comes to embody meaning, as opposed to re-presenting it with language; and one's meaning is a paradoxically fulfilling, edifying nullity. They continue through the cathedral in pitch-blackness and, at one point, a traveler brushes against an "iris whose delicate flower let out a sustained wail, terrifying in the darkness and silence, as if some small and lovely creature but a few steps away were telling them it was about to die" (53). Here there is room not only for the inevitability of death and impermanence, but the "darkness," comparable to that which inhabits Sonny, that necessarily precedes a quieting orientation of self-effacement.

The father and his companions feel compelled to remain still for seven hours – far longer than an eternity to the easily distracted – from fear of "[toppling] the massive mechanisms of Stillness and Silence," which insure that "time was both very long and very short" (54). Eventually the cathedral will dissipate, its walls and spires of fog never to return; its apparatus will cease operations in keeping with the reality of death. It survives, of course, in Willems's narrative in which he creates a "home" for the "mechanisms" of genuineness. Gone is the chaos of Ligotti's "other world;" here, "perfect harmony" (55) presides as a result of processes ("Stillness," "Silence") that cultivate Being and direct awareness of time's immanent dimensions over and against the blunt inertia of "stone," the density of self-absorption. The author's language – his poesy, his capitalizations – doubtless remains in the realm of representation, though it advances the power of "ceaseless textual intervention" by paradoxically explicating the essential ephemerality of its core subject matter, and thus of itself as a mere terminal, a layover through which meaning, and more importantly, experience may be achieved. The cathedral, in view of the narrator's father, is a "miracle," the "tangible evidence" of which "can never be erased quickly enough. Miracles belong only to the moment, and live on only in memory" (56). The "miracle" of "perfect harmony" emerges in an exceptional moment of time, while its "evidence" remains in the consciousness of its observer, to do with what she, he, or they will.

The stirring, fleeting alterity of Willems's cathedral and the text as a whole, an elegant paean to death in life, is most likely drowned out (in American letters, at least) by louder voices, those that adhere to aesthetic and thematic conventions, incorporate the current theoretical trends and concerns into fictional narratives, or practice some form of sexy, experimental prose/verse hybridity. Such voices are not inherently *déclassé*, but they are not necessarily prone to alterity in the sense of radical, contemplative otherness. More often than not, they are regurgitations of accepted standards that in turn inform identity, perhaps on a mass scale. Alterity is not merely alt-personality, alt-sexuality, hipster fashion, chic nihilism, alt-bigotry. Genuine, dissident alterity and the quiet orientation of living from this state of Being comprise the cornerstone of authenticity. It is suffering, sacrifice, and redemption. In its development, the legion of booming, often manufactured voices, all competing for dominance in the desperate psychology of a self, may be observed and abnegated with effort. What is redeemed is nothing short of emptiness, the void or the nothing we attempt to fill with infinite distractions and a monolith of selfhood like the antiquated, confederate monument certain voices are intent on preserving. Healthy, selfless alterity transforms emptiness by making it "beneficent," a space in which to *be* in "harmony" with the moment, or to become the "truth" of a given point in time; in the mist, where the miracle of death may find its proper home.

Bibliography

Augé, Marc. In the Metro. Trans. Tom Conley. Minneapolis: University of Minnesota Press, 2002.

———— No Fixed Abode. Trans. Chris Turner. London: Seagull, 2013.

Badiou, Alain. The Century. Trans. Alberto Toscano. Malden, MA: Polity, 2007.

———— Ethics: An Essay on the Understanding of Evil. Trans. Peter Hallward. London: Verso, 2012.

———— In praise of Love. Trans. Peter Bush. New York: The New Press, 2012.

Badio, Alain and Barbara Cassin. Heidegger: His Life and His Philosophy. Trans. Susan Spitzer. New York: Columbia UP, 2016.

Baldwin, James. The Fire Next Time. New York: Vintage, 1992.

———— "Sonny's Blues." The Longman Masters of Short Fiction. Trans. Andrew R. MacAndrew. Eds. Dana Gioia and R. S. Gwynn. New York: Longman, 2002.

Barthes, Roland. A Lover's Discourse. Trans. Richard Howard. New York: Noonday, 1993.

———— Roland Barthes By Roland Barthes. Trans. Richard Howard. New York: Hilland Wang, 1977.

———— . S/Z. Trans. Richard Miller. New York: Hill and Wang, 1974.

Beauvoir, Simone de. The Second Sex. Trans. Constance Borde and Sheila Malovany Chevallier. New York: Vintage, 2011.

Blackwood, Algernon. "The Man Whom the Trees Loved." Ancient Sorceries and Other Weird Stories. New York: Penguin Books, 2002.

Bove, Emmanuel. Armand. Trans. Janet Louth. Evanston, Il: Marlboro Press, 2000.

Cage, John. Silence. London: Boyars, 1987.

The Dark Descent. Ed. David G. Hartwell. New York: Tor, 1987.

Darrieussecq, Marie. Being Here is Everything: The Life of Paula Modersohn-Becker. Trans. Penny Hueston. Cambridge, Mass.: Semiotext(e), 2017.

Deleuze, Gilles. Essays Critical and Clinical. Trans. Daniel W. Smith and Michael A. Greco.Minneapolis: University of Minnesota Press, 1997.

———— Negotiations. Trans. Martin Joughin. New York: Columbia University Press, 1990.

—————— "Vincennes Session of April 15, 1980, Leibniz Lecture." *Discourse: Berkeley Journal for Media Studies and Culture.* Volume 20, Issue 3 (1998), pp. 77-97.

Deleuze, Gilles, and Félix Guattari. *A Thousand Plateaus.* Trans. Brian Massumi. Minneapolis: University of Minnesota Press, 1987.

—————— *Kafka: Toward a Minor Literature.* Trans. Dana Polan. Minneapolis: University of Minnesota Press, 1986.

DeLillo, Don. *The Body Artist.* New York: Scribner, 2001.

Eagleton, Terry. *On Evil.* New Haven: Yale University Press, 2010.

—————— . *Radical Sacrifice.* New Haven, CT: Yale University Press, 2011.

Eliot, T. S. *The Cocktail Party.* New York: Harcourt, Brace and World, 1978.

—————— . "The Four Quartets." *The Complete Poems and Plays, 1909– 1950.* New York: Harcourt, Brace and World, 1971.

Etchison, Dennis. *Halloween III.* New York: Jove, 1982.

—————— "It Will Be Here Soon." *The Dark Country.* New York: Berkley Book, 1984.

Ettinger, Bracha. "Laius Complex and Shocks of Maternality. Reading Franz Kafka and Sylvia Plath." *Interdisciplinary Handbook of Trauma and Culture,* eds. Y. Ataria et al, NY & Heidelberg: Springer, 2016.

Fugazi. "Suggestion." *7 Songs.* Washington DC: Dischord Records, 1988.

Goethe, Johann Wolfgang Von. *The Sorrows of Young Werther.* Trans. Michael Hulse. New York: Penguin, 1989.

Goffman, Erving. *The Presentation of Self in Everyday Life.* New York, NY: Doubleday, 1959.

Grant, Charles L. *Dialing the Wind.* New York: Tor, 1989.

Hallward, Peter. *Badiou: A Subject to Truth.* Minneapolis: University of Minnesota Press, 2003.

Han, Byung-Chul. *The Agony of Eros.* Trans. Erik Butler. Cambridge, Mass: MIT Press, 2017.

Hasan, Ihab. "Toward a Concept of Postmodernism." In *Postmodernism: A Reader.* Ed. Thomas Docherty. New York: Columbia University Press, 1993.

Hval, Jenny. "Female Vampire. *Blood Bitch.* New York: Sacred Bones Records, 2016.

Hawthorne, Nathaniel. "Young Goodman Brown." *The Longman Maters of Short Fiction.* Eds. Dana Gioia and R.S. Gwynn. New York: Longman, 2002.

Heidegger, Martin. *Basic Writings.* Ed. David Farrell Krell. London: Harper Perennial, 2008.

—————— *Being and Time.* Trans. John Macquarrie and Edward Robinson. London: Harper Perennial, 2008.

Hendrix, Grady. *Paperbacks from Hell: The Twisted History of '70s and '80s Horror Fiction.* Philadelphia: Quirk Books, 2017.

Jackson, Shirley. *The Haunting of Hill House*. New York: Penguin, 1987.

———— "The Summer People." In *The Dark Descent*. Ed. David G. Hartwell. New York: Tor, 1987.

Janicker, Rebecca. *The Literary Haunted House: Lovecraft, Matheson, King and the Horror In Between*. Jefferson, NC: McFarland Books, 2015.

Jay, Martin. *Downcast Eyes: The Denigration of Vision in Twentieth-Century Thought*. Berkley: University of California Press, 1994.

Kafka, Franz. *Booklore*. Zagava. https://zagava.de/shop/booklore?edition=8

Kristeva, Julia, Philippe Sollers. *Marriage as a Fine Art*. Trans. Lorna Scott Fox. New York: Columbia UP, 2016.

———— *The Powers of Horror: An Essay on Abjection*. Trans. Leon S. Roudiez. New York: Columbia University Press, 1982.

Lacan, Jacques. *Écrits*. Trans. Alan Sheridan. New York: W. W. Norton, 1977.

———— . *Four Fundamental Concepts of Psychoanalysis*. Trans. Alan Sheridan. Ed. Jacques-Alain Miller. New York: W. W. Norton, 1998.

Levinas, Emmanuel. *Ethics and Identity*. Trans. Richard A. Cohen. Pittsburgh: Duquesne UP, 1985.

Ligotti, Thomas. "The Frolic." *Thomas Ligotti: Songs of a Dead Dreamer and Grimscribe*. New York: Penguin, 2015.

———— "In the Shadow of Another World." *Thomas Ligotti: Songs of a Dead Dreamer and Grimscribe*. New York: Penguin, 2015.

Lovecraft, H. P. *Supernatural Horror in Literature*. New York: Dover, 1973.

Machen, Arthur. "The White People." *The White People and Other Weird Stories*. New York: Penguin, 2011.

Matheson, Richard. "Blood Son." *The Best of Richard Matheson*. New York: Penguin, 2017.

Motte, Warren. *Fiction Now*. Champaign: Dalkey Archive Press, 2008.

———— *French Fiction Today*. Champaign: Dalkey Archive Press, 2017.

Ndiaye, Marie. "Interview with Marie Ndiaye." *The White Review*. March 2021. www.thewhitereview.org/feature/interview-with-marie-ndiaye/

———— *Self-Portrait in Green*. Trans. Jordan Stump. San Francisco: Two Lines Press, 2014.

Maharaj, Sri Nisargadatta. *I am That*. Ed. Sudhakar S. Dikshit. Trans. Maurice Frydman. Durham: The Acorn Press, 2016.

O'Brien, Mahon. *Heidegger and Authenticity: From Resoluteness to Releasement*. London: Continuum, 2011.

Ouspensky, P.D. *In Search of the Miraculous*. San Diego: Harcourt Brace Jovanovich, 1976.

———— *The Psychology of Man's Possible Evolution*. New York: Vintage, 1981.

Nothomb, Amélie. *Strike Your Heart*. Trans. Alison Anderson. New York: Europa Editions, 2018.

Phillips, Thomas. *T.E.D. Klein and the Rupture of Civilization*. Jefferson, NC: McFarland, 2017.

Plath, Sylvia. *The Bell Jar*. London: Faber and Faber, 2005.

The Sacrifice. Dir. Andrei Tarkovsky. Kino, 1986.

Salinger, J. D. *Franny and Zooey*. New York: Bantam, 1981.

Seltzer, David. *The Omen*. New York: Signet, 1976.

The Shining. Dir. Stanley Kubrick. Warner Brothers, 1980.

Schopenhauer, Arthur. *The Essential Schopenhauer*. Ed. Wolfgang Schirmacher. New York: Harper Perennial, 2010.

Silverman, Kaja. *The Threshold of the Visible World*. New York: Routledge, 1996.

Smith, Paul. *Discerning the Subject*. Minneapolis: University of Minnesota Press, 1988.

Sollers, Philippe. A Strange Solitude. Trans. Richard Howard. New York: Grove Press, 1959.

Thacker, Eugene. *Tentacles Longer Than Night*. Washington: Zero Books, 2015.

Thrower, Stephen. *Beyond Terror: The Films of Lucio Fulci*. Surrey, UK: Fab Press, 1999.

Toomer, Jean. "Fern." *Cane*. New York: W.W. Norton and Company, 1988.

Toussaint, Jean-Philippe. *Self-Portrait Abroad*. Trans. John Lambert. Champaign: Dalkey Archive Press, 2010.

Wakoski, Diane. "The Belly Dancer." In *Emerald Ice: Selected Poems*. Santa Rosa, CA: Black Sparrow, 1988.

Willems, Paul. *The Cathedral of Mist*. Trans. Edward Gauvin. Cambridge, Mass: Wakefield Press, 2016.

Wiskers, Gina. *Horror Fiction: An Introduction*. London: Continuum, 2005.

The Witch. Dir. Robert Eggers. A24, 2016.

Woolf, Virginia. *A Haunted House and Other Short Stories*. New York: Harcourt, Inc., 1966.

Zoline, Pamela. "The Heat Death of the Universe." *The Heat Death of the Universe and Other Stories*. Kingston, NY: McPherson and Company, 1988.

Endnotes

[1] Nathalie Sarraute's *Tropisms*, a defining text of the *nouveau roman*, is a compelling reference point for this composite.

[2] See Thomas Phillips, *T.E.D. Klein and the Rupture of Civilization: A Study in Critical Horror*, McFarland, 2017.

[3] Perhaps it is useful to conceive of Ndiaye's focus on her writerly identity in such terms.

[4] Heidegger is clearly averse to reliance upon anthropocentricity or metaphysical speculation, though his concept of Being is one that transcends the socially-constructed subject, as opposed to a self whose cognitive and somatic integrity allow for greater access to the time of life and death than might otherwise be available.

[5] For a lively examination of Heidegger's marriage and his extra-marital relationships with other women, predominately his students, see Badiou and Cassin, *His Life and His Philosophy*.

[6] See Deleuze and Guattari's *Kafka: Toward a Minor Literature*, University of Minnesota Press, 1986.

[7] Badiou scholar Peter Hallward argues that "to be modern is to be fully contemporary with what is truly taking place in your own time, without yielding to the temptations of routine or regret" (*Badiou* 158), "routine" being perhaps the most insidious antagonist of authentic being. In contrast, the "truth" of said modernity can only be such in so far as it is "internal to [a given] situation" (258), as opposed to conditional "routines" being foisted upon the current event.

[8] In the U.S., current right-wing notions of the 2020 election being stolen, along with subsequent violence enacted in reaction to this and other conspiracy theories ("simulation[s] of truth"), appear indicative of such a process.

[9] The important caveat here, of course, is that those for whom gender is aligned with normative, binary heterosexuality, also, probably unconsciously, perform gender as well, and do so with blanket affirmation from the larger culture. Those individuals who, in the vein of Judith Butler's arguments concerning performativity, *consciously* enact gender may do so in the service of nurturing personal, psychological health and well-being, not to mention broadening the cultural scope of gender, and thus our collective access to greater understanding, benevolence, and social justice.

[10] See Silverman's *The Threshold of the Visible World*, Routledge, 1996.

[11] For an analysis of "Don't Tread On Me" from a Lacanian perspective, see Thomas Phillips, *T.E.D. Klein and the Rupture of Civilization: A Study in Critical Horror*, McFarland, 2017, pgs. 20-27.

[12] For an overview of Gurdjieffian methodologies, see P.D. Ouspensky's *In Search of the Miraculous*, Houghton Mifflin Harcourt Publishing, 1965, and Kathleen Riordin Speeth's *The Gurdjieff Work*, Penguin, 1988.

[13] There is an argument to be made here regarding the mutual awareness of death between two or more people as fundamental to authentic relationality, that which recognizes Being, as shared actuality, at its center.

[14] See Jacques Lacan, "The Mirror Stage as Formative of the Function of the I." *Écrits: A Selection. Trans. Alan Sheridan. Norton, 1997.*

[15] Regarding the work of Patrick Deville, a writer whose most recent novels examine the power and failures of poltical revolution, Motte observes how in the novelist's view, "literature must be promoted as literature, but also as a way of coming to terms with a world and a reality that can be very oppressive indeed. Literature is, and must be, both artifact and tactic" (*French* 131).

[16] Cage was gay but, as with Marie DNiaye's "blackness," elected not to make this a centerpiece of his public life. Whether he chose such discretion out of fear of ridicule during an era that did not look kindly upon homosexuality or because he deemed it insignificant to his aesthetic life would make for a fascinating study.

[17] In our experience, general education students tend to either detest Fabre's novel on the basis of its being tedious or they find it uniquely compelling, as though experiencing mundane otherness for the first time.

[18] Found footage horror would seem to contradict this claim, though in the wake of the highly original and compelling *The Blair Witch Project* (1999), the multitude of protagonists documenting their terrifying adventures is now considerably less uncanny than it may have originally been.

[19] John Carpenter's Haddonfield in *Halloween* (1978) or, outside the domain of horror in 1979's *Over the Edge*, New Granada, a suburb devastated by its teen inhabitants whose boredom escalates into violence, exemplify a profound lack of security where refuge from the grit of existence would seem most apparent.

[20] As Hallward explains, the site of an event "comes *from beyond*, undeserved, unjustified, and unjustifiable" (our italics, *Badiou* 115) to the degree that it operates as an anomaly in the context of psychological, social, or ethical convention. Notably, it may also be perceived as "sinister and threatening" (ibid.).

[21] Prior to her realization that something ominous is definitely awry, Liza is driving along a seemingly endless bridge to nowhere when she encounters a lone woman and her seeing eye dog blocking her way on the otherwise deserted road. The ghost that is Emily knows Liza's name and will warn her,

having read of a zombie apocalypse in the dreaded book *Eibon*, to leave town and thus leave the hotel quietly and safely abandoned.

[22] In a remarkable display of what Kristeva might expect from the current "selfie" memoir, Eleanor thinks "what a complete and separate thing I am ... going from my red toes to the top of my head, individually an I, possessed of attributes belonging only to me. I have red shoes, she thought – that goes with being Eleanor; I dislike lobster and sleep on my left side and crack my knuckles when I am nervous and save buttons. I am holding a brandy glass which is mine because I am here and I am using it and have a place in this room. I have red shoes and tomorrow I will wake up and I will still be here" (83). This could easily be the typical thought press of a 21st century user of social media "liking," posting, and plugging in the carefully chosen details that make "me" me.

[23] See Sigmund Freud, *The Uncanny*. Trans. David McLintock. London: Penguin, 2003.

[24] See Viktor Frankl, *Man's Search for Meaning*. Boston: Beacon Press, 2006.

[25] These categories are from Ihab Hassan's "Toward a Concept of Postmodernism." *Postmodernism: A Reader*. Ed. Thomas Docherty. New York: Columbia UP, 1993.

[26] For Peterson, this tendency presumes the absolute veracity and legitimacy of patriarchy and capitalism, while Eagleton stands firm against any orientation that would negate material, social realities in favor of what he observes (not always without a particularly delightful accuracy) as shallow preoccupations.

[27] There are always exceptions, a point that is both easy and pleasurable to concede.

[28] Jeremy Thorn is a wealthy industrialist and presidential economics advisor, while Katherine Thorn initially attracted him with her "haunted eyes, begging for someone to protect her; the role of protector suiting his needs as well" (Seltzer, *Omen* 4).

[29] Like the following "becoming-animal," this process confers "the power, not to conquer what is other than the self, but to transform oneself in perceiving difference" (Colebrook 133), what Deleuze and Guttari call a transversal "anomalousness" (*Thousand* 243) that diverges from normative Being without the weight of prejudice.

[30] Consider any novel by *nouveau roman* writer Natalie Sarraute, for example, whose texts offer fragments of discourse that gesture towards rather than parsing narrative detail, stripped of conventional character development and context as they are. Remarkably, and often beautifully, these fragments contain revelations, not unrelated to a painterly impressionism, of great insight and relatability.

[31] From *A Thousand Plateaus*: "We know nothing about a body until we know what it can do, in other words, what its affects are, how they can or cannot enter into a *composition* with other affects, with the affects of another body,

either to destroy that body or be destroyed by it, either to exchange actions and passions with it or to join with it in composing a more powerful body" (our italics, Deleuze and Guattari 257). See also their examination of Freud's Little Hans in this respect (257-59).

[32] See Woolf's *A Room of One's Own*. New York, NY: Mariner Books, 1989.

[33] This is not to essentialize, though the alignment of what might be deemed "essential" to a person's Being-constitution is worth consideration over and above, or beneath, the more or less apparent rudiments of a given personality.

[34] When Lucien joins Armand and Jeanne for lunch, the narrator notes "it was decided that we would have coffee in the drawing-room. I was trembling as I did after every meal" (22).

[35] Lucien to Armand: "Anyone who behaves like you can well be generous. But it will not make you happy. You have to play fairer than that in life. Do you hear" (78)?

[36] In this respect, it could be instructive to consider the Gurdjieffian exercise known as "Stop," when a teacher suddenly yells the word with the expectation that students will arrest their movement, regardless of what they are doing or the awkwardness of a position, with the aim of "forcing" self-awareness by freezing potentially drifting thought processes.

[37] The qualities that the narrator perceives in (or projects onto) Sonny – "dreamlike," "weird and disordered" – attest not only to a druggy state but a "beyond" that, in relation to Guillaume's notion of "being and exchanging," assumes a "spectral" quality (*Radical* 28). It should comes as no surprise that spectrality appears as frequently as it does here given its association with both a simulated form of being (human) and a mode that is potentially more authentic than its human counterpart waking sleep.

[38] It is worth considering that Joan is not a perspective character in Plath's novel, and thus prone to the "flattening" of interpretation, and this reductive, symbolic reading of Plath's story, not the experiences of real love between women.

[39] Here, Heidegger's description of the path to the Revelation of the Nothing brings to mind the famous Zen Koan that annihilates ambition: "If you see the Buddha walking along the road at night, kill him."

[40] See the concluding chapter for a discussion of language's limits and potentialities.

[41] Aldous Huxley's Sebastian, in his early novel *Time Must Have a Stop*, is another excellent example of such a figure.

[42] "Passionate detachment" exerts a logic akin to Zen paradoxes or a related, Cageian notion of "purposeful purposelessness" intrinsic to aleatoric music that allows room for some degree of improvisation.

[43] The current Covid-19 death toll in the US has surpassed 1,000,000.

[44] What is meant by "language" without the qualifier of "vulgar?" Beyond the usual suspects, to what else could this warning refer? Perhaps terms that were once part of common discourse but are no longer acceptable? What might it say about this culture that the broad category of "language" can be sandwiched between "fear" and "gore" as a potentially foreboding hazard to one's well-being?

[45] She lives with her uncle, her aunt, her grandmother, and her tutor, the household of which is largely governed by James.

[46] Donald Trump's notorious comment to Hillary Clinton earned the ire of any self-respecting critical thinker in 2016, compelling many women to don ironic t-shirts with the designation. The breadth of Elizabeth's "nastiness," however, immersed in occult violence and, perhaps more importantly, entirely bereft of sentimentality as it is, precludes appropriation.

[47] For a curious parallel to this scenario, see Pascal Laugier's film *Martyrs* (2008).

Index

Printed in the USA
CPSIA information can be obtained
at www.ICGtesting.com
JSHW011316240624
65298JS00020B/538/J